The Seamless City

"Rick Baker made possible the politically impossible. He's a socially and fiscally conservative Republican who won reelection by over 70% of the vote, in a city with 29% registered Republicans, and carried every single precinct against the Chairman of the county's Democratic Party. The lesson? Inspired leadership that works is universally popular."

–Adam Goodman, President of The Victory Group

"This is a city that reduced property tax rates by almost 20%, more than tripled emergency reserves, reduced staffing by 10% while increasing the number of uniform police officers on the street, lowered violent crime rates, dropped the murder rate to the lowest level in decades, saw high school graduation rates and student achievement scores rise dramatically, revitalized its downtown core, dramatically improved its most economically depressed area, became Florida's first Green City, improved service levels, and added quality of life amenities like playgrounds, libraries, bike paths, kayak trails, dog parks, and countless others. Wow!"

–Mike Sittig, Executive Director, Florida League of Cities

"Under a different mayor, such attention to downtown might have worsened a political fault line between neighborhood advocates and downtown interests. But if anything, Baker has paid even more attention to St. Petersburg's neighborhoods. His brand of inclusiveness is one reason why a reliably Democratic city re-elected this Republican mayor in 2005…"

—*Governing Magazine*

"Rick Baker: Lessons from a successful Florida mayor: Stick to your principles and make government work are mantras for St. Petersburg's GOP chief executive."

—*Christian Science Monitor*

"St. Petersburg ... has blossomed from a city struggling with its historical identity as a haven for middle-class retirees into a diverse, livable community with a vibrant downtown and arts scene....Under former Mayor Rick Baker, the city welcomed downtown development and also moved aggressively and notably to redevelop the largely minority Midtown district..."

—*Florida Trend*

"The arts are everywhere in St. Petersburg, from world-renowned, such as the under-construction Salvador Dali Museum...and the newly expanded Museum of Fine Arts, to the private art galleries that line its downtown streets."

—*American Style*

"...Mayor Rick Baker is showing how city CEOs, without taking over the governance of a school district, can improve local schools...Baker has become almost a rock star in his city's public schools, which make up a third of the 108,000 students in the Pinellas County School District."

—*Detroit Free Press*

The
Seamless City

The
Seamless City

A Conservative Mayor's Approach to
Urban Revitalization That Can Work Anywhere

Rick Baker

Since 1947
REGNERY
PUBLISHING, INC.
An Eagle Publishing Company • Washington, DC

Library of Congress Cataloging-in-Publication Data

    Baker, Rick (Richard Murray), 1956-
      The seamless city / by Rick Baker.
        p. cm.
      Includes index.
      ISBN 978-1-59698-197-3
      1. Saint Petersburg (Fla.)--Politics and government. 2. Municipal government--United States--Case studies. 3. Baker, Rick. I. Title.
      JS1420.S4B35 2011
      975.9'63--dc22

                    2010054142

Published in the United States by
Regnery Publishing, Inc.
One Massachusetts Avenue, NW
Washington, DC 20001
www.regnery.com

Manufactured in the United States of America
10 9 8 7 6 5 4 3 2 1

Books are available in quantity for promotional or premium use. Write to Director of Special Sales, Regnery Publishing, Inc., One Massachusetts Avenue NW, Washington, DC 20001, for information on discounts and terms or call (202) 216-0600.

Every good faith effort has been made in this work to credit sources and comply with the fairness doctrine on quotation and use of research material. If any copyrighted material has been inadvertently used in this work without proper credit being given in one manner or another, please notify the publisher in writing so that future printings of this work may be corrected accordingly.

Distributed to the trade by:
Perseus Distribution
387 Park Avenue South
New York, NY 10016

To Joyce, Julann, and Jacob,
who shared the adventure

What is
a Seamless City?

In a seamless city, when you go from one part of town to another, you never cross a seam—whether a street, interstate overpass, or railroad track—and enter a place where you do not want to be…where you feel the need to reach over and lock your car door; an area with boarded-up buildings, broken windows, and large tracts of urban blight, with drug dealers on the street corner.

All parts of the city are not the same, and that will always be true. Some areas have large houses and big lots, while others may have duplexes and apartments; but all parts of a seamless city should have certain things in common. They should be safe and clean and should have the services, retail, and public infrastructure that adequately accommodate the people who live there.

A seamless city is an attitude that we are all in it together. It means that we do not pit one area against the other, but work toward advancing the entire city by addressing the needs of the parts.…It's connecting everyone with bike paths, and encouraging the community to gather together at dog parks and playgrounds.

A seamless city looks for ways to help the homeless turn their lives around while not allowing them to adversely impact others, and has a downtown that becomes the gathering place for all who live there. Such a city works with neighborhood leaders so that the residents define and help execute their own ideas for progress. A seamless city also understands that our public schools are not islands to be left drifting on their own. They are vital to the city's success and should be supported by everyone.

No area in a seamless city should be crime ridden and blighted. All of our children should grow up in neighborhoods that are safe and clean; that have libraries, parks, athletic fields, banks, shopping centers, and grocery stores; and where every boy and girl can share in the pride and success of the entire city!

—Rick Baker
February 7, 2011

Contents

Foreword

by Governor Jeb Bush

Among the many wonderful sayings of Ben Franklin, there is one that I associate with my friend Rick Baker: "Little strokes fell great oaks."

When Rick Baker was elected mayor in 2001, he had a clear vision for the future of his hometown: "Make St. Petersburg Best," and he went about consistently and constantly executing on that vision. The net result after almost nine years of "little strokes" was that his beloved St. Petersburg was a better place to live, work, and prosper.

From his first day in office, Mayor Baker worked tirelessly to turn his vision into reality. Like all great leaders, he started with a plan. With blueprint in hand, he advanced policies and programs to accomplish the ultimate goal.

First on the list, improve public safety. Keeping streets free from crime—so children can play outside and elders can live without fear—is the foundation of a vibrant community. By his last year in office, St. Petersburg was safer city, with significantly lower violent crime rates and a murder rate that fell to the lowest level in decades. There were more uniformed police on the street, the number of arrests were up—including a substantial increase in drug arrests—and police response times were reduced.

Second, promote economic development. A healthy and growing economy produces prosperity and raises the standard of living for citizens. Under Rick Baker's leadership, the economy of St. Petersburg flourished. Downtown experienced an unprecedented renaissance, while several businesses moved or expanded their operations in St. Petersburg, creating thousands of jobs for Floridians. Among the top job generators were Raymond James, Bright House, Progress Energy, Home Shopping Network, and ValPak.

During my time as Governor, every announced trip would secure an invitation from Mayor Rick Baker to see the extra efforts undertaken to revitalize the poorest sections of the city's urban core—Midtown St. Petersburg. He worked to bring in amenities that many of us take for granted—a full-service post office, a brand-name grocery store, and banking services—to spark rebirth in that area.

Rick's third priority was to support public schools. A quality education can change an individual life and provide the catalyst for a robust economy. Many students gained the knowledge and skills to succeed in school and beyond during Rick's terms in office. The number of high performing schools in St. Petersburg—those graded A or B under the state's accountability system—increased a whopping 260 percent ... no small feat, given the state raising the bar for earning these good grades multiple times during this same timeframe. Mayor Baker's "little strokes" included an ambitious mentoring program, a rewards program for schools that improved, and involving the business community deeply in schools.

Fourth, build strong neighborhoods. Creating the opportunity for neighbors to meet and interact brings individuals together to form a community. As mayor, Rick undertook major initiatives to bring people together to enjoy their city. He empowered residents to improve their own neighborhoods, nurturing local leaders and supporting over 100 active neighborhood associations. The city expanded outdoor recreation to appeal to every sector of the diverse population—waterslides at the city pools for the kids, a kayak and canoe trail system branded "Blue-Way" Trails for the adventurists, athletic fields for teams, skateboarding parks for teens, greens for golfers, courts for tennis players, and bike paths for everyone. The city built playgrounds within a safe walking distance of 78 percent of the children in the city and built dog parks where pet owners could let their dogs run loose. St. Petersburg became Florida's first designated Green City and went from being one of the most dangerous cities in America for pedestrians to one of the safest.

Fifth, improve government operations. Few challenges are as difficult, or as rewarding, as changing the bureaucracy to better serve the people. At the end of Rick Baker's service, city government was smaller and smarter. Property tax rates were cut by almost 20 percent and government positions were reduced by 10 percent.

Mayor Baker was an outstanding leader. He led by example. Before he recruited people to serve as mentors in public schools, Rick became a mentor himself. And he led with a servant's heart. His constituents came first. Their problems were his problems.

The Seamless City tells Mayor Baker's story, but it also provides a road map. It is an example of how preparation, planning, persistence, and a passion for service can move America's cities closer to the goal of becoming seamless—places where citizens in all neighborhoods enjoy safe streets, reliable infrastructure, a high quality of life, and the opportunity to pursue their dreams.

Introduction

A Great Nation Needs Great Cities

*America is a shining city upon a hill whose beacon light
guides freedom-loving people everywhere.*

—RONALD WILSON REAGAN
(FROM JESUS CHRIST'S SERMON ON THE MOUNT: MATTHEW 5: 14–16)

Cities are important.

The history of America is really the accumulation of the histories of its cities, towns, and villages. If you want to learn about our country's past, study America's cities. Towns developed around transportation centers—rivers, coasts, railroads, and roads. The story of the railroad coming in 1888 to the village that is today's St. Petersburg, Florida, and a town springing to life, is the same story that was repeated across the nation in different eras from the beginning of America's history.

While the history books have to put a universal perspective on things, the great events in our nation's history were all lived out by individual people in their various hometowns and cities. In the 1940s, in Baltimore, St. Louis, Portland, and Jacksonville, young men packed up their clothes, kissed their parents good-bye, and left from train stops across America to save the world from Nazi tyranny and Japanese imperialism. Back home their families and sweethearts collected old tires, bought savings bonds, worked in defense plants, and joined civil defense forces to protect the homeland. The Civil Rights campaigns of the 1960s were carried out in cities by the people who lived there. Lunch counter sit-ins, movie stand-ins, and sanitation worker protest marches took place on main streets from Memphis to Tallahassee.

The mass movement from farms to cities in the 1800s, the suburbanization of our country after World War II, and the anxiety after September 11, were all personally felt in America's cities. The national government and state governments have many roles to play, from defending our country to building highways. Their influence and authority have expanded over the course of American history, and it is likely that this trend will continue. Yet when you want to know how the country is doing, you don't go to Washington, D.C. You visit the coffee shops and little league fields in cities and towns. You ask the clerks, teachers, and soccer moms.

As the cities of our country succeed, the United States becomes a stronger nation. Our collective future is dependent on the cumulative strength and passion of our cities and towns. America is Broadway, South Beach, the French Quarter, and the Golden Gate Bridge. It is the St. Louis Gateway Arch and Chicago's State Street; the Mall in Washington, D.C.; Beale Street in Memphis and the Pike Place Market in Seattle. Our country's pulse is felt in the factories, office buildings, museums, ball fields, and busy sidewalks of its urban centers. If America is to continue to embody Ronald Reagan's vision of the shining city on a hill, then *our great nation must have great cities!*

Retail Government

Before I ran for mayor of St. Petersburg, Florida, my wife Joyce and I had dinner with Bob Martinez and his wife Mary Jane. Bob Martinez is a highly respected Floridian who had served two terms as mayor of Tampa before being elected as our state's second Republican governor since reconstruction. After completing his term, Governor Martinez joined President George H. W. Bush's Cabinet as America's drug czar.

I was pleased to have a chance to talk with Governor Martinez and receive some advice about my upcoming campaign. During our talk, I asked the former mayor and governor which job he enjoyed the most. He smiled broadly and responded without hesitating, "Being mayor, of course!" Then he gave me a brief description of the job that I would embrace for the next nine years.

Mayors are retail government.

Cities, led by mayors, are responsible for keeping people safe, with police officers to fight crime, fire fighters to keep homes and businesses from burning down, and emergency medical rescue teams to save lives when someone has a heart attack or an auto accident. Cities build the local roads and handle traffic control. They pick up trash, fix the sidewalks, provide drinking water, and treat sewer water.

Cities build and maintain playgrounds, athletic fields, swimming pools, skateboard parks, and gymnasiums for children. They provide dog parks, people parks, and bike paths. Cities trim trees in alleys and roads and manage rainwater runoff. They build performing arts theaters, professional sports facilities, and downtown activity centers. Cities are home to our factories, colleges, hospitals, and museums. City governments provide most of the government services that the average citizen sees and uses on a regular basis.

Cities are important.

People relate to their city in a special way. When the city receives positive publicity by hosting a presidential debate, the World Series, a Grand Prix, a college bowl game, or an NCAA basketball tournament, the people who live there feel better about their town and about themselves. Similarly, when a city experiences a crisis, the people who live there feel the effects, and they focus on the need for solutions.

If a community experiences a series of convenience store hold-ups, an approaching hurricane, a water line break, or the potential loss of a major employer, the media look for someone to respond and assure the public that the leaders are on top of it—that they have a plan. They won't call the local congressman or state senator; they will contact the mayor.

People view their mayor differently than they view most elected officials. Unlike their relationships with presidents or governors, citizens feel that they know their mayor on a personal level. Residents see the mayor on television or in the newspaper almost daily, and they may also run into him or her at the local grocery store or a youth soccer game. Even if they have never met the mayor, they feel like they have. They also feel that they have the right to hold the mayor accountable for solving the city's problems.

A mayor does not need a sophisticated survey to know how the city is doing. He does not even need to read the emails to city hall or letters to the editor, although he should. He need only conduct what I call the "Home Depot Poll." Just by going to Home Depot, or the local diner, drug store, youth soccer game, McDonalds, or even church, he learns a lot.

When things aren't going well, the mayor can feel a chill in the air as he walks through the mall or stands in the grocery store check-out line. Occasionally someone may say something unpleasant, but the negative comments made in person are not common, at least in my experience. When I was in real trouble, I knew it because friends and even perfect strangers would come up to me, grab my hands, and look at me with concern saying: "We're praying for you!"

The good news is that when things are going well, people enjoy introducing themselves, talking about how much they love the city, and expressing their thanks for your willingness to take on the job of mayor. Sometimes they want to address a specific issue that's easy to handle, like paving an alley or lighting a dog park. Other times the problems are more difficult, but they warrant action, such as a parent's concern that someone is selling drugs in a parking lot down the street, or a neighbor's problem of flooding in front of her house at high tide.

My wife joked that, when I was mayor, it took me an hour and a half to buy a screwdriver at Home Depot.

A Servant's Approach

Former United States Transportation Secretary Norm Mineta tells the story of an experience he had when he was mayor of San Jose, California. It was nearing the end of the day, and he heard some commotion at his receptionist's desk. A lady had arrived without an appointment and was demanding to see the mayor. Mineta describes how he approached the door and quietly leaned his ear against it so he could hear the conversation going on in his lobby. The receptionist kept offering alternate members of the staff for the lady to see, but the visitor only became more irate, finally demanding in a loud voice: "I want to see the mayor and I will see no one lower than the mayor!"

At that moment Mayor Mineta slowly opened the door, poked his head into the lobby, and said to his constituent, "Madam, there is no one lower than the mayor."

Mayor Mineta was right. When someone works for a city, whether their job is to be mayor or a worker in parks maintenance, it requires a servant's approach, a desire to be a helper. There are some who seek an elected job predominantly because they want to "be" in the office. They desire the status and attention of the position. There are others who run for office principally because they want to "do" something with the position. They understand the great responsibility and capacity to change people's lives for the better that comes with an elective trust. Every mayor falls on the continuum line somewhere between wanting to "be" and a desire to "do." In each case there is some element of ego and some element of wanting to help.

This book is written for those mayors, along with all others involved in changing the world, who take on their job primarily because *they want to do something*. They want to get something accomplished that will tangibly improve the quality of life for other people. They recognize that they are servants, and that they are there first and foremost to serve those who elect them.

The job of city-building and development is never done. The job of mayor, like all leadership jobs within the community, is not a marathon or a sprint. It is a relay race. We take the baton from our predecessors, with all their cumulative strengths and difficulties. We then run with all our might, hopefully building up a strong lead for the community, knowing that someday we will pass the baton on to the next leader.

Why do some cities work while others—we could all name them—do not? City success does not occur through evolution, luck, or timing; the difference is leadership. The successful cities typically have neighborhood, business, community, faith, and political leadership that unite and rally around the effort to make their town better. You can tell when it's working because the taxi drivers, waiters, and store clerks are eager to tell people about the greatness of their city. When it's not working, you can tell by the boarded-up buildings, graffiti, and the general sense of hopelessness—the universal feeling that those in charge have given up.

In this book, I have outlined some initiatives that moved our city forward. While St. Petersburg has made significant progress in the recent past, I recognize that we have more work to do. In fact, the job of city-building is never done. Our city still has challenges common to major cities across our country.

Although many of the ideas in this book came from the experiences in the city that I led, I know there are many other cities with their own success stories. I have studied them and, at times, followed their lead. My hope is that the examples of our approach to "Making St. Petersburg Best" will help other cities as they work to improve the quality of life for the people who live in their communities.

Chapter 1

Day One

April 1, 2001

When the burdens of the presidency seem unusually
heavy, I always remind myself it could be worse.
I could be a mayor.

—Lyndon B. Johnson

On Sundays, my wife Joyce and I sometimes liked to grab some chicken and bring our children, Julann and Jacob, to play in the water and watch the sunset on Pass-a-Grille. It is a beach that reminds you of Key West with sea oats, white sand, and Caribbean cafes. There is a snack shack on the water with picnic tables and a bell used by the Clapper Club.

One of our outings was on an unusual day, when Julann was five and Jacob four. It was Sunday, April 1, 2001. Earlier in the afternoon, at one o'clock, I was sworn in to office as mayor of Florida's fourth largest city. I had been elected the previous Tuesday. I'd lost twenty pounds during the campaign, mostly from stress, and was exhausted by election night. But I still had the energy to sing James Brown's "I Feel Good" (our unofficial theme song) with everyone else at the victory party celebration. The next day was filled with television and radio interviews, and Thursday and Friday were my transition period to turn over my law practice to my

1

now former partners and get ready to put together a new city government.

Now, as my college sweetheart and I sat on picnic tables at the beach, eating corn on the cob and watching the kids splash in the water, I was uneasy about the coming days. Although I had succeeded in a campaign with nine candidates and thirty-four debates, I felt unprepared. I had led a medium-size law firm, the chamber of commerce, and some charities, but today I had 3,000 employees in 34 departments including police and fire, water and sewer, sanitation, parks, and roads. The city had many challenges that we debated during the campaign, and those challenges were now mine to tackle. I was excited about the opportunity, but my nervousness would drive me to spend many days during the next few months coming into the mayor's office before 6:00 a.m., trying to get up to speed.

As the sun lowered on the horizon over the Gulf of Mexico, several members of the Clapper Club were enjoying the moment at a table near ours. The club is an informal group that gathers from time to time at Pass-a-Grille to watch the sunset. The name "Clapper Club" comes from the clapper of the bell that hangs from a rustic pole on the deck overlooking the water. They ring the bell as the sun dips into the Gulf of Mexico.

One member of the Clapper Club got up and walked over to ask if I was the new mayor of St. Petersburg. They had seen me on television. When I nodded, he said that they had been having a discussion at their table, and agreed to give me the honor of ringing the Clapper Club bell as the sun set that night. He added that, as the honoree, I would also get to sign and date the Clapper Club book after ringing the bell.

I called Julann and Jacob up from the water, explained the tradition, and suggested that we all ring the bell together. Our family sat with our new friends from the Clapper Club and talked about the excitement of the day, how lucky we were to live in this corner of Florida, and how one never gets tired of sunsets.

Then the leader of the group, whose business card designated him the "Head Ding Dong," became very serious, and his voice dropped to a whisper. He told us he felt the conditions might be right for a "green flash sunset." Although I had lived in Florida since I was ten, I had never heard of a green flash sunset. The salty Clapper Club member explained that the phenomenon occurs only on very, very rare nights, if the conditions are just right. As the top of the sun drops into the Gulf and disappears from view, the entire horizon flashes green for an instant, the color seeming to move in both directions from the disappearing sun. It is considered to be a very positive omen, and a sign that good fortune will follow.

Our new friends admitted that none of them had actually seen a green flash sunset at Pass-a-Grille, and I mentally placed the notion in the large file of Caribbean legends.

By now the kids were back in the water and playing in the white sand of Florida's West Coast. We started to pack up. My thoughts began drifting again to the days ahead, and I wondered if I was up to the job. In many of my life's adventures, I have been motivated by a lack of confidence in my ability to tackle a new challenge. It makes me work as hard as I can to over-prepare. Sitting in the salty sea breeze on Pass-a-Grille that afternoon, I questioned whether I had bitten off more than I could chew this time. I was taking on a whole city!

As my thoughts wandered and I gazed out over the Gulf, I noticed that the sun was beginning to touch the water, so I called Joyce, Julann, and Jacob up to the bell. My small children stood on a chair, and the four of us reached together for the clapper, ready to ring the bell. We were all focused on the horizon.

Then it happened!

As the sun vanished into the Gulf of Mexico, the horizon flashed a bright green hue that I had never seen before. The light seemed to be spreading across the sky in slow motion, but it actually came in an instant. Then the color was gone as quickly as it had arrived.

We rang the bell, and there was a moment of stunned silence followed by excited looks and chatter, each of us trying to confirm that we weren't the only one who had seen what we thought we saw. As the Clapper Club members excitedly shook my hand, they assured me the good fortune predicted by the green flash meant that my term as mayor would be blessed with great success.

My mind raced back to the hectic days of the campaign. It was an exhausting—at times terrifying—period filled with debates, media, direct mail, consultants, speeches, and fundraising. At moments I wondered whether I had made a mistake, taking this sharp turn in my life. But it seemed that when I needed it most, God sent a sign that He was with me. I didn't know it then, but I would experience many similar moments as I faced the challenges of the next nine years.

But few messages would be as clear as the one received on the eve of my first day in office. I signed the Clapper Club book: "Mayor Rick Baker, April 1, 2001, a green flash sunset."

Chapter 2

Four Years Later

Election Day 2005—A City United

*This City is what it is because our citizens
are what they are.*

—PLATO

Election Day is a mayor's report card. A mayor receives input on how he is doing throughout his term, from the media, interest groups, and the general public; however, the ultimate test of his performance comes when the voters decide whether or not to keep him around for another four years. The report card on my first term as mayor of St. Petersburg, which had begun in 2001, was scheduled to be delivered on November 8, 2005. It was Election Day, and I was seeking a second term. During the previous four years, we had experienced hurricanes, budget challenges, and crises of various types and sizes. We had also welcomed a renaissance unmatched in our city's history. Now, we were about to find out if the voters agreed with the direction we were going.

After the polls closed, my supporters enjoyed a party downstairs at the St. Pete Clay Company in Midtown. I gathered with my family and campaign leaders—Jim Koelsch, Adam Goodman, Mike Gilson, Deveron Gibbons, Terry Brett, and others—in an upstairs room to watch the online returns come in. Although our team had felt for some time that I would be reelected for a second term, we did not take the effort lightly. I have always believed in the campaign adage that there are only two ways to run for political office: unopposed or scared! We had an opponent who put a lot of energy into the race, and we worked hard on our campaign as well.

Four years earlier, when I ran and was elected to my first term as mayor, the wounds of division within our city were still fresh. In 1996 St. Petersburg had been ripped apart by two separate nights of riots following a police shooting and killing of an African American suspect at a traffic stop. There had been many years of conflict: racial discord, clashes within the police department, downtown versus neighborhood debates, feelings in the west part of the city that they were underserved, and unhappiness over large scale city building projects and the resulting tax rate increases. Mayoral elections during those previous twenty years tended to be very close and contentious. Each race seemed to be for the soul of the city.

During our first term of office, we worked to bring people together by including every corner of the city in the progress. We placed a strong emphasis on redeveloping our most economically depressed area (now called Midtown), along with a focus on bringing downtown to a new level of vibrancy. We paid attention to our schools and neighborhoods and targeted resources and efforts throughout the community, all at once. We also worked to bring property tax rates down while we improved public service. In 2005, we wanted to win reelection, but we also wanted to demonstrate that our city had come together and overcome many of the issues that had previously divided us.

Many saw me as an unlikely urban champion. As a Republican who is conservative both fiscally and socially, I governed during my first term as mayor with these philosophies, although without stressing a partisan approach. After serving for four years, I ran for reelection against the county chair of the Democratic Party in a city where less than 30 percent of the population are registered Republicans. Needless to say, my opponent stressed his partisan roots during the campaign. As we awaited the returns on Election Day 2005, I hoped for the best, but I understood the political realities we were facing.

When the final online returns appeared on the computer screen, they revealed a stunning victory. *We won every single precinct in the city with a 70 percent overall victory margin.* Remarkably, we also won over 90 percent of the vote in the core Midtown precincts, where an overwhelming number of voters are African American Democrats. Over 90 percent of the Midtown voters chose a conservative Republican! By comparison, in my 2001 mayoral primary election, these same core Midtown precincts had been won by the chairman of the African People's Socialist Party.

The next morning's front page headline in Florida's largest newspaper, the *St. Petersburg Times,* proclaimed, "A City United." It was an election result so unusual that I was invited to breakfast in the U.S. Capitol's Senate dining room with Bill Frist, the Republican Majority Leader of the United States Senate. Over coffee, Senator Frist asked me to share ideas on how our party could reach out to broaden our base of support. My summary reply was simple: listen, do what you say you will do, and genuinely care about the future of every child.

The unabridged answer to the Senator Frist's question is a bit longer, and it is the subject of this book: people respond to results. Successful city-building is not the product of a magic formula or a faddish, quick-fix solution. It comes from deliberate, focused hard work applying the fundamentals of a good plan, solid practices, and passionate leadership. The effort must be aimed at improving every part of the city, leaving no one behind.

The chapters that follow present an approach to making cities better. It starts with the development of a strategic plan. The plan is not static or left to gather dust on a shelf in the city clerk's office. It comes to life through the crises, opportunities, achievements, and heartaches experienced by any mayor who takes on the responsibility for improving a major city in America. It is one of the most challenging and rewarding enterprises to which someone can commit a portion of his or her life.

Chapter 3

Define the Mission, Set Goals, Become the Best

Where there is no vision, the people perish.

—KING SOLOMON, PROVERBS 29:18

O ne of my favorite figures in history is Winston Churchill, who united a nation and the world against the cruel Nazi regime. Churchill clearly grasped the historic nature of his challenge and understood the importance of the past in guiding his present decisions. The leader on whom so much depended counseled his generals that their best chance at success was to gain perspective and context by understanding history, or as he specifically said: "*The further backward you look, the further forward you can see.*" With Churchill's advice in mind, during the 1990s, I studied St. Petersburg's history and wrote a book on it. It is helpful to take a brief look at that history before describing our plan to move the city forward.

In 1528, Panfilo de Narvaez landed a Spanish expedition in today's St. Petersburg, a city located on the Gulf Coast of the Florida peninsula.

Narvaez's expedition would be the first European group to cross the American continent. After Narvaez, there would be little European activity for many years on the peninsula that comprises today's St. Petersburg. The native population died out in the early 1700s. Scattered settlements arrived in the mid-1800s, and the railroad came in 1888, about the time that the town plat was filed. The town was named after St. Petersburg, Russia, the major city in the homeland of Peter Demens, who built the railroad.

St. Petersburg officially became a city in 1903, followed by the election of Robert H. Thomas as its mayor. Thomas was from Illinois, southwest of Chicago. John Williams, the town's founder, was from Detroit, Michigan. His father had been the first mayor of Detroit. Thomas and Williams were the earliest among many Midwesterners who, in years to come, would travel by train to visit and settle in St. Petersburg. Eventually U.S. Highway 19 and U.S. Highway 41, followed by Interstate 75, would funnel in visitors and new residents from Pennsylvania, Ohio, Illinois, Wisconsin, Indiana, and Michigan, giving the city a Midwestern feel.

U.S. Highway 1 and Interstate 95, conversely, each began in Maine and brought visitors and new residents from America's Northeast to Florida's lower east coast and Miami. North Florida cities like Tallahassee and Pensacola sit near the borders of Georgia and Alabama: they have a distinctly Southern feel—so much so that an expression that took root some time ago still has a ring of truth: in Florida, the farther north you go, the farther south you get. In recent decades, Miami has become an international city, and Orlando has brought the world to see Mickey Mouse, so the cultural dynamic has become more complicated.

St. Petersburg's early industries included citrus, fishing, and tourism. The city was a military training town during World War II, a status that brought the defense industry to the city after the war. Later, the city entered the suburban period of America, building shopping centers, malls, and residential developments away from the city center. The tourism industry shifted from downtown to the beaches, and the downtown ceased to be a vibrant area.

By the day of the mayoral election in 2001, St. Petersburg had a fairly diverse business base, and there was a desire to bring more employers to downtown and the major business parks of the city. Many of the commercial corridors were in need of an upgrade. The city's downtown, which was showing some new signs of life, still struggled despite an enormous effort to bring vitality. The public schools were not faring well under the state's new grading system. The crime rate had come down during the 1990s, but there was continued pressure to reduce crime more, especially violent crime and murder rates.

Tax rates rose significantly during the 1980s, following expensive efforts to revitalize downtown. Many neighborhood leaders decried the expenditures and tax rates, while many chamber and civic boosters vigorously defended the downtown efforts. Mayoral and city council races in the late 1980s and 1990s were close, and the investments in downtown were vigorously debated. In the late 1980s, two efforts reflected the frustration felt by many in the city: there was an attempt to recall the mayor and the entire City Council; and a west side neighborhood tried to secede from the city due to rising tax rates.

The 1993 mayoral election was one of the closest in city history. The bitterly fought campaign ended with a vote so close that multiple recounts were required, predating the famous 2000 presidential race in Florida. The split vote reflected a highly divided city. The 1993 election also resulted in a change in the city's charter to usher in the "strong mayor" form of government, under which the mayor no longer sat on City Council. Instead, the mayor became the generally elected chief administrator and political leader of the city.

In the late 1990s, city leaders achieved better neighborhood relations and some tax rate relief, but there was still room for improvement on both fronts. Tax rates, although lowered, still significantly exceeded the rates in most of Florida's major cities. Some neighborhoods felt detached and underserved, including those on the city's west side, which would be described as "prickly" by *Governing* magazine. Many western precincts had not backed the winning mayoral candidate in years. Residents of those neighborhoods tended to feel they got little in return for the real estate taxes they paid.

In 1996, St. Petersburg suffered worldwide bad publicity with two nights of race riots in the south-central part of town. The disturbances followed a police shooting of an African American suspect at a traffic stop. By the end of the decade, efforts to improve the poorest parts of the community had been tried, but there had been little progress. During the 2001 campaign, resentment was expressed by many African Americans living in these economically depressed parts of the city.

The 2000 census showed St. Petersburg to be the 4th largest of Florida's 400 cities, larger than Orlando and Ft. Lauderdale, and smaller than Jacksonville and Miami. In that census, St. Petersburg was the 68th largest of America's 20,000 cities—a city big enough to experience the issues common to the nation's other major cities, and small enough that its leaders can get their arms around problems and test out new programs quickly. The city was in the process of transforming from a retirement community to a more balanced economy. As of 2000, the city's average age had dropped considerably, and the number of residents over 65 fell to about 17 percent of the city, which was less than the Florida average.

By 2001, St. Petersburg had made progress on many fronts, but there was still much work to do. The residents of St. Petersburg did not boast much about their town; they wanted it to do better. We won the 2001 election by 14 percentage points, following two decades of mayoral elections that were highly contentious battles resulting in many razor-thin victories. Our margin of victory was enough to declare a mandate for action—but it would be of no value unless we figured out a way to move our city to the next level of urban success. We needed a plan.

A Strategic Plan for the City

It can be challenging to develop a strategic plan for a city because it has so many diverse functions, and many are not easily susceptible to measurement. What are the goals of a water or sanitation department?

How can you quantify whether the parks or traffic effort is successful? City responsibilities include sewer treatment, police and fire protection, permitting, codes enforcement, recreation, libraries, economic development, and dozens more. The diversity and intangible nature of many of the operations make it hard to set goals and measure success. Nevertheless, that is exactly what should be done.

While the priorities and programs within a strategic plan will change from city to city, the core elements of the plan should contain the following:

(1) Define the city's mission
(2) As a community, develop a plan of action to accomplish the mission
(3) Communicate the plan clearly to the public
(4) Unite around the effort—build a seamless city
(5) Work toward accomplishing the plan
(6) Measure and report on progress
(7) Keep getting better by adjusting the plan and developing new strategies based on performance

(1) The City's Mission

A strategic plan must start with a mission. What are we trying to accomplish? In a business organization, the mission may relate to its service level, product quality, profitability, and increase in shareholder value. If a business is not profitable, ultimately it will not survive.

In the case of a city government, the mission may seem harder to define, but in my mind it is actually easier: the purpose of any city government should be to make its city the best. This effort is accomplished by constantly seeking and acting on ways to improve the quality of life for the people who live there. This is, admittedly, a very broad objective. But I believed that, in the case of my town, if we viewed every decision through the prism of whether or not a chosen path would "Make St. Petersburg Best" by advancing our city's quality of life, ultimately we were on the right track.

I understand that "becoming the best" is an intangible idea, but I am also certain that it must be the goal. Who is going to be inspired by an effort or follow a leader whose goal is to become the third best city in Florida, or the eighth best city in the country? People are naturally drawn to an effort that strives for excellence. They want to be part of something that is important. When you empower people by believing in them and their ultimate success, you can lift an entire city. Every city in our country should measure progress toward increasing its quality of life; and each city's goal should be simple: *to become the best city in America!*

(2) Develop a Plan of Action

The next step is to develop a plan of action, the roadmap to improve the quality of life for the people who live in the city. Obviously, if you are trying to come up with an improvement plan, it is helpful to have a pretty good idea of how the organization operates and what it is presently doing. It is also a good idea to learn what other cities are doing, and whether they are having success in improving the quality of life for their citizens. To do this, it is critical to receive input from the people who live in the city. As time goes on, the residents will ultimately decide if the plan is right, and whether their city will continue to follow it.

While preparing to run for mayor in 2001, I set out to find out more about other cities around the country. I started with the book *21st Century City*, written by Mayor Steve Goldsmith of Indianapolis. I lived in Indianapolis growing up, and I considered it one of the more successful cities in the country, so I wanted to find out more about how the place developed. I was impressed with Mayor Goldsmith's businesslike approach to running a city, including his "marketization" of public services. I began to ponder ways I could make our city operate more efficiently and reduce tax rates, but I also did not know what I did not know. What else were other cities in America doing?

Mayor Goldsmith's book was copyrighted by the Manhattan Institute, an entrepreneurial city think-tank in New York. I learned of other publications of the Manhattan Institute, especially their magazine *City Guide* and the pamphlet book *Entrepreneurial City*. The *Entrepreneurial*

City is an amazing compilation of best practices on city issues including finances, education, public safety, economic development, and others. It is written by accomplished mayors in some of America's most successful cities. Although it is only about one hundred pages long, it took me days to go through it. Each topic area contains annotations at the end with lists of additional reference reading on the topic and lists of people to talk to in the contributing mayors' cities. I found myself in telephone conversations with city clerks and budget officers in cities across the country learning more about topics highlighted by their mayors.

Entrepreneurial City was so valuable that, after I became mayor, we acquired a copy for every manager in the city government. Each was required to read the book and participate in a half-day team meeting exploring ways to incorporate its lessons into our city's operations.

In addition to studying the practices of cities around the country, I also studied my city's past. If you want to help set a course for the future, then you should have a firm grasp on where you have been and how the community got to its current point. Most cities have a number of books available for study on the community's history. Each city is unique. It would be a mistake simply to adopt programs from a list of best practices without first considering whether they fit in your city. What works in New York City or Chicago may not work in Charlotte or St. Petersburg. It is important to have a solid grasp of the history, challenges, and civic fabric of your city before trying to develop a plan for its future.

Finally, after a great deal of time spent talking with people throughout the community, studying best practices of other cities, learning the history of our city, and reviewing the present priorities and conditions, I completed a ten-page plan of action, which was entitled "Making St. Petersburg Best." The plan synthesized my understanding of the history, businesses, neighborhoods, and community groups in our city, along with my study of best practices underway in cities across America. This understanding became the springboard of the plan for the future, which included areas of focus and ideas for improving the quality of life for the people of our city. The mission and plan of action were ready to launch ... or so I thought.

(3) Communicate the Plan Clearly

In late 2000, I stayed up late one night working on the fine points of the plan to "Make St. Petersburg Best." I wanted to make sure it was in good shape for my meeting the next day with Adam Goodman. Adam is one of a talented breed of political media consultants in the country. Prior to our meeting, he was featured in *USA Today* as Rudy Giuliani's U.S. Senate campaign media consultant. With his national experience, I knew Adam would be a great asset to my campaign, and I was pleased that he had agreed to work on it. I was very eager to hear his thoughts about my plan.

Working with campaign consultants can be a little unnerving, especially at first. They often appear to have attention deficit disorder. As you talk, they are constantly looking around the room, repositioning themselves in their chair, answering their cell phone, or sending text messages. But the most frustrating part is their thought process. You might spend ten minutes trying to explain a very important problem to them and fail to isolate their focus for even a few moments—then suddenly, they stop the peripheral motion, look you directly in the eye, and give you a recommendation ... which you immediately recognize is the exact right thing to do.

My meeting with Adam Goodman was my introduction to this approach. After fielding a few cell phone calls, and talking for awhile about everything other than my campaign, he finally let me present my plan for making St. Petersburg the best city in America. I slid my impressive ten-page plan across the table, feeling quite proud of my aggressive goal.

Adam seemed surprised, but not impressed, that I had prepared this text. I sat back to allow him time to go through the plan, and he glanced at the title on the cover. Then, to my annoyance, he slid the plan back across the table to me without even cracking the binder. Before I could speak, he ordered me to summarize my plan in one sentence without taking a second breath.

I almost jumped across the table at him. I have never cared for "big picture guys" who think they can run an organization or effort without ever getting into the details of driving the train.

In a great display of self control, I did not strangle my new media consultant. Instead, I took a deep breath and tried to summarize my plan in one sentence. For the next thirty minutes we went back and forth, with me summarizing the points and Adam telling me that I talk too much. My annoyance finally reached boiling point, and it showed in my expression. Adam waved his hand back and forth in my face like he was hailing a taxi and ordered me to stop talking.

With the patience of a drill sergeant teaching kindergarten, he slowly explained to me what he was trying to accomplish. Most people are not going to read my lengthy plan, he told me. It is not that they do not care about the city or are not thinking people. But they are busy with their lives, their jobs, and their kids. Their electric bill is due. They have a parent in the hospital. Their child has a cold and their boss gave them a project that will take the weekend to complete. Their primary focus is not going to be on my campaign—and that is okay. Studying my vision is not their responsibility. It is my job to clearly and consistently tell them my goals for the city in a way that they can quickly understand.

Once he explained his rationale, I understood and agreed—though I still wished that he would read my very impressive plan. We continued our back and forth until we had boiled my approach down to four points:

(1) Improving public safety
(2) Promoting economic development—especially in Downtown and our economically depressed area (now called Midtown)
(3) Supporting public schools
(4) Building strong neighborhoods

"The Baker Plan," Adam said.

I remember thinking: How does this guy make a living coming up with such stupid names? It would be egotistical for me to promote a plan for the city's future named after me. People would not take me seriously. My drill sergeant patiently responded that, with nine candidates, I was going to have to build name identification for my candidacy and separate myself from the crowd with a simple, measurable, easy-to-communicate plan. I am not sure whether Adam convinced me or just wore me down, but I decided to quit arguing with him.

The Baker Plan became our platform. I repeated the name and four points relentlessly in every speaking engagement, interview, and debate. Opponents and reporters began to mouth the words as I spoke, either out of boredom or as a way to mock my singular focus—but something else happened. The Baker Plan stuck with the public. Other candidates began receiving questions about elements of the Baker Plan, and a couple of them adopted some of the points. Entire gatherings would nod as I listed the four points that were to become the guideposts for our city's future.

By the time I was elected, we had more than a campaign victory. We had a strong consensus on our direction and a mandate to make St. Petersburg the best city in America by executing four easy-to-explain, specific strategies. During the next nine years we would research, adopt, and refine programs that advanced these strategies, and we would constantly measure our progress, communicating the results to the people we served. We would also add a fifth strategy, *improving government operations*, which is at the core of providing good service to our community.

(4) Unite around the Effort— Build a Seamless City

There can be no boundaries limiting the scope of the effort, whether geographic, racial, economic, education level, ethnic, or other. Everyone and every aspect of the city must be part of the effort and part of its success. Resentment will build if any part of the city is left behind, and the effort will collapse because it is imbalanced. Of course, the most underdeveloped parts of the city are especially in need of improvement; however, positive change can and must be experienced by every region in the community, and the goal must be to make the city *seamless*!

In a seamless city, when you go from one part of town to another, you never cross a seam—whether a street, interstate overpass, or railroad track—and enter a place where you feel the need to reach over and lock your car door: an area with boarded-up buildings, broken windows, and large tracts of urban blight, with drug dealers on the street corners.

All parts of the city are not the same, and that will always be true. Some areas have large houses and big lots, while others may have duplexes and apartments, but all parts of a seamless city should have certain things in common. They should be safe and clean and should have the services, retail, and public infrastructure that adequately accommodate the people who live there.

The creation of a seamless city requires an attitude that we are all in it together. It means that we do not pit one area against the other, but work to advance the entire city by addressing the needs of all the parts. On the west side of our city, it meant building a library, recreation center, and pier on Boca Ciega Bay, to prove that the government had not forgotten the residents of that area. In the north, a new public pool, recreation center, and an expanded nature center were added. In our most economically depressed area, now known as Midtown, we had to make an unprecedented effort to reverse decades of decline and create a new level of vibrancy, services, and hope. A seamless city connects everyone with bike paths, and encourages the community to gather together at dog parks and playgrounds.

If you seek a seamless city, you must look for ways to help the homeless turn their lives around while not allowing them to adversely impact others. You create a downtown that becomes the gathering place for all who live here. You work with neighborhood leaders throughout the city so that the residents define and help execute their own ideas for progress. You also understand that public schools are not islands to be left drifting on their own, but are vital to the city's success and should be supported by everyone.

Finally, in a seamless city it is not acceptable to have places that are crime-ridden and blighted. All our children should grow up in neighborhoods that are safe and clean, that have libraries, parks, athletic fields, banks, shopping centers, and grocery stores, where every boy and girl can share in the pride and success of the entire city.

(5) Work toward Accomplishing the Plan

A city is a complex organism with interdependent parts. Each part requires a unique focus, but the multiple efforts must be viewed as a collective enterprise. Developing strategies for reaching the city's goals requires a deep understanding of the city's history and a grasp of its present diverse interests. It also requires buy-in from the community.

Shortly after taking office in 2001, we invited residents throughout the city to a process called "Vision 2020," where we collectively identified the qualities of the city we wanted to become in twenty years. The resulting plan was woven together by the projects that would be tackled. We avoided mushy, "feel-good" programs (programs that are politically attractive, but are ineffective and can even harm the very people they are supposed to help) and focused on strategies that made common sense and could project a path that would lead to success in addressing the needs of the whole community.

Because every city is different, priorities will vary, but the five areas of concentration that we adopted will be among the core priorities of any successful city:

(1) Improving public safety
(2) Promoting economic development
(3) Supporting public schools
(4) Building strong neighborhoods
(5) Improving government operations

The five goals are interconnected and must fit together like puzzle pieces if the city is to reach its potential. The public schools must be strong for the sake of the students, and this in turn will encourage people to move into the city's neighborhoods and bring businesses to the city. The community must be safe if neighborhoods and businesses are to thrive. Taxes cannot be too high, and government services like water, sewer, and sanitation must be reasonably priced, dependable, and high quality. We need jobs so that people can live in the neighborhoods and the tax base can support the public safety needs. Advancing each of these goals must be the constant focus of the city's leadership.

(6) Measure Progress toward Success

There is no better reflection of a city's priorities than its metrics, which are collected and communicated to the public. What matters gets measured! The performance measures should be tied to the city's goals and strategies. They should be communicated to the people being served in a clear, timely, and honest manner. If you are serious about accomplishing something, you must measure whether or not you succeed. It is a simple concept that is often overlooked in public life.

(7) Keep Getting Better

No matter how successful an effort, it is never complete. If the city's performance measures are honest and published for the public to review, they will reveal the effort's shortcomings as well as its successes. Progress can be determined, and adjustments can be made in policy and programs in order to continuously get better. The best programs can always be improved, and everyone involved must be constantly challenged to find new ways to enhance the quality of life for the people who live in the city.

Chapter 4

Public Safety
Is Job No. 1

When a sparrow dies in Central Park, I feel responsible.

—Fiorello La Guardia

Mayor, New York City 1934–1945

I t was a Tuesday morning, and it began with the familiar routine. Early in my term I often started my work day before 6:00 a.m., in an effort to learn all I could about how to run the city. I love mornings. There is something renewing about the sun coming up over the bay as I take my run through North Shore Park. Each morning is a brand new opportunity, a fresh chance to start again, to finish what we didn't get done yesterday and to set new goals for tomorrow. I drive my wife and daughter—who are not morning people—crazy as I hop out of bed, singing enthusiastically while getting ready for the day. (On the other hand, by 10:00 at night I am beginning to melt while my wife and daughter are just warming up!)

Since this particular morning was a Tuesday, I had a City Hall Cabinet meeting at 7:30 a.m. The Cabinet consisted of the police chief, fire chief, first deputy mayor for administration, deputy mayor for neighborhoods, deputy mayor for Midtown, internal services administrator (water, sanitation, finance, storm water), development services senior administrator (facilities, economic development, permitting), school programs administrator, general counsel, city services administrator (parks and recreation), and the information systems administrator. Later in my term we would also invite the marketing and communications director to the Cabinet meetings.

I tried to keep the Cabinet meetings informal. We went around the table having each member give an update on pressing issues in their departments. One job of the deputy mayor for neighborhoods was to provide a survey of the phone calls, emails, and online complaints or comments coming into the city. I often opened up the meeting for a general discussion when a major decision was needed, or when we were considering a new initiative. The Cabinet meetings were held on the second floor of City Hall. After the Cabinet meeting on that particular Tuesday, we reconvened downstairs with the directors of many of the city's departments to review the upcoming City Council agenda.

As directors calmly reviewed various agenda items that day, our fire chief rushed excitedly into the room. He told us an airplane had flown into the World Trade Center in New York, and turned on the television that was mounted high in one corner of the large room to show us the footage.

The scene on television was total chaos as reporters speculated on whether or not the airplane crash was an accident. As we watched in amazement and horror, another plane struck the second tower. I rushed to my office where I was joined by Herb Polson, our government relations director, along with a visitor from Orlando. We were supposed to be talking about a high speed rail connector to St. Petersburg, but the news from New York changed everything, including our focus for that day. We watched the scene unfold on my office television. Another plane struck the Pentagon. A fourth plane crashed in Pennsylvania. The president left Sarasota for an undisclosed location, and speculation was rampant about other possible targets.

It was September 11, 2001, and our country was at war. We didn't know who the enemy was and we didn't know who would be attacked next, or the method of terror that would be used. The events continued to play out—people jumped to their deaths from the towers; the Pentagon was on fire; the twin towers crumbled one at a time. The television screen showed pictures of the air control screen for the nation, eventually showing no aircraft over America. I felt a cold chill in my body.

America's cities were under attack from an unknown enemy. Because of the magnitude and urgency of the crisis, there would be no advice or help coming from Washington in the near future. And I was responsible for the safety of hundreds of thousands of people. What should our response be? How could I protect our city?

Just as defending our country is the national government's most important role, the first job of any city and its mayor is public safety. Protecting the city took on new prominence after September 11, because our police, fire, and emergency medical personnel became first responders in a global war against terror.

In the days following the attacks, our city established a homeland security task force, updated our emergency plan to cover terrorism, and evaluated the hardening of facilities in the city. We took measures to strengthen the safety of potential targets, increase security, and react to the evolving threat.

We responded to an anthrax scare following national reports that envelopes sent to *NBC News* and the *New York Times* had St. Petersburg post marks and contained powder. Our emergency response and hazardous materials teams were inundated by concerned callers with suspicious packages.

We also worked with state and federal authorities to provide a coordinated approach to homeland security. Weeks after the attack, I flew to Washington, D.C., landing one night at an empty Ronald Reagan National Airport, which had just been reopened for the first time since September 11. The purpose of the Washington trip was to meet with federal authorities and other mayors around America to discuss ideas to protect our communities. Homeland Security became a new part of our vocabulary and an addition to the city's core responsibility of public safety. Our nation's cities contained many vulnerable targets, and we needed to make efforts to strengthen their protection, although many would still be exposed. Anyone responsible for the safety of a city understood that, if we were to avoid another September 11, the national government needed to improve intelligence gathering and go after our enemies wherever they were.

Public safety is not only the primary job of a city government—it is also the most difficult one. Whether the issue is one of national defense, as we dealt with after the September 11 attacks, or fighting crime in our city's neighborhoods, the city government is responsible for keeping the people within the community safe. No matter how low your crime rate, if it is over zero, then someone has been the victim of a crime. To that person, the crime rate is 100 percent. As described below, our violent crime rate and homicide levels dropped considerably between 2001 and 2009; but that is not good enough for the family member or loved one of a 2009 victim. One violent crime, one murder, is too many!

If someone hears an intruder stalking outside, or their house is on fire, or their loved one has suffered a heart attack, then they aren't thinking about the water service or the park system, or even their tax rates. They are counting on their city to save lives and protect property. This is a serious responsibility. The occurrence of crime, medical emergencies, and fire have such a profound impact on both the individual and the city that there is tremendous pressure to constantly adjust to the evolving issues and to keep the community safe. The pressure is appropriate because city officials and public safety officers, no matter how good they are, should constantly be reminded that people's lives are in their care.

● ● ●

August 6, 2009, was scheduled to be another busy day for me, starting out with an early meeting to discuss a developing opportunity to bring a Chihuly Collection, with remarkable glass art, to downtown St. Petersburg. Following the meeting, I went to the opening of the City Council meeting, but I had to leave a little before 9:00 a.m. for my speech at the downtown Hampton Inn about our Green St. Petersburg environmental programs. I then returned to City Council to speak on an agenda item before leaving again, this time for the Mud Wars.

The Mud Wars occur each year at the end of the summer. Young adults and teens from our recreation department, part of our great TASCO group, bring truckloads of mud to Spa Beach Park downtown and create a venue for several competitions involving teens from recreation centers throughout the city. We have mud football, tug-of-war in the mud, mud dodge ball, jousting over a mud pit, and other challenges. The highlight of the event is a mud obstacle course complete with a slide, climbing wall, rope barriers, pipes to crawl through, and tires to run in—all in mud that can pull your shoes off if you don't use duct tape to keep them on. Each year I was in office, I chose a team of teens and we competed against a team chosen by one of our recreation center leaders. I participated in the event every year for nine years.

I should have stopped after the eighth year.

Before leaving City Hall that 2009 day, I changed into shorts and an old t-shirt. Generally, whatever I wore to the Mud Wars had to be thrown out after the event. I chose my team, including my son Jacob and his friend Shane, and went to the starting position at the top of the slide. After the whistle blew to start, I raced down the slide into a mud pit. I stood up to begin the run, but I slipped, catching myself with my hands as I fell into a barrier. I knew right away that I had hurt my right hand, but I didn't want to let the team down, so I continued through the course, lifting myself over the ropes and walls with my left hand. Although my performance was terrible, the rest of my team was quick enough that we won the race.

After the victory picture I got some ice for my hand and drove home so I could shower before going to the hospital for X-rays. By 6:00 a.m. the next day, Friday, I would be at St. Anthony's Hospital preparing for surgery on a broken hand, requiring a plate and seven screws to become a permanent part of my body; but while driving home from the Mud Wars, I still hoped that the injury would heal with some ice. I walked up to my house, covered in mud, wearing my shorts, t-shirt, and gym shoes. My right hand was swollen and throbbing. Unfortunately, the challenges of that particular day were just beginning.

As I approached the side door of my home I tried to put my key into the lock using my left hand, which was a little cumbersome. As I struggled, I noticed that something was wrong. A panel in the door had been kicked in, the window next to the door was open, and I heard someone in the house. My family was still at the Mud Wars, so I knew they were safe, but it was clear that burglars were in my house. I backed away from the door and tried to think quickly through my next step.

I didn't know if the crooks in my house were armed, and they had probably heard me messing with the door lock. Having been in my current job for over eight years, I also knew that the day would soon become a media circus amid reports of the mayor's house being broken into. I realized that the only good ending to this story would be to catch these guys.

My first instinct was to get them out of my house, so I hit the emergency key for my car that set off the car alarm. I then looked around for the burglars' getaway car, which I found in the alley behind my house. I quickly memorized the license number and car description and went down the alley to look for a neighbor at home so I could call the police. (Since I was still in shorts and a t-shirt covered with mud I didn't have my cell phone on me.) Hearing the alarm, the thieves rushed out the back of my house and over the fence, with my television in tow, and took off in their car.

By the end of the day the police tracked the license number to the car used in the break-in, and had the thieves in custody. Thirty minutes after the break-in, the street in front of my home was filled with television trucks from every regional network, broadcasting the news. The police had arrived a few minutes after I called, and I went upstairs to shower.

I was anticipating the media onslaught. By the time I finished changing clothes, the television stations began to arrive, so I walked across the street for interviews. As I stood in front of my home being interviewed by several stations, trying to ignore a broken hand that had become very swollen and sore, each of the reporters asked if I was angry.

My answer surprised them, and it made me realize something that I had not completely thought through before. I confirmed that I was angry and outraged, but no angrier than I was any time anyone in our city has their home broken into. Whether it is the mayor's house or anyone else's home, the intrusion and personal invasion is an outrage in all cases!

When I took office, I developed an ongoing sense of anger and outrage for everyone in my city who became a victim. New York Mayor La Guardia once summarized the feeling: *When a sparrow dies in Central Park, I feel responsible.* It is difficult to understand the depth of this statement unless you have served as a mayor or police chief of a major city.

When someone sprays bullets down a neighborhood street or conducts a spree of break-ins in people's homes, those responsible for the public safety of the city feel it personally. In our city, I was called by our police chief each time there was a murder; that is a call you never get used to.

The feeling of responsibility described by Mayor La Guardia extends to every criminal act, and it produces a passion to work constantly to make the city safer. It is the city's first and most important mission. Like all other efforts of the city, public safety success does not come as the result of luck or timing. Those responsible must have a plan—an approach to crime that includes both effective law enforcement and attention to the community efforts that reduce the likelihood of criminal activity.

The Approach to Crime

The fire, natural disaster, and emergency medical functions of a city are all critical, but there is no area of city responsibility that evokes more emotion and community focus than the city's role of protecting people from crimes. Becoming a victim is a life-changing event, as anyone who has been victimized knows. For the mayor, reducing crime rates is not enough. Until crime rates are zero, a city must continually be looking to steer people away from a criminal life and provide certainty and severity in punishment for those who choose crime.

Volumes have been written on making cities safer, and I will not attempt to repeat them here. However, I do believe that there are certain principles for successful efforts:

(1) Maintain an adequately sized, well-equipped, well-trained police force with excellent investigative and administrative functions.

(2) Maintain close communication with neighborhood groups, crime watch, and other community organizations in order to gain information on activity and encourage confidence in the effort. An important part of this element is encouraging citizens to testify as witnesses when crimes do occur.

(3) Constantly evaluate the success of the effort through statistics and community feedback, providing accountability for those involved and adjusting tactics and deployment to address evolving challenges.

(4) Develop targeted programs focused on speeding, drugs, prostitution, and violent crime.

(5) Work to steer young people, especially young men, away from a criminal life through mentoring, public school support, athletics, city recreation, and other programs.

(6) Change the environment of the poorest areas of the city to create an atmosphere where the community takes pride in itself and does not tolerate activity that promotes crime.

With respect to the fifth principle, we worked with young people through our recreational, educational, and athletic programs (discussed in chapters 8 and 9). Advancing the sixth principle, we made great progress in turning around the environment of our poorest areas (as outlined in chapter 7). The importance of these programs in making the city safer cannot be overstated. The law enforcement effort and the work to change the conditions and prosperity of our residents go hand in hand. With respect to the first four principles described above, we took steps to increase staffing, team up with our neighborhoods, instill accountability into the process, and attack the drug trade.

(1) Maintain A Well-Equipped Force

While police work is important everywhere, it is especially critical in our major urban centers where some of the nation's difficult public safety challenges manifest themselves the most. A well-equipped force is important both for the protection of the community and for the safety of the police officers on the job. To advance that effort, our police chief Chuck Harmon established a recruitment and retention task force, which included officers among the members, to identify issues important to ensuring that we met our staffing requirements. We reviewed compensation and benefits, and we analyzed policies related to hiring. We discovered that we were in a small minority of departments requiring two years of college with no exceptions, a fact that hindered our recruitment effort. Many departments required no college, or a lesser amount, while some had the two-year requirement but allowed exceptions for applicants with military or prior police experience. We wanted to maintain our high standards, so we continued to require two years of college, but we opted for the military and police experience exception. We left it up to the department's hiring personnel to determine if the alternative experience provided the background we wanted.

Over the years, we also increased compensation and benefits for our police officers in an effort to become more competitive with other jurisdictions. These public safety increases accounted for a large percentage of our general fund budget growth during my first term, but we felt it was necessary. We had unacceptably high attrition rates, and nearby departments paying more were regularly hiring away our officers.

One of our less tangible efforts was outreach. I held meetings in my office for officers representing the nine police sectors in the city. Each meeting included ten to fifteen officers from the particular sector to talk about public safety and other issues in our city, and ideas on how to move the department forward. I attended the swearing in ceremonies for new officers at the court house with the chief judge, police chief, and new officers, along with their families. The events became celebrations. Family members lined up to take pictures of the young officers, along with the presiding officials.

Over time our efforts paid off. Our attrition numbers went down and staffing levels went up. By July 2009 our department's actual level of employed uniformed police exceeded the full 540 authorized strength level, the highest level of police staffing in the city's history.

Another part of having a well-equipped force is making sure that we are taking full advantage of technology. We engaged in a major effort to provide our dispatchers and officers on the street with the latest technology at their fingertips so they could do their job better and more safely. We expanded the direct in-patrol car access to databases through wireless, using current technology and advanced computer-aided dispatch/records software. The result was efficient dispatch and the availability of file and criminal records for the officer to retrieve while sitting in his or her cruiser.

(2) Working with Our Neighbors

The most effective way to ensure that crime problems within neighborhoods are addressed properly is with a community policing strategy that ensures neighborhood and crime watch leaders have quick and direct access to officers who are familiar with their neighborhood. The program must also have a system of accountability in place so the senior management at the police department can monitor whether or not the community officers are responding quickly to emergencies.

In the 1990s, St. Petersburg had a system in which our community police officers acted like independent contractors within the neighborhoods they represented. It worked well as long as the officer was self-motivated, but we had problems in many areas where neighborhood leaders complained that their officers were non-responsive. So we evolved to a team-based system, with requests and concerns being documented and channeled through a reporting system before being assigned. The overall police effort became more responsive, and the neighborhoods saw the results. Our senior police management had the ability to evaluate the responses by our community officers, and the community policing effort was integrated into the entire department.

In addition to the overall community policing effort, we constantly challenged ourselves to work more closely with our neighborhood leaders in the goal of making the city safer. One example was "CAPE," Community and Police Engagement, where our officers knocked on every door in targeted neighborhoods, talking to residents about public safety on their block. The result was better communication, more information on criminal activity, and a sharp reduction in violent crimes within the surveyed areas. Another example was allowing people, especially teens, to use their cell phones to send text messages of crime reports and other communications to our police department.

In the effort to team up with the neighborhoods on the law enforcement effort, we worked to expand and support neighborhood associations, crime watches, and business groups throughout the city. We followed through with back-up support. Neighborhood plans, developed by the local associations in conjunction with city staff, included action items to reduce speeding and enhance safety.

The neighborhood associations and crime watch groups in our city were our partners. We regularly held breakfast meetings in my office with five to ten neighborhood presidents to talk about their neighborhoods' problems and opportunities. City staff attended the meetings with me in order to ensure turnaround of identified issues. Police personnel would attend often as well, especially when public safety issues had been identified. Community police and code enforcement personnel attended neighborhood meetings throughout the city, and the police chief had regular gatherings in different regions to give an update and respond to input.

(3) Responsiveness—Accountability

No matter how effective the law enforcement effort, there will be times when a series of criminal acts come in rapid order, and the law enforcement effort and City Hall need to be nimble in responding. This is true whether the trend is an increase in taxi hold-ups or auto thefts. The police must be prepared to spot the trend and respond quickly. Even an uptick in graffiti instances must be addressed right away, for if unchecked, the activity broadcasts a tolerance for behavior that can lead to other crimes.

After a series of convenience store robberies in 2009, police officers met with store owners to provide tips on safety, and City Council passed an ordinance requiring various safety measures within the stores. The new requirements included a prohibition against putting signs on windows that blocked the view of the cashier area, and a requirement that electronic locks be installed in stores open after 11:00 p.m., so patrons had to be allowed in by the clerk.

Some small businesses raised concerns about the cost of electronic door locks, so our police department set up a grants program for the locks. The grants were funded with money that had been seized by the police department during arrests—from arrestees who used the cash in the course of criminal activity, often drug sales. Solid investigative and surveillance police work were the core responses to the convenience store robberies, but the efforts to increase the security of the properties combined to make the community and the store clerks safer.

Factors beyond the police department's direct control can affect the public safety effort, such as incidents when the state's court and prison systems return arrested people to the street without rehabilitation or much (if any) time served. Financial trends also have an impact. St. Petersburg experienced its share of the national recession that began in 2008, and unemployment rates rose locally as they rose nationally.

Simultaneously we experienced a sharp increase in property crime, which drove up the overall crime rate in 2009. Even when crime events are influenced by uncontrollable factors, it is important to take proactive steps to stem the tide. In 2009, police responded to the property crime uptick by increasing the number of burglary detectives, increasing the size of the special investigation unit, distributing information on steps the public could take to avoid becoming victims, developing strategies in response to break-ins at vacant properties (whose numbers had increased due to the increase in foreclosures), and increasing the attention given to recycling companies and pawn shops which sometimes purchase stolen items.

One response to the property crime spike began in December 2009. Our police department identified forty youths suspected of being responsible for many of the auto thefts and other property crimes in the city at the time. A detective and a crime analyst were assigned to keep tabs on the youths, many of whom were repeat offenders. The detectives introduced themselves to the youths' families; they had school resource officers notify them if the youths were absent from school; and they were informed if any of the youths were arrested. The police officials tracked down the youths who didn't go to school, went with them to court dates, and checked their homes at night to see if they were violating court-ordered curfews.

The program was not voluntary, and the youth knew they were being watched. At the end of eighteen weeks, auto thefts went down by 37 percent. Within six months, property crimes fell by 14 percent. With the strong support of my successor, Mayor Bill Foster, the police chief expanded the program in 2010 to include more youth.

Like every other department in the city, it is important to keep track of the success of our efforts to make the community safer. Crime and arrest statistics are the best indicator of progress, and we tracked them on our web-based City Scorecard. It is important to ensure that the information presented for the crime statistics reports is accurate and consistent, as there can be variations in interpretation on how statistics should be kept, and thus differences among jurisdictions about whether a particular event constitutes a crime. As an example, if ten cars are broken into at a football game, one jurisdiction may treat all ten break-ins as one crime, while another may report the incident as ten crimes. Because the most important indicator of progress is the comparison of a city's current crime rates to its past rates, the methodology for keeping the statistics must be consistent in order to be relevant.

(4) Targeted Programs

Speeding

Among the crime issues most commonly raised at a crime watch neighborhood meeting, depending on your location in the city, are speeding, drugs, and prostitution, with speeding the most widespread issue. One approach to speeding—often suggested by frustrated neighborhood leaders—is to put a police car at every intersection in the city and give out tickets. Obviously this is an impractical solution in a city with thousands of intersections. Although we deployed speed traps and wrote tickets, we also worked with neighborhoods to develop plans to modify roads in such a way as to increase speed limit compliance by drivers, an approach known as "traffic calming" in city planning circles.

Traffic calming started in our city in the 1990s, beginning with the addition of more stop signs, an approach that had limited impact. In fact, it annoyed most people and increased incidents of people running stop signs. Alternatives were introduced, such as speed bumps and intersection "plateaus," although these also can annoy the driving public a great deal if not done correctly. Traffic circles are often suggested and are sometimes good solutions, but they tend to look better on paper than they are in practice. I found that narrowing roads through landscaped medians and "neck-outs" from the curb are often the most effective method of slowing traffic while having a low level of disruption for drivers. They have an added benefit of street beautification.

Traffic calming can be controversial. People do not like slowing down or driving over bumps in the road. Our approach was to work through neighborhood associations in an effort to develop a consensus where possible, and hold public meetings to get broad input before moving forward. We avoided traffic calming on major corridors except for landscaped medians. Generally, traffic calming has been an effective tool in slowing people down and making the neighborhood roads safer for our children and everyone else. While it is hard to directly quantify the impacts of our traffic calming and other road safety efforts, we know that the number of traffic accident investigations decreased by almost 12 percent from 2001 through 2009, as reflected in the City Scorecard.

Drugs

One morning, I left my house at about 3:00 a.m. to head to the Coliseum, our large historic dance hall downtown. Our police department had been working for months with the Drug Enforcement Agency (DEA) and Alcohol, Tobacco and Firearms (ATF) in advance of the arrests that were about to take place. As I walked into the Coliseum, the scene resembled an army about to embark on an invasion. About 300 law enforcement personnel, the largest number being our police department, were going through pictures of suspects, confirming the timing sequences of the raids, and checking their weapons and body armor. Hours of surveillance and undercover work had produced warrants for individuals suspected of providing much of the crack cocaine in our city.

I had been asked to talk to the group before they began their operation. As I looked over the personnel, all dressed in full protective gear, I was struck by the significance of the moment. I assured them that there was no more important job in America than the one they were doing that morning. The poison of drugs in any city takes lives, tears apart communities, and destroys the future for children. Their efforts would provide hope to law-abiding people who feel trapped in their own neighborhoods. I thanked them for their service and wished them a successful morning. After I finished, I worked my way to the back of the room. I leaned against the wall and silently prayed for protection for the officers who would be protecting us all that day.

As the morning progressed, the combined forces raided homes, made twenty-one arrests, and confiscated large quantities of firearms and drugs. I drove along on one of the raids. Once the police entered the house, there were some tense moments until the police flushed the suspects out. I watched as our officers led handcuffed prisoners out of the house and stacked up an extensive pile of seized weapons in the yard by the home. They also seized quantities of crack cocaine and other illegal drugs.

We loaded up into the police van after the raid to head back to the command center. As we pulled onto the road I saw something that left a significant impact on me. Two blocks away from the house where the raid took place, a young mother was walking her elementary school-aged children to the bus stop. The children were carrying their books and supplies, while their mother shepherded them to keep them out of the street.

It was like a scene from a Norman Rockwell painting, a simple activity that could take place anywhere in our city or in America—but the scene was not occurring just anywhere. It was two blocks from a house which, until this morning, had been filled with illegal drugs and a stockpile of firearms. No child in St. Petersburg or in America should have to live in that environment. We have a moral responsibility to work aggressively to rid our communities of the poison of illegal drugs, as well as the violent cloud that surrounds them.

Over the following years, we developed an expanded focus on drug arrests, consolidating efforts into a Street Crimes Unit and then expanding both that unit and our undercover Special Investigation Unit. I personally visited the regional U.S. Drug Enforcement Agency officials to express my commitment and desire to work with the DEA, ATF, and other agencies to aggressively pursue the drug trade.

Through these combined efforts, our department increased the number of annual drug arrests by 50 percent—over 1,000 additional arrests each year—but we didn't eliminate the problem. City leaders must combine an aggressive effort at drug arrests with programs providing alternatives for our kids who are exposed to drugs if we are to succeed. And we have to acknowledge that we cannot arrest our way out of all crime problems. We must also strike at the underlying causes, by addressing the education, employment, mentoring, and other youth-oriented efforts described throughout this book.

Prostitution

Historically, in neighborhoods along certain commercial corridor sections of St. Petersburg, prostitution was a persistent problem. While complaints remain, we experienced a significant reduction in reported instances, largely due to a combination of factors: the good work of our Police Street Crimes Unit described above; the tenacity of neighborhood and business leaders along the corridors; and the success of our economic redevelopment attempts in the areas prostitutes previously frequented—such as run-down motels converted to alternative uses.

Another effort that helped us make progress was the move to provide drug rehabilitation services to female offenders. Police officers regularly tell me that virtually all prostitutes are supporting a drug habit, and prostitution arrests are a revolving door when jails are overcrowded with violent offenders. If we could address drug addiction and lack of job prospects as underlying contributors to the prostitution activity, then we might make better progress. The alternative is to continue the frustrating process of arresting people today who will wind up back on the street tomorrow.

Drug Rehabilitation

My first scheduled appointment as mayor was with Watson Haynes, an old friend who had come to solicit support for the Davis Bradley center, a building which was intended to be a drug rehabilitation facility in Midtown. The group that was putting the project together had obtained the building but had not obtained the funds for renovation or operations of the center. During my campaign, I had come to believe in the need for additional drug rehabilitation services in the city. We envisioned a residential program where nonviolent drug offenders would be placed in drug rehabilitation and job training instead of jail. The idea, which is not a new one, is to try to get them straightened out and productive before they proceed down a more dangerous criminal path. In addition to the criminal justice component, the center was also hoping to obtain funding that would permit non-offenders to obtain drug rehabilitation services.

On my second day in office, I flew to Tallahassee to obtain state funding for the Midtown drug rehabilitation facility. After several meetings with Governor Jeb Bush and others, along with follow-up efforts in the coming weeks, we were able to get the funding to have the center opened by the private company designated to operate the facility. Its initial funding was to support seventy-five residential beds for men only, and the services would be for drug rehabilitation along with job training and placement.

During the following years, we worked to expand Davis Bradley funding to include a residential component for female offenders. This effort was related primarily to prostitution. We believed that it would be extremely difficult to stop women from engaging in prostitution when they are supporting drug habits. We needed a mechanism to help them break the cycle by getting them off drugs and into a job where they could support themselves. After many failed attempts, we finally obtained state funding and opened twenty-five beds for female offenders. I attended and spoke at a graduation of the six-month program, and had the chance to speak to a number of the graduates. The courage and grit it takes to rise out of the prostitution lifestyle is remarkable, but the drug treatment and job training approach had a meaningful impact on the lives of the women who chose to change, and it reduced the number of prostitutes on our streets.

Guns Used Illegally

Early one April morning in 2009, on the Sunday of the Honda Grand Prix of St. Petersburg, I received a call from Police Chief Harmon. It was very bad news. A dispute in a Midtown neighborhood had turned deadly. A group of young men in a car had stopped in front of a house and shot fifty rounds from a semi-automatic weapon into the building, targeting another young man who lived in the house. An eight-year-old girl named Paris was in bed when the firing began. She tried to run from her room in fear, but was struck dead by three bullets as she ran. It was a ruthless attack by cowards, and the community reacted with appropriate outrage.

There is an unwritten code against "snitching" in many of America's communities, which protects those who deal in drugs and commit violent criminal acts. But Paris' murder brought about a call from throughout the neighborhoods to turn in those who do us all harm. Four hundred people joined us for a march and rally led by the NAACP and Southern Christian Leadership Conference in opposition to violence. There was a general call for young and old alike to turn in the thugs in our city who harm people with guns and drugs.

At the rally, we announced a Gun Bounty program: a $1,000 reward for those who provided information that resulted in an arrest, recovered a gun, and led to a weapons charge. If the charge involved an assault weapon, the reward was $1,500. The informer could remain anonymous. The money for the rewards would come from the police seizure fund, and from private contributors. I was able to raise over $50,000 in private money commitments on the first day. The program was administered through a non-profit group called Crime Stoppers.

The only chance for any city to significantly reduce violent crime is for the people who live in the neighborhoods to decide that they have had enough and are willing to stand up to the criminals. Our Gun Bounty poster read: "It's the right thing to do for your family, neighborhood and community." Within a couple weeks we made our first arrests from a Gun Bounty tip, and we seized firearms and a large quantity of cocaine. We would also make arrests in Paris's murder. As of this printing, one suspect had confessed and the others were awaiting trial.

We continued to receive tips and information as the program progressed. Although our program focused only on illegal guns and guns used illegally, I received some pretty harsh comments from a few people who felt it was an attack on gun ownership. One out-of-state email called me a tyrant and threatened: "I hope you die in a hail of gun fire." Fortunately, the large portion of our community understood that the program focused only on the *illegal* use of guns, and we received widespread support for the effort.

● ● ●

The combined efforts of the men and women who serve in our police department and our neighborhood, business, community, and city leaders have made St. Petersburg a safer city. Crime rates for 2008 were at the lowest level in thirty years. In Midtown, an area with historically high crime rates, total crime was reduced by 12 percent, and violent crime was reduced by 23 percent. For the 2009 FBI statistic year, violent crime rates continued to fall, while property crime rates increased following the dramatic increase in national, state, and county unemployment rates. As discussed above, the police department's response to the property crime increase brought measurable results within six months.

The homicide rate for 2009 was the lowest level for which the city has uniform crime data (at least thirty-eight years), and was a reduction of almost 50 percent from the 2001 level.

During the same period, from 2001 to 2009, the number of arrests for all crimes committed increased by 43 percent (11,525 to 16,543); and the number of arrests for drug-related offenses increased by over 60 percent (from 1,924 to 3,150).

Response times for police calls improved considerably from 2002 (when we started tracking the number) through the end of 2009. Priority 1 response times (the most serious calls) decreased by 22 percent, from 7.2 minutes to 5.6 minutes. Priority 2 and 3 response times showed similar reductions. From 2001 to 2009, the number of citizen complaints against police department personnel decreased by over 50 percent (from 122 to 60).

Despite the great progress made, the job was not done. As long as there is one victim of crime in the city, leaders must continually look for ways to change the path of those who are heading toward a criminal life and punish those who choose to commit crimes.

Fire and Rescue

I like to start the day early, but I still need a fair amount of sleep, so I usually try to get to bed by ten. One Wednesday night in March 2007, at around eleven after I was already in bed, the phone rang.

Typically in a mayor's house, if the phone rings after 9:00 p.m. it's not good news. No one calls at 2:00 a.m. to report that a new business is coming to town or that we got the major federal grant we wanted. It might be that a hurricane has turned our way, or a significant violent crime has taken place or, worse, that a police officer or firefighter has been injured on duty. As I got up and approached the phone that night, a familiar voice inside my head told me that I should just let it ring.

The caller ID flashed the number of the fire chief.

Fire chiefs and police chiefs, if they're good, always remain calm (at least on the outside) when something big is happening. Fortunately, our Police Chief Chuck Harmon and our Fire Chief Jim Large both fit into that category. That Wednesday night, in a very level voice, Chief Large advised me that a tanker truck had overturned on I-375, one of the prime interstate feeders coming into downtown, causing a major fire. He didn't have many details and was on his way to the scene. He didn't bother to ask if I was going to come—we'd worked together for some time by this point, and he knew I'd be there. He just recommended the best place to try to park.

Within five minutes, I had let Joyce know what was happening, put some jeans on, warmed up instant coffee in the microwave, and was in my car heading downtown. I was still several blocks away when I saw smoke rising and the glow of the flames on the northwest corner of our urban center. The tanker truck had overturned on an interstate exit ramp into downtown. The ramp, several stories high, was directly above one of our storage areas for city heavy equipment, and next to our water department headquarters buildings, labs, and other facilities.

The scene was still in the chaos phase of the crisis as I approached. Police had arrived to close down the interstate overpass that was engulfed in flames, several stories above us. The fuel from the truck (which we later learned was diesel), had spilled from the interstate into the equipment yard, and several items of heavy equipment were also on fire. Fuel from the truck had also flowed into the interstate's storm water drainage system that runs through the overpass support structures, feeding directly into our underground storm water sewer pipes, causing fires underground.

As I toured the facility with the fire chief, we heard underground explosions every few seconds. Vibrations from the blasts underneath our feet were a constant reminder of the danger. It had the feel of a combat zone as our fire leadership set up two command posts. One was on the overpass to deal with the tanker fire, and the other was on the ground to handle the equipment yard and underground fires. The multi-level fire also had multiple layers of risk to the community. As the fire and fuel flowed along the interstate, into the downtown, and through the sewer system, there were risks of injury to people and an expanded zone of damage. Containing the damage, putting out the fire, avoiding injury to the public and emergency personnel, and preventing the flow of the fuel through the storm water system and into the bay, were all priorities.

After surveying the scene, I called Mike Connors, our administrator over the storm water system, to let him know about the situation. Mike sprang to action when I called, contacting his staff and driving to the fire. After reviewing the underground maps of the drainage system, our team directed firefighters to pump fire-containing foam into manholes upstream from the underground fires. We had storm water crews put flotation booms downstream to keep fuel from floating into other parts of the city, and eventually into Tampa Bay.

Our fire, police, hazardous materials, storm water, and other teams worked in great coordination handling the event, which was managed from a make-shift emergency operations center we established in a water department meeting room. The fire was controlled and extinguished. Our group did well in containing the damage, which was extensive. Among other needed repairs in the area of the fire, the elevated interstate feeder had to be replaced.

Early in the morning, we held a makeshift press conference a couple blocks from the fire, giving a factual update, assuring the community that the event was contained, and giving instructions on traffic in the downtown area. We also expressed condolences for the loved ones of the tanker driver who died. We had not yet identified the driver, the truck company, or the type of fuel on board. It had been a long night, but the good work of our first responders contained the disaster and helped us avoid more extensive damage.

Hurricanes

The effort to contain the tanker fire was an example of the moments of quick response that are made possible by the hours of preparation that go into the public safety enterprise. It is important when a fire is blazing or a heart attack victim is waiting for emergency medical services to arrive. In St. Petersburg, it is especially important when our most significant natural disaster threat is driving up Florida's Gulf Coast.

In 2004, Hurricane Charley was moving north with a storm track projected to make a direct hit on St. Petersburg. It was the beginning of two years of storms that would mark the most intensive hurricane period in Florida's history. On Thursday, August 12, over 380,000 of our county's residents were ordered to evacuate their homes. It was the largest evacuation in our history. By early Friday morning, August 13, our main emergency operations center (EOC) in the city was fully activated. We had our reserve fuel tanks filled and our generators on standby. Storm water and parks crews had swept the low areas picking up debris that could block drainage. Sanitation trucks picked up trash until the latest time possible in an effort to keep bits of garbage from becoming missiles during the storm. Parks crews with front-end loaders were assigned to fire stations so they could be prepared to clear the roads for emergency vehicles after the storm.

Hundreds of tasks within the emergency operations manuals were completed and checked off. Our police, fire, water, storm water, roads, and other emergency operation sub-centers were also activated. As an example, when the electricity goes out, our water crews need to get the generators running for the pumps that keep the water coming to our homes, and the pumps that keep the lift stations moving sewer flow away from homes.

We were fully activated. We even had an omen to confirm that we were in trouble. Hurricane Charley was projected to hit us on Friday the 13th, which was also the birthday of our emergency operations director. His name was Charley, the same name as the major hurricane that the weather stations predicted would directly strike us in the afternoon.

Friday morning, a few hours before the projected landfall, I decided to tour the operation sub-centers to see how we were doing. I left the main EOC under the charge of First Deputy Mayor Tish Elston and headed out with a fire fighter and Mike Connors. Mike was directing many of the operations critical to our hurricane response. As I traveled to the various centers, I talked with staff about their preparations and concerns. I learned about problems that I could not address that day, but which would be helpful to know later as we modified our emergency plans. Driving through the city, I tried to picture what it would look like in twenty-four hours, after the storm went through. What community and personal tragedies would come? How long would it take us to recover? I thought about my interview on CNN the night before. National media had already called to schedule post-storm interviews to discuss response and clean-up operations.

Early in the morning I kissed my young children and wife goodbye and left them at the hurricane shelter located at Tropicana Field. It was the hardest moment of a very hard few days.

As I drove through the town, I said a prayer for our city, and I girded myself for some tough times. I toured the police emergency operation sub-center and checked the status of their preparations in the city. We talked through the pre- and post-storm issues and predictions of storm strength. As part of our preparations, we constantly compared the land-fall time predictions to the high tide time charts in order to estimate what areas would be under water. I thanked everyone and started out to the next sub-center when someone shouted: "*It's turned!*"

These may have been the two most important words uttered during my almost nine years in office. Everyone in the room raced to the television set. A reporter was excitedly describing the changed storm path. Hurricane Charley, now a category 4 storm that had been within a few hours of landfall in St. Petersburg, had taken a sharp turn toward the east and was heading toward Port Charlotte. Unless it turned north again, the storm would miss us completely!

It was a stunning moment. We were prepared for an invasion, and the enemy had changed course. Still, the city stayed on full alert until it was clear that we were out of danger. Hurricane Charley struck Port Charlotte, seventy miles south of St. Petersburg, drove through central Florida, and exited by way of the Atlantic Ocean. Some of our residents who evacuated to Orlando had to ride out the storm in the bathrooms of their hotel rooms as the hurricane swept through central Florida. Port Charlotte and other areas were severely damaged, but St. Petersburg escaped any impact from the storm. It was an unbelievable change in fate.

After the storm we sent our Urban Search and Rescue team to Port Charlotte to help in the recovery. I spent a day in the impacted area with St. Petersburg's police and fire personnel observing the damage and response efforts in order to learn for our future planning. We would make many changes to our emergency plans as a result of the lessons learned. After observing the Charlotte County Emergency Operations Center, which was severely damaged during the storm, we resolved to find a stronger EOC for St. Petersburg. We would later revise our plans for construction of our city's water administration building to make it hurricane hardened, and to co-locate our EOC in the water building during storms. Many other observations during that trip helped us to do our jobs better in the coming years.

We were threatened and impacted by three other storms in 2004—Frances, Ivan, and Jeanne. None would strike us directly, but they came close enough to cause damage. We had electric lines down, flooding in low areas, and damage from wind and tide. The hours of preparation by our public safety team, led by Fire and Rescue, resulted in professional, quick response. After each event, our team evaluated how we did and improved our ability to respond to the next storm.

Prepare

In St. Petersburg, the fire department is responsible for the fire and emergency medical response. Leadership, training, staffing, and equipment are all important. When an auto accident occurs or a house catches on fire, our citizens expect a quick response from professional, well-equipped personnel. Response times are important, as is the quality of the response.

A dependable water system is critical, deployed both in buildings and hydrants throughout the city. Training and equipment are as important to the fire effort as they are to the police—both for the daily job of responding to fire and medical emergencies, and for the unexpected events. After September 11, our Hazardous Materials team was a vital part of the Homeland Security effort as reports of anthrax were widespread, and the city was the subject of national news surrounding packages with white powder being mailed out of St. Petersburg's post office. There was no time to learn how to respond. We had to rely on the training of our team.

The skill of our fire, police, storm water, and other city departments in responding to the tanker fire and 2004 hurricanes was a testament to the character of the individuals, along with the hours and years of training that came before the successful moments of response.

• • •

I have enormous respect for the men and women who serve us in the public safety arena. Whether it is firefighters dealing with a blazing tanker truck filled with fuel, or the precision with which drug search warrants are delivered by our police officers in very dangerous circumstances, the skill with which these professionals handle their jobs in an emergency is remarkable. And the actions they take in moments of crisis reflect the character of the individual, along with the training and preparation that preceded the crisis.

I will never forget standing late one night with our police chief and a young wife as we watched an operation on a closed circuit television screen in the emergency room nurse's station. The woman's husband, an undercover police officer, had been shot while apprehending criminals fleeing from a convenience store robbery. The doctors in the operating room next to us were calmly putting our officer back together. The surgeon, Dr. Stephen Epstein, is a legend in our police department, known for his talent and commitment. Our emergency response medical team was lauded for the quick work they did to stabilize the officer at the scene of the shooting. Thankfully, the officer recovered well.

These moments remind me of the difficult nature of our work to keep a city safe. I have come to realize that the scenes I observed reflect something beyond the quick action of the moment. Hiring public safety personnel who have character, commitment, and talent is critically important. Thorough training and preparation must follow. When it works, the city has the ability to effectively respond to the public safety need, whether it is to put out a tanker fire, respond to a hurricane, carry out warrants, or provide emergency medical care in response to a wounded officer. It is a difficult, often risky, and imposing effort, and it is one that every city must take seriously.

After all, public safety is our number one job!

● ● ●

Slightly over one year after I left office, on January 24, 2011, Sergeant Thomas Baitinger and Officer Jeffrey Yaslowitz of the St. Petersburg Police Department were shot and killed while attempting to apprehend a criminal. They were the first St. Petersburg police officers killed in the line of duty in over thirty years. It was one of the saddest days in our city's history—and a vivid reminder of the courage and sacrifice required to keep the citizens of the city safe. I consider both of these men—and the families they left behind—to be heroes.

Chapter 5

Downtown

Rebuild the City's Heart

When you're alone and life is making you lonely
you can always go ... downtown.

— "DOWNTOWN," PERFORMED BY PETULA CLARK

O ne of my fondest memories from my childhood in Indianapolis was going to the Circle at Christmastime. It was the early 1960s, and I was in elementary school, but I still remember the sights and feelings as though they were last Christmas.

The Circle is a roundabout in the center of downtown Indianapolis. In the middle of the roundabout is the State Soldiers and Sailors Monument. The Circle Monument is almost as tall as the Statue of Liberty and, among other impressive images, is adorned with large statues of soldiers, cannons, winged birds, an angel of peace, and a goddess of war. It has water fountains on the sides, an observation deck several stories high, and a Civil War museum underneath. On the top sits the thirty-eight-foot-high statue "Victory," nicknamed "Miss Indiana" by some locals. There are four forty-foot-tall bronze candelabra around the perimeter, and steep staircases leading up to the large bronze doors of the monument.

At Christmas, the city hangs strings of lights from Miss Indiana at the top to the pavement below, encircling the Monument. Christmas trees line the base, and poles around the monument are striped like candy canes. Imagine the fascination and excitement of a seven-year-old boy looking up at the Christmastime Circle Monument. Then imagine the same scene covered with a blanket of fresh snow.

Around the Circle were shops and places to eat, wonderfully decorated for the holidays. I can remember my mother walking me past the window displays decorated for Christmas, and we'd stop to eat at a lunch counter in one of the stores. It was a festive experience. At times, my dad would drive the whole family downtown to see the lights and cruise around the Circle. I can remember all of us singing Petula Clark's "Downtown" while we drove around and looked at the sights.

There was always something neat about being downtown, at any time of year, but especially at Christmas. People walked briskly, going in and out of shops, enjoying the museums, the Circle, and the scene. When I was downtown I always felt like I was part of something very special—not just a location but a community, a sense that this place belonged to everyone. We're all part of it. Somehow we took pride in ourselves because we were proud of our town.

Downtown is the heart of the city. It is the place where our crossroads come together, our common bond. Picture in your mind's eye a city you have visited. You are probably not thinking of the suburbs, shopping malls, or industrial parks—you are picturing the downtown area.

View the skylines of Chicago or New York, or visit Independence Hall in Philadelphia. Walk the Freedom Trail in Boston. Enjoy the parks, fountains, museums, cafes, and bustle of the urban centers around America. Downtown is more than a location on a map. It is where a city defines itself, and it is the prism through which the outside world views the city. Downtown is a city's heart, so if a city is to thrive, its heart must be strong.

A downtown with a large commercial, office, and residential base will contribute significantly to the tax rolls of the city with the effect of reducing the tax burden on residents in the city's neighborhoods, helping residents throughout the city save money. But downtown is more than just a revenue producer. The city center contains many of the community's businesses, apartments, restaurants, parks, and museums. The major events typically occur there. When it works, downtown becomes the gathering place for the entire city and the surrounding areas.

I left Indianapolis when I was ten years old. Fifteen years later, following law school, I arrived in St. Petersburg. Although I had resided in different cities since leaving the Midwest, I had not lived in a place that had a downtown that replicated the feeling of my boyhood Indianapolis city center. Following the suburbanization of our country in the 1960s and 1970s, with the rise of shopping malls, retail strip centers, and secluded neighborhoods, we lost ground in our nation's downtowns.

St. Petersburg was no exception. The city's own newspaper regularly used the word "moribund" to describe the activity and vibrancy level of downtown. At one point in the early 1980s, there was not a single hotel room downtown. Other than the private Yacht Club, there were only a couple restaurants, and they were not of the type to draw people into the city. The big downtown employer, Florida Power Corporation, had fled to the suburbs in 1972, a move that accelerated the urban core's decline and made it difficult to reverse. Downtown had some level of activity during the weekdays, although not what you'd call vibrant. On weekends, there was little going on unless there happened to be an event in the parks. At night there was rarely a reason to be downtown, and it could be scary.

The city's heart was sick!

A first step in turning around any part of a community is to inventory the assets presently in place. It is surprising to see how many good things already exist. These assets become the foundation around which to build.

Despite the challenges of downtown St. Petersburg in 1981, the urban center also had strengths. Major employers included the newspaper, law firms, accounting firms, and banks. Unfortunately, over the next decade many of our banks and accounting firms consolidated with state and national firms. The mergers usually resulted in the corporate headquarters and professional offices moving out of the city.

Other 1981 downtown assets included a general aviation airport, a municipal pier, a small port, and a civic center, all of which were in need of significant upgrade and repair. There were a number of historic structures, although many were closed and boarded up—the most significant being the 1888 Detroit Hotel and the 1926 Vinoy Park Hotel. The Vinoy was a majestic waterfront structure from the Roaring '20s, but it was now abandoned and all its windows had been broken out. The hotel had been closed since 1973. Birds now inhabited the structure that once boasted prominent visitors from the north, including Jimmy Stewart, Alf Landon, and President Calvin Coolidge.

The most important physical asset of downtown St. Petersburg thirty years ago was its waterfront park. During the early 1900s, there was a contentious debate in the city between those who favored a working, industrial waterfront and those who wanted to acquire partially submerged waterfront lots, assemble them together, dredge and fill the land, and create a large waterfront park system. Led by the Board of Trade (today's chamber of commerce) and William Straub, the newspaper's publisher, the "waterfront park" faction prevailed. On Christmas Eve in 1909, a deal was put in place that would result in the foundation of our core waterfront park system, today's Straub Park. The *St. Petersburg Times* called the 1909 arrangement the "best Christmas present St. Petersburg ever gave itself."

The desire to preserve a beautiful, open, active downtown waterfront park system would become a central ethic of the city to be reconfirmed over the next 100 years by preservation, referenda, and additional park expansion. On Christmas Eve in 2009, exactly one hundred years after the 1909 plan was put in place, we held a ceremony in the newly created Albert Whitted Park to dedicate three additional parcels of land as permanent waterfront parks. My hope and belief is that the city's commitment to waterfront parkland will continue for the next hundred years.

In the early 1980s, the people of St. Petersburg were not proud of their city, but they wanted to be. Many had visited or lived in other cities and had experienced the downtown feeling that I knew in my boyhood Indianapolis. They wanted the same for St. Petersburg. The downtown area possessed an intangible quality that would ultimately produce one of the country's best urban core turnarounds of the past thirty years. This quality was a feeling shared by a large number of people that something needed to be done to give our citizens a vibrant city center.

The city leaders started with a plan.

Plan

In 1982, the City Council adopted the Intown Redevelopment Plan, designating core sections of the downtown for redevelopment. The stated objectives of the plan were:

- Encouraging and reinforcing development
- Creating an integrated movement system for vehicles, transit, pedestrians, and parking
- Maintaining the historic, cultural, and aesthetic integrity of the area

The plan would use taxes derived from increased downtown values to finance improvements—a process called tax increment financing—and the city's condemnation powers to drive the effort.

The activities of the city to redevelop downtown over the following twenty-eight years were extensive, and could be the subject of an entire book in their own right. The effort consumed substantial portions of the city's tax revenues, community energy, and political capital during that period. At times, the city was sharply divided on the costs associated with the effort and the lack of success. For almost two decades, conflicts over the wisdom of the downtown redevelopment efforts dominated the debate in each mayoral campaign.

The elections were close and, with the exception of one two-year period, the more pro-downtown mayoral candidate always won. While the downtown redevelopment had many components over a twenty-five-year period, the single effort which most galvanized those seeking a vibrant downtown, and angered those upset about rising property taxes, was the decision to build a domed, multi-purpose stadium in the hope that the city would attract a major league baseball team.

St. Petersburg began its affinity for major league baseball in 1914 when the St. Louis Browns arrived for spring training at Sunshine Park. For the next three years, Mayor Al Lang convinced the Philadelphia Phillies to make St. Petersburg their spring home. Spring training was seen as an economic and image boost to the city.

Over the course of the next eighty years, the Boston Braves, New York Yankees, St. Louis Cardinals, New York Giants, New York Mets, and Baltimore Orioles all found their way to hold spring training in the city. Baseball legends like Babe Ruth, Dizzy Dean, and Joe DiMaggio delighted local crowds. Eventually, perhaps predictably, the city leaders decided that summer ball would provide an even greater economic impact. In the late 1970s the Pinellas (county) Sports Authority was formed for the purpose of going after a major league baseball team.

By the late 1980s, the city had a downtown domed baseball stadium under construction, which would open in 1990. There were high hopes that its presence would convince major league baseball to award a team to St. Petersburg. The stadium effort sharply divided the city between those who hoped the stadium/baseball effort would spur economic revitalization of the sleepy downtown and those who were angered at tax rate increases required to pay for the stadium, which had no ball team, along with the other city downtown investments.

Frustration set in as attempts to lure other teams to town failed, including negotiations with the Chicago White Sox, Seattle Mariners, and San Francisco Giants. In 1991 Major League Baseball overlooked St. Petersburg in its expansion effort. Finally, in 1995, a team was awarded to a local ownership group. The team was called the Tampa Bay Devil Rays. Eventually "Devil Rays" was shortened to the "Rays," but the Tampa Bay name stayed and resulted in constant confusion and an assumption by national media that the team played in Tampa. This was hardly the image enhancement St. Petersburg leaders had sought. The team played its first game on March 31, 1998. The presence of the team sparked a new confidence within the city, but the franchise suffered through ten years of losing seasons and low attendance until 2008, when both trends changed as the Rays went to the World Series and welcomed many sold-out crowds at the St. Petersburg stadium, which was named Tropicana Field.

In the end the bet on baseball cost a great deal. It also returned many benefits to the city. While the effort to construct a stadium and attract the team was expensive and divisive, it created part of the energy that led to further downtown development efforts. Unfortunately, the team's failure to name the franchise after St. Petersburg reduced the image impact for the city from the team, although there is some, albeit limited, association of the team with the city. There are economic benefits to local hotels and shopping from visiting teams, media, and fans, especially when the Rays are winning. The economic value of the team to the city, and the branding of St. Petersburg as part of the franchise, will likely be discussion items as the team advances their desire for a new stadium, a conversation that they began at the onset of their eleventh season in Tropicana Field.

One element of the city's 1982 Intown Redevelopment Plan was the development of a "unified retail program" proposed for eight blocks in the core area of downtown. In May 1987, just six months after breaking ground on the construction of the domed baseball stadium, the City Council approved the "Bay Plaza" contracts that were aimed at fulfilling the retail objective. The thirteen-year agreement named Bay Plaza Companies, controlled by Kansas City-based J. C. Nichols Co., as downtown's master developer. Bay Plaza was to manage the Bayfront Center (arena), the Mahaffey Theater, the Pier (a festive marketplace), and the stadium. Also, Bay Plaza was to develop a nine-block area in the heart of downtown into a major retail center, a planned one million square feet of development. The city would build parking garages and walkways.

Bay Plaza was an ambitious plan with an experienced developer. Both the city and developers spent millions of dollars on the project. City expenditures would include substantial renovations to the Pier and Mahaffey Theater, along with the construction of parking garages. After years of effort, the parties managed to acquire key blocks of downtown, but Bay Plaza failed to attract major retail stores. Maas Brothers, the only major department store downtown, closed in 1991. In 1995, six months after St. Petersburg was awarded a major league baseball team, Bay Plaza announced that it was pulling out of the city.

Although the Bay Plaza project did not reach its intended retail development, the attempt succeeded in assembling several core blocks for development. By 1999, the city announced plans with a local developer partnership for the construction of three blocks within the core of the former Bay Plaza area to include a parking garage, retail, restaurants, and a twenty-screen movie theater. By late 2000, the development branded "BayWalk" opened to large crowds in the heart of downtown.

The combined Bay Plaza and dome projects tested the community's patience. By 1990, the city's property tax rate had increased significantly, yet the early 1990s brought multiple disappointments on both the baseball and retail fronts. Mayoral and city council races in the late 1980s and 1990s were close, and the investments in downtown were vigorously debated. Fortunately for the city, candidates who favored staying the course ultimately prevailed. Still, two efforts in the late 1980s reflected the frustration felt by many in the city: first, an effort to recall Mayor Bob Ulrich (a mentor of mine, and a leader strongly committed to reviving the city's heart) along with the entire City Council; and second, an attempt by a west side neighborhood to secede from the city due to rising tax rates. Both attempts failed.

By 2001, several blocks of downtown remained vacant. Few people lived downtown, and the activity level was still lacking, but progress had been made. I was chairman of the Chamber of Commerce during the 1999 announcement of BayWalk, and I was quoted in the newspaper comparing the foundations of downtown redevelopment to a three-legged stool: "The Vinoy [hotel] had to come back, we had to get baseball, then we needed some sort of entertainment and retail area." With the foundation pieces in place in 2001, it was time to develop a plan for taking downtown to the next level.

The Plan

One of the world's great philosophers is Winnie the Pooh. I loved to watch the cartoon with my children when they were young. One day Pooh Bear and Christopher Robin were wandering aimlessly through the Hundred Acre Wood, climbing trees, chasing butterflies, and *doing nothing*—when Pooh asked Christopher Robin: "What exactly is doing nothing?" Christopher Robin replied, "It's when people say 'What are you two doing?' and we say 'Oh nothing.'" It's "going along, listening to all the things you can't hear and not bothering." Winnie the Pooh later concluded that Tigger, Eeyore, and Piglet were his *best* friends because he could do anything with them. But only Christopher Robin was his *best, best friend* because he was someone Pooh *could do nothing with*.

The introduction of major league baseball and BayWalk provided much-needed forward progress for the downtown effort, but as I took office in 2001 our city center was not yet close to the level of vibrancy and activity that our leaders had sought for decades. We needed a Winnie the Pooh "best, best friend" downtown. *It should be a place where there is so much going on that people will come even if, like Winnie, they have nothing particular in mind that they want to do, confident that they can simply come "downtown" and pick from a variety of activities once they get there.*

In order to accomplish this objective we focused our efforts on a mission to:

(1) Expand the number of recurring events along our waterfront park system and work to maintain those we had—with an emphasis on events that fill our downtown hotels.

(2) Develop and expand the fixed activity generators downtown like medical complexes, marine research, education, general business, hotels, shopping, and restaurants.

(3) Support and expand the cultural amenities downtown, setting a goal of the city becoming the cultural center of Florida.

(4) Make Beach Drive, along the park on the waterfront, a café and retail activity attractor and tie the district to the other downtown activity centers.

(5) Improve access to and around downtown.

(6) Focus on making downtown a desirable place to live and work to attract more residential living in the city center.

(1) Events

When I lived in Indianapolis as a child, I grew up within earshot of the speedway. I literally could hear the roar of open wheel racers from my front porch. By the time I was nine years old I had been to the Indianapolis 500 Mile Race and attended the time trials several times. I could name the recent winners of the world's premier race. I knew the words to "Back Home again in Indiana," which was sung before each race, and had my own small checkered flags in my bedroom. Although I moved to Miami when I was ten, I have experienced every race since I left in 1966 either by listening to it on the radio, watching it on television or, on two occasions, returning to the brickyard. I am an Indy racing fan!

It was my love for Indy car racing, and my understanding of what it can do for a city, that convinced me to call Tony George in April 2003. Tony was the head of both the Indianapolis 500 and the Indy Racing League. The purpose of my call was to make an outrageous proposal to Tony: that the Indy Racing League should veer from their long-term tradition of oval racing to run IndyCar's first-ever street race in downtown St. Petersburg.

During the prior two decades, St. Petersburg had a few failed efforts at establishing street racing downtown. When I took office I put a team together in our economic development department with the specific charge of reviving the race effort, but changing it to establish the audacious goal of bringing Indianapolis-style open-wheel racing to our city. In 2003, with the help of local promoter Tom Begley, we were able to land an open-wheel Champ Car series race. The 1980s races in St. Pete were fun, but were literally not in the same league as major open-wheel racing from the perspective of the racing, crowd, or media coverage.

Our 2003 Champ Car race was a step toward the big leagues of open-wheel racing. It established a waterfront circuit (a race course) designed by Chris Pook, who had been involved in the Long Beach open-wheel race. The circuit would be hailed by drivers as one of the best street race courses in the world. Unfortunately, Champ Car went into bankruptcy shortly after our race.

The city's past efforts and my childhood memories were both in my thoughts as I settled into my chair to place the call to Tony George. Kevin Dunn, the city head of our racing effort, was making the call with me. Ken Unger, Indy Racing League's senior vice president for business affairs, was on the line with Tony in Indianapolis. I had decided ahead of time that I would not begin the conservation by pitching the city; rather, I would try to convince them that I was a fan.

I started by telling the head of the Indianapolis 500 that I had watched or listened to every one of his races since I was seven years old. We talked about the racing legends of the past and present. My point to him was that I understood the importance of the race to a city: the vibrancy, the economic impact, and the sense of pride it instills. I wanted him to know that if he brought a race to St. Petersburg, I would make sure that it succeeded here. It was more than an economic development project to me. It was a passion.

Years later, Ken Unger shared with me Tony's response at that point in the conversation. After I described my enthusiasm for Indy racing, Ken put their phone on mute, and Tony exclaimed to Ken: "I like this guy already!" The next few years, establishing and building a race, were a blur of activity with several bumps along the way. Andretti Green Promotions—initially led by Barry Green, Michael Andretti, Kevin Savoree, and Kim Green—agreed to promote our race, and Indy Racing League (IRL) became the sanctioning body.

The first Honda Grand Prix of St. Petersburg, a race through the streets of downtown, ran in 2005. Since the IRL had only run oval races in the past (a track dubbed one long left-hand turn), St. Petersburg became the first place where IndyCar racing made a right-hand turn. By the time of our fifth Honda Grand Prix of St. Petersburg in 2009, the race was hailed as one of the most important IRL races, and a catalyst for reuniting open-wheel racing in America. We were attracting crowds of 150,000 people, filling hotels throughout the region, and enjoying worldwide television coverage in over 200 countries for two days of racing.

The race, which evolved under a five-year rolling contract with the city, established St. Petersburg as a race town. It brought an impact to our city that the director of our county's visitor's bureau compared to having the NCAA Final Four in town every year, and it became something more. It wove its way into the heart of our city. People planned trips around the race; they held parties; they attended the race parade; and they took pride in the fact that it is part of the life of St. Petersburg. My children could even hear the roar of open-wheel race cars from our front porch, twenty blocks north of downtown.

With the Grand Prix as a model, we set out on a focused effort to attract events to the city. The objective of every event was to:

(1) Favorably impact the city economically, hopefully by filling hotel beds that in turn provide visitors who spend money on taxis, restaurants, shopping, and visiting other places in the city. We tracked the growing number of major chain or "flagged" hotels in the city on our City Scorecard.

(2) Provide image enhancement, often with television coverage that positively shows off the city.

(3) Introduce an activity that our community can enjoy, improving the quality of life and making us all feel even better about our town.

Understanding the importance of our downtown waterfront parks as venues for events, we protected them from attempts to expand buildings onto green space, and we added two new event parks on the waterfront: Albert Whitted Park and the Park Plaza by the Progress Energy Center for the Arts. We also recognized the importance of maintenance of activities. Sometimes we had to work as hard to help a struggling enterprise recover, from events to museums, as we worked to attract new ones to the city. A save is as important a victory as a win!

By 2009, we had about 400 events in our downtown waterfront parks each year. Weekend festival events were popular with people throughout the region and drew tens of thousands of attendees. Among these events are Bluesfest, Ribfest, Taste of Pinellas, Folk Fair, Crawfish Festival, Snowfest, Caribbean Carnival, and Arts in the Park. As an example, Ribfest is a three-day (Friday to Sunday) event in Vinoy Park with rock concerts, lots of ribs, and a children's carnival area. It attracts up to 25,000 people for nightly concerts and raises tens of thousands of dollars for local charities. The festivals typically do not produce national media coverage, and they attract smaller hotel room use than some other events, but they create overflow activity downtown, and they provide the city with gatherings that enhance our quality of life.

Other events are targeted at media coverage and out-of-town visitors, in addition to the enjoyment of our local community. Rays baseball and the Grand Prix are the best examples of this, and there are others. We recruited the St. Petersburg Bowl, a post season college bowl game held by ESPN that is played in Tropicana Field. By 2009, its second year, the Beef 'O' Brady's St. Petersburg Bowl had a title sponsor with a multi-year agreement, a sold-out crowd, a national broadcast, and a direct economic impact in the city that included selling out every downtown hotel and most on the beach.

We also recruited and landed the annual Miss Florida Scholarship Pageant, a televised Miss America preliminary event that fills many hotel rooms in the city for many nights each year. The pageant's tenacious leader, Mary Sullivan, was the driving spirit behind the move. Our annual waterfront Boat Show expanded to include both sail and motor boats, and is a great draw. Our running events don't attract large crowds of fans, but many of the thousands of competing athletes who travel to the city stay at our hotels. In addition to our established running events, the largest being the St. Anthony's Triathlon, an Olympic qualifying race, we welcomed the Women's Running Magazine Half Marathon, the Iron Kids Triathlon, and others.

We enjoyed four downtown parades each year, including a Santa Parade, Festival of States Day Parade, Grand Prix Night Parade, and the Martin Luther King Jr. Day Parade, which is one of the country's largest. The parades are special traditions and memories for our kids. We also worked to attract events that were not annual, such as the Republican Presidential CNN/YouTube Debates, the Cirque Du Soleil traveling shows, the Tall Ships Festival, the Offshore Power Boat Championships, and others.

Finally, we attracted and supported annual events that became part of the fabric of our community, what we call being "Very St. Pete!" One of my favorites is the Saturday Morning Market, a weekly happening that grew to be the Southeast's largest farmers' market, regularly drawing over 10,000 people. It has live music, booths with fresh fruits and vegetables, crafts, and stands to get breakfast and lunch. When it started, the organizers asked me to play guitar and sing at the market with Sam Stone, a local rock and beach musician, in order to attract publicity for the event. We had so much fun that we played together at the market every six weeks or so. I loved the surprised look on people's faces when they realized that the mayor was singing songs by Crosby, Stills, Nash, and Young (admittedly "old guy" rock and roll).

Other "Very St. Pete!" events included the Fourth of July celebration that fills the entire four-mile length of our downtown waterfront parks; the downtown-wide First Night family-oriented celebration on New Year's Eve; the First Friday street party held on Central Avenue each month; the monthly Gallery Walk showing off our arts community; American Stage in the Park, a multi-week theater production under the stars; Florida Orchestra in the Park; the Friday Night Shuffle, a weekly night of pot luck, shuffleboard, lawn bowling, volleyball, and more, enjoyed by singles and young families at our historic downtown St. Petersburg Shuffleboard Club—a facility we upgraded after a grassroots effort came together to launch the Shuffle; Summer Solstice Yoga, watching the sunrise on Straub Park overlooking the downtown waterfront; and many more. Each event started small, but they all persisted and built on success. Many required help along the way, and we often rallied the business community and individuals to provide the support when needed.

Our city's marketing department was responsible for coordinating the park events, but relatively little city money was spent to host them. The collective impact of these events is often underestimated. They added significantly to the enjoyment of living in St. Petersburg, and they became a primary driver in moving our city's downtown to the vibrancy level that had long been sought.

(2) Ongoing Activity Generators

In 1972, Florida Power Corporation moved out of downtown St. Petersburg and into a new campus along a federal highway away from the city center. Before moving, there had been an effort to keep them downtown in a major planned multi-use development, but protracted legal challenges and delays ultimately resulted in a corporate leadership decision to move. The loss to downtown of its major employer, in my mind, set the downtown on a downward course from which it was difficult to recover. Then, in the late 1990s, the company sold its suburban campus, disbursing its employees into leased space in different buildings while moving its corporate offices and some employees into leased space in a downtown building that had originally been built to house a department store.

When Florida Power Corporation was later merged with a Raleigh, North Carolina-based power company to become Progress Energy Corporation, there were fears that even the remaining activity of our once major corporate citizen would melt away. The threat seemed imminent when I learned that Progress Energy had decided to consolidate their disbursed offices. I had heard that they were looking both inside and outside the city.

It was a crisis—and an opportunity.

The future of Progress Energy Florida—and of downtown St. Petersburg—was the focus of my thoughts as I drove to my meeting with Bill Habermeyer, a retired Navy admiral and the chosen CEO for the Florida division of our power company. It was to be my first lengthy meeting with Bill, and it was held while a tropical storm was brewing outside. We both were on-call. As we talked, I was immediately impressed by a broad range of his qualities. He was smart, deliberate, and polished, but he also possessed a sincerity and courtesy that, based on my own roots, I associate with the Midwest. Even though we did not know each other well, I immediately sensed that I could trust Bill.

As we turned to the subject of the Progress Energy Florida headquarters, I pulled out the book *Mangroves to Major League,* which I had written on the history of our city. I read out loud to Bill the portion of the book that discussed the 1972 move by Florida Power Corporation to the suburbs. I shared with him my belief in the importance of downtown as the city's heart, and the injury to the heart that came from the 1972 move of his company. I felt that we had a real opportunity to correct a mistake of the past by consolidating the power company offices back downtown, and returning it to the place of corporate prominence in the city.

Thankfully, Bill agreed. He valued the importance of corporate citizenship and he agreed with the concept of strengthening downtown's heart. He would need to evaluate all options in order to make sure that his shareholders got the best value, but his preference would be to consolidate downtown if the right deal could be made. As I left the meeting, I sensed that Bill was one of the special individuals I would work with during my term as mayor: a man whose handshake I could trust. This judgment turned out to be correct.

Over the course of the coming months and years, we worked to consolidate Progress Energy Florida's offices in the heart of downtown. It turned out to be a very complicated jigsaw puzzle to put together on a double city block. The final transaction required the city to acquire dozens of underlying ownership interests relating to a ground lease that we possessed, move the Florida International Museum, sell land for the establishment of a new St. Petersburg College campus, get state approval for the unprecedented transfer of existing cultural liens on the property, sell part of the land to a major hotel developer, and sell the remaining land for the construction of Progress Energy Florida's new corporate headquarters.

One observer described the result as a perfect downtown block with a corporate headquarters, another historic office building, a college campus, a museum, and a major hotel with restaurants and shops. Later the block would also boast a new performing arts theater and the Florida Orchestra's headquarters.

When we sat down to complete the paperwork prior to construction, Bill Habermeyer pulled out his copy of *Mangroves to Major League,* which I had given him several years before. He turned to the 1972 page where Florida Power Corporation moved out of downtown and asked if we could both sign the book on that page to show that a new day had come. We did!

After the new building was completed, I cut the ribbon with Jeff Lyash, Bill's successor and a nuclear engineer who possesses the same strong character qualities that made me come to trust Bill. At the ceremony Jeff presented me with a poster-size new page for my history book. It described the March 2007 ribbon cutting for the consolidation of Progress Energy Florida's headquarters offices in downtown St. Petersburg, with almost 700 employees. It was clear that our power company once again understood their importance in strengthening the heart of downtown.

The Progress Energy Florida effort is a reminder that a downtown is built and rebuilt one project at a time. Most of the efforts are difficult and complicated. Many will receive opposition from multiple directions, and many will not succeed—and it's all too easy to overlook the efforts that do not succeed. For example, we spent considerable energy to attract an arts education college to downtown in order to compliment our growing cultural programs, recruiting both the Savannah College of Art Design and Full Sail University. Neither came, although the effort to bring education and arts together resulted in St. Petersburg College putting many cultural programs together in our downtown.

As another example, we assisted some major housing and hotel projects, which became stalled with the national economic downturn in 2008. We also put considerable energy into obtaining Corps of Engineers channel dredging in order to establish our port as a cruise ship destination and the Pier as a cruise ship port of call. We also worked for years to bring a federal courthouse downtown. It was an effort that continued beyond my two terms of office. While these attempts did not succeed by my terms' end, they were not wasted time. They were the investment we made that may ultimately result in projects going forward.

Fortunately, the efforts where we succeeded far outnumbered those that have not yet succeeded. Each attempt is the reminder of the importance of tenacity. Rebuilding a city, project by project, is difficult work, and there are many setbacks, both in general and specific to each project. It is critical not to give up when you hit a wall. Rather, step back, regroup, develop a new strategy, and move forward again ... and again and again.

The result of this approach has been an increase in activity level downtown. Under the leadership of Congressman Bill Young and former University of South Florida Marine Science Dean Peter Betzer, the city assembled a powerful marine science center, branded the St. Petersburg Ocean Team, around Bayboro Harbor downtown. The group includes the National Oceanographic Atmospheric Administration, U.S. Geological Survey, University of South Florida College of Marine Science, SRI St. Petersburg—Marine Science, Florida Institute of Oceanography, Center for Ocean Technology, Coast Guard Sector St. Petersburg, Florida Fish and Wildlife Research Institute, the Tampa Bay Estuary Program, and the International Ocean Institute. None of these groups came downtown by accident. There are stories for each, which entailed considerable efforts—sometimes second, third, and fourth efforts—before they landed or expanded in St. Pete.

By 2009, two of our major downtown hospitals (Bayfront Medical Center and St. Anthony's) had been expanded and updated, and the third, All Children's Hospital, had been completely rebuilt, along with a new medical office building, resulting in a combined construction project that was one of Florida's largest at the time. We opened new and renovated national brand hotels downtown, along with many downtown bed and breakfast hotels and inns. Additionally, plans had been filed for three more major hotel construction projects at the end of 2009, although they would be delayed by the national recession.

We added a new college campus downtown for our local state college, St. Petersburg College. Also, downtown's University of South Florida St. Petersburg added new dorms, a bookstore, parking, and a Science and Technology Center. Plans developed for an expanded USF St. Petersburg campus at the former Dali Museum building. We have dramatically expanded our cultural footprint and have added shopping and retail as further described elsewhere in this chapter.

The medical, educational, and research employment base downtown supplements historic employers like banking and insurance, law firms, accounting firms, newspaper, power company, and a growing group of technology organizations. As it turns out, companies and their employees are as attracted to the quality of life downtown as the people who come for the activities. When I was hired by a St. Petersburg law firm in the early 1980s, we regularly left the downtown area in order to find something to eat at lunchtime. This has changed. By 2009 our economic development office counted over 120 restaurants within the downtown interstate feeders.

As the vibrancy improved, more businesses wanted to be nearby. This happens when employees see working downtown as a company benefit, especially if the city center has activities for them to enjoy in their free time. One of those activities became a main focus for our efforts. It is an attractor whose economic muscle is significant, but is often overlooked: arts and culture.

(3) Cultural Center of Florida

I made a visit to New York City in 1996. As my taxi drove south through Manhattan toward the Battery Park area, I watched the famous scenes roll by and tried to walk mentally through my upcoming meeting. RMS *Titanic*, the luxury ocean liner that sank in 1912, had been located in 1985. Many of the artifacts from the ship had been recovered and were scheduled to be displayed in a magnificent exhibition, which would be larger than many entire museums. The exhibition would have galleries portraying areas of the ship and would likely be one of the most popular exhibition presentations in recent history. I was attempting to line up St. Petersburg as the second city to host the exhibition, after the opening venue in Memphis. The success of our effort was critical to the future of the Florida International Museum, but more importantly it would turn out to be a pivotal moment in downtown St. Petersburg's renaissance.

The Florida International Museum (FIM) was established in the 1990s by a group of St. Petersburg business leaders, led by Templeton Mutual Funds executive John Galbraith. Despite herculean efforts, downtown still struggled, and the FIM founders felt that bringing major museum exhibitions to the city could help spark the turnaround that had proven so elusive. They believed cultural attractions could be the stimulus to economically turn around downtown.

In January 1995, the first exhibition—Treasures of the Czars—included over 270 artifacts from Moscow's Kremlin museums. It drew about 600,000 attendees over a five-month period. The attraction brought in people who had never been downtown before, and helped start positive momentum. It filled restaurants and generated hope. Unfortunately, the following two exhibitions—Splendors of Ancient Egypt and Alexander the Great—brought significantly fewer people and lost considerable amounts of money. It was critical for FIM and downtown that the next exhibition be successful, or it would be the last.

It was December 1996, more than four years before I would become St. Petersburg's mayor. As a lawyer I had represented Templeton Mutual Funds and gotten to know John Galbraith well. John, chairman of FIM, now asked me to develop a plan for moving FIM forward. I worked closely with Dick Johnston, an FIM board member, and CPA to develop the plan. Our search eventually led me to the offices of RMS Titanic, Inc. near Manhattan's Battery Park. Upon my arrival in New York, it soon became apparent that the negotiations would be very complicated, with a need to reconcile the various interests of RMS Titanic, Inc., the Wonders Exhibition series in Memphis, FIM, and the City of St. Petersburg. It was equally clear that we had no back-up plan for regaining FIM's momentum. After assembling a complicated puzzle, we were able to pull it off, and Titanic: The Exhibition came to St. Petersburg in November 1997.

The results were remarkable. Our showing of the exhibition coincided with the blockbuster *Titanic* movie, and people flocked to the museum and downtown. During the final days of the exhibition, lines of people circled outside the building until late at night. People bought tickets with reserved times, and our attendance was only limited by the number of people we could physically send through the museum during opening hours. It drew over 830,000 people in about six months and was one of the nation's largest attended exhibitions. Titanic: The Exhibition was overwhelmingly profitable for FIM, and it did something more: it proved that people would come to downtown St. Petersburg if there was something to see. After the results from the *Titanic* exhibition became apparent, the developer of BayWalk would credit this success at FIM as a catalyst in convincing him to build the BayWalk project downtown.

FIM was a dramatic example of how culture can drive economic development in a city, but it was not the only example. The Salvador Dali Museum brings hundreds of thousands of people into the city each year, a large number of them international tourists. Our various museums, performing arts companies, galleries, and cultural events have had a profound impact on the renaissance of downtown. Recognizing the importance of the arts in moving our downtown forward, we supported a large array of projects: the waterfront move of the new Dali Museum, new headquarters offices for the Florida Orchestra, the redevelopment of the Palladium Theater, the expansion of the Museum of Fine Arts, and the construction of the new American Stage live theater.

One of my favorite programs is Creative Clay. The group links local artists with developmentally disabled children. Artists teach the children how to paint, sculpt, and create other visual art. Creative Clay sells the children's art at their downtown gallery, and the proceeds provide a substantial portion of the financial support for the program. It is a unique concept that blends art, social service, and an entrepreneurial approach.

The city government's support of the various cultural programs took different paths. At times the city was the main financial support, as was the case with the reconstruction of the Mahaffey Theater, a city-owned facility. The city supported Class Acts, a program that features theater productions for our school children, as well as school-arts outreach. The city provided space in the historic Sunken Gardens buildings for the relocation of our children's science museum, Great Explorations. We lobbied for state grant funding for Creative Clay and played a leadership role in the larger lobby effort for the Dali Museum. We suggested the waterfront site for the museum. We supported the effort to obtain voter approval to give rights on two parcels of land, and helped negotiate with the neighboring FAA, Grand Prix, and other interests impacted by the move. The city also moved a storm water main. It was a great effort with many partners, and it was one of the most important projects in the city's history.

I traveled to Seattle to sign a commitment with glass artist Dale Chihuly to bring his collection to St. Petersburg. For the Fine Arts Museum's major exhibition space expansion, the city built parking and moved a storm water main. The opening of the Chihuly Collection downtown in July 2010 was one of St. Petersburg's newest cultural opportunities. It is a large and magnificent permanent collection of Chihuly glass art. Although the effort had many bumps and curves along the way, thanks to the tenacity of the Arts Center's committed board and staff, as well as the enthusiasm of Dale Chihuly's organization, we were finally able to accomplish our goal.

Our "public arts" program was coordinated by a committee of representatives from the arts organizations and general community. We dedicated a percentage of city construction projects to arts projects to be placed at new city building sites. Public arts programs, selected by an independent committee, are often controversial, but we had relatively few complaints. Although I had veto power over the projects, I never exercised the option. My general rule was that I would not substitute my view of art for the committee's decision, so long as I felt that the art did not offend the character of the city.

Eventually we organized the leadership of our various cultural groups into an association called St. Pete Arts. City staff developed a website for St. Pete Arts and linked it to our city's website home page. The Arts site provides links to the various cultural organizations' websites, contains a description of our various groups, includes a calendar of arts and cultural events in the city, and acts as a news source for updates on the arts world in St. Petersburg. By organizing and focusing the effort, we have increased both enthusiasm and momentum for the independent cultural efforts in the city.

Early in the process we announced that St. Petersburg was "the cultural center of Florida," and then we set out to make the claim a reality. Victories like those described above mounted up, along with other wins like the creation and ongoing success of the SunScreen Film Festival, the Mainsail Arts Festival, the new Dr. Carter G. Woodson African American History Museum, St. Petersburg Little Theater, the St. Petersburg Historical Museum, the Florida Holocaust Museum, Studio 620, and the Florida Craftsman Gallery. We established a rotating gallery in the Mayor's reception area for local artists, appointed a Poet Laureate for the city, and held a contest for songwriters to create songs about St. Petersburg.

When you add to the mix hundreds of downtown events, and venues like the State Theater and Jannus Landing courtyard providing music and entertainment for all sorts of people of all ages, the result is an eclectic arts culture that is woven into the fabric of the city. This culture is an activity generator without a limited season, and it has been one of the primary drivers of our downtown's success.

In 2010, *American Style* magazine ranked St. Petersburg the number one Arts City in America (populations 100,000 to 500,000) in their annual "Top 25 Cities for Art" reader's poll, ahead of New Orleans, Charleston, Pittsburgh, Salt Lake City, Minneapolis, Cleveland, and every other Florida city. Our claim of becoming Florida's cultural center had become a reality, as was confirmed by a national, independent competition.

(4) Beach Drive—Play to Your Strength

St. Petersburg has one of the world's most beautiful downtown waterfronts. It is lined with parks going north and south from the city center. These parks are the sites of hundreds of festivals, concerts, and community events each year. The Pier, a five-story festive marketplace in the shape of an inverted pyramid, protrudes from the parks into Tampa Bay. It has an aquarium, a rooftop Caribbean restaurant, the historic Columbia restaurant on the fourth floor, and many shops and eateries along the first level. Outside there is a boardwalk for fishing and a place to feed fish to the pelicans. During the winter months the HMS *Bounty* sailing ship replica docks alongside the Pier. It is a great place to bring kids and visitors.

Beach Drive runs along the downtown waterfront parks on the landside. In 2001, Beach Drive was a beautiful but underutilized stretch of downtown. It had a few shops and one restaurant, but I believed that its potential was far greater. Having traveled Europe with Joyce while in college, I experienced the ambiance and gathering-place attraction of sidewalk cafés—and I pictured Beach Drive lined with umbrella-shaded tables on the sidewalks for restaurants and cafés that overlook the parks, waterfront, Pier, and downtown vistas. If we really wanted downtown to succeed, we needed to play to our strengths, and the Beach Drive waterfront was clearly one of our major strengths.

Our opportunity came with the real estate boom of the early 2000s, which brought condominium towers to four of the five waterfront blocks, and two hotels to the fifth block. One hotel was new, and one was a renovation of the 1920s-era Ponce de Leon Hotel. In each of the developments, the city applied rules requiring setbacks of the towers so they don't hang over Beach Drive, and required parking garages to be hidden in the middle on the larger lots, or set in the back side away from Beach Drive for the narrower lots. We required that shops and restaurants be on the waterfront side along with one other amenity: sidewalk cafés.

Bob Churuti, a retail developer in two Beach Drive blocks, recalls how he started conversations with potential tenants: "The mayor wants to see umbrellas!" Bob was referring to my push for sidewalk restaurants, cafés, and coffee shop seating along the Beach Drive waterfront. My hope was to create a European atmosphere of sidewalk café seating, park events, and waterfront vistas. Beach Drive became a gathering place—our trendsetter was Steve Westphal who started two great restaurants with sidewalk dining: 400 Beach Seafood and Parkshore Grille.

We felt that horse and buggies would add considerably to the downtown waterfront ambiance, so we learned about the horse-related ordinances in effect in other cities, along with the groups providing horse and buggies in places like Charleston and New Orleans. Eventually, a couple of brothers, Woody and Leland Allenbrand, who had a large horse and buggy business in Kansas City, decided to expand to St. Petersburg. We worked with them to provide downtown storage for their buggies, which included one lighted Cinderella carriage. These became a special part of downtown's charm. We later added a mounted police unit downtown that provided a more visible police presence and added to the overall ambiance.

We lighted about sixty waterfront park trees with LED string lights, resulting in a festive nighttime scene. Along with the low energy LED lights, we traded out our high pressure sodium street lights for induction lighting. When we completed the new lighting system, the parks were brighter and more inviting, yet we were using less electricity than before making the improvements.

Eventually we developed the Beach Drive Connector Plan to link the sidewalk café boulevard to other downtown restaurant districts—Bay-Walk, McNulty Station, Jannus Landing, and the Pier. By 2009, BayWalk had gone into decline, so we developed the BayWalk Redevelopment Plan. Working with the new owners, we developed upgraded security and pedestrian links of BayWalk to the other emerging downtown activity centers in an effort to support BayWalk's continued success.

As part of the connector plan, we created a more pedestrian-friendly area by adding brick paver crosswalks, enhanced lighting, widened sidewalks, and pedestrian walkway signage. We also changed many of the one-way roads to two ways, which slowed down through traffic and made crossing the street by foot much safer. We added countdown signals at each intersection. It was a small change that also gave the pedestrians a safer trip across our busy downtown streets. As if to cap off a perfect waterfront boulevard, Dale Chihuly agreed to let us house his major collection of magnificent glass art in the heart of Beach Drive.

For our sidewalk cafés, we passed Florida's first sidewalk café dog ordinance, allowing man's best friend to join the crowd. Now ice cream parlors and restaurants keep water dishes on the sidewalks and dog treats by the cash register. Beach Drive became a magnet that attracts visitors who have nothing specific to do. They stroll, pet a horse, go on a carriage ride, eat ice cream (or gelato), shop, have a meal, or simply enjoy the scene.

(5) Improve Access to and around Downtown

It is basic to the development of any downtown that, for it to be successful, people have to be able to get there easily and move around within the area quickly. This requires attention to those steps that can be taken quickly to ease flow, as well as long-term efforts. The nature of transportation improvements is that it takes many years to develop ideas, plan solutions, rally support, identify funding, and execute the program. Most major improvements will not be completed by the same political leaders who start the ball rolling. That is the nature of transportation leadership: it requires a focus on the long term and a willingness to invest current political capital for projects that will not be completed until much later.

St. Petersburg is the largest city in Pinellas County, a densely populated peninsula on the West Coast of Florida. Thanks to the efforts of Congressman Bill Kramer, and later Congressman Bill Young, today's Interstate 275 comes into the city from the east across a bridge over Tampa Bay, then south through the city to its southern tip. I-275 then travels across the Sunshine Skyway Bridge toward Bradenton and the lower West Coast of Florida. The expressway, including Interstates 175 and 375 which provide access to downtown, was completed in the 1980s.

During the 1960s and 1970s, two separate efforts were entertained to develop an additional expressway for the county that would eventually have connected I-275 in St. Petersburg to the north portion of the county, including Clearwater, Tarpon Springs, and a significant portion of the upper Florida Sun Coast. Unfortunately, both these efforts failed politically for various reasons, resulting in much of our county, and the highly populated areas to the north, being cut off from expressway access to St. Petersburg and our downtown. Just as a strong heart needs clear arteries to move the blood in and out, a vibrant downtown needs free moving transportation corridors to bring people into the city center. We needed to find a better way to connect people from the north.

I had read about the prior efforts to obtain a county north-south expressway while I was preparing to take over as chair of the St. Petersburg Area Chamber of Commerce in the late 1990s. The name that kept popping up in my reading was Don Crane, a former state legislator who had been one of the leaders of the movement in the 1960s and 1970s. Since I felt it was time to reopen the north county access issue, I looked Don up and met with him at a downtown restaurant for lunch. Despite the difficulty of the past failed efforts, Don was surprisingly eager to dive back into the issue. We opened up a AAA map on our lunch table and used a highlighter to draw proposed routes for a road. The options included the old proposed paths and one crazy idea of going into the bay and up an existing waterway. (This last idea would never have worked environmentally, and it was quickly abandoned.)

After many meetings we settled on an option of tying in with an effort that was already underway by the county government to convert U.S. 19 to a controlled access (no stoplights) road south toward St. Petersburg. By looking at our maps, and having discussions with the regional head of the State Department of Transportation, we concluded that we could connect the improved U.S. 19 to I-275 in St. Petersburg at 118th Avenue North, the place where the roads were closest together in the middle of the county. The result would be an expressway from north Pinellas County through St. Petersburg with multiple access points to downtown.

Thankfully, the county-elected officials and staff supported the idea. Eventually the county transportation board and State DOT officials also backed the plan. The price tag for the total project would be hundreds of millions of dollars. It required a team effort of city, county, and state officials to advance each phase. From the initial meeting with Don Crane in 1998, it was hoped that the project would be completed in the late 2010s. If it is in place within twenty years of our AAA map lunch, it will be light-speed in transportation terms. When complete, it will have been worth the effort and wait, since easy access to downtown is critical to the city's success.

Other long-term efforts underway for the downtown are plans for Bus Rapid Transit and a regional rail transit system that would tie together the many counties around us. These are long-term, major efforts that are passed from administration to administration in each of the local governments. In our city, Council Member Jeff Danner and our transportation department staff, along with others, played an important role in moving these projects forward.

Some programs that advanced the community's access to downtown took less time to accomplish. The CityTrails bike paths (described in chapter 9) included four major bike trails and routes emanating from downtown: the North Bay Trail heading north; the South Bay Route going south to Pinellas Point; the Downtown to Beaches Route heading west; and the Downtown Trail, which starts on the waterfront downtown and goes west to link with the Pinellas Trail, which travels all the way to Tarpon Springs. We built a considerable amount of bicycle parking downtown and added temporary bike parking for our major events. We evolved our downtown trolley systems into three routes. The systems were popular and provided access and a quaint method of getting around.

Other access efforts included the installation of way-finding signs throughout downtown that direct visitors to the major centers, the upgrade of interstate signage that also directs travelers to our downtown events and centers, the change of many one-way roads to two-way in order to make the city center easy to navigate for visiting drivers and pedestrians, the development of plans for a new bus terminal downtown, and the upgrade of our downtown general aviation airport.

Airport improvements included a new terminal (with restaurant) for our visitors who arrive by small planes. We also expanded our downtown marina, one of the country's largest municipal marinas, for those who arrive by boat. As part of the marina improvements, we added temporary boat parking, with parking meters for those who wanted to boat downtown for a meal or event. Whether people chose to come to our downtown by air, sea, or land, we worked to make the journey more pleasant.

(6) Living Downtown

At some point the various pieces of downtown feed each other. The arts receive support from the businesses, and the waterfront events bring people to our other attractions. Students are regularly seen studying at our coffee shops, along with employees from the medical and research campuses. While activities that bring people into the downtown are important, we needed more people living there if we wanted to fill the activity gaps and give downtown a neighborhood feel. We were fortunate to have strong residential areas surrounding the downtown core, but the core itself needed more people living there.

The most important way to entice people to live downtown is to make it a nice place. Among other efforts, the city government needs to participate in making the area attractive. Beautification efforts are as critical to downtown residential success as they are in the neighborhoods. Investments in sidewalks, paved crosswalks, decorative streetscaping, mast arm traffic lights, and downtown parks pay off. They improve the environment and convince private investors that the city is serious about downtown development.

If the area is safe and pedestrian-friendly, and has retail, dining, and fun events, people will want to be part of the downtown neighborhood. We encouraged the Sembler Company, a local developer who built a major grocery store and retail center in the heart of downtown. The availability of grocery and other shopping within walking distance, along with downtown's quality urban feel, made it much easier to attract people to live in the core.

Early in my term, I visited Miami to meet with a developer who was considering building rental apartments downtown. His argument for downtown living was compelling: If he builds another rental complex in the suburbs, the amenities he can offer are a swimming pool and tennis courts. If he builds rental apartments downtown, the amenities he can sell are movie theaters, restaurants, night clubs, museums, galleries, performing arts, the Pier, Major League Baseball, the Grand Prix, the St. Petersburg Bowl, and hundreds of waterfront events—all within walking distance of each other. We even built a playground in Albert Whitted Park and a climbing rock in Straub Park for downtown dwellers and visitors with children.

By 2009, our number of new residential units downtown approached 2,000. The additions included ten new condominium towers along the waterfront—impressive developments such as the Signature Place, Ovation, Parkshore, 400 Beach Drive, the Vinoy Place, and others. We regularly met with the developers of the projects as they were being considered and progressed, and we put together a team of city staff who made sure that the projects proceeded smoothly. Off the waterfront many new townhomes, lofts, apartments, and smaller condominium projects brought people to live in the urban center who also work, shop, eat, and attend the cultural, festival, sports, and other events. They enjoy the downtown life!

The people who decided to move downtown helped St. Petersburg hit a tipping point. During the first decade of the 2000s, we experienced the largest amount of construction downtown in our history: office, residential, hotel, retail, educational, and cultural. The total value of property in the Intown Tax Increment District, the largest district downtown, more than tripled! We began steering the downtown progress, not just fueling it, as the city had been required to do in prior decades. But maintaining momentum requires a constant focus on improving. At the end of 2009, there was still a need for more corporate offices and retail in the downtown core.

• • •

At Christmastime in St. Petersburg, Straub Park is decorated for the holidays on the waterfront next to Beach Drive. The scene includes a forty-foot lighted tree, many lighted holiday scenes that are up to 35 feet tall and 120 feet wide, and an outdoor ice skating rink. The rink is actually "glice," which is a synthetic ice for Florida's winter skaters. Visitors enjoy hot chocolate and a Santa's sleigh, complete with Santa who hears wish lists from our younger citizens each night. Santa's North Pole mailbox receives letters from children all season long. There are spotlights on the two large banyan trees, a broad Kapok tree, and a manmade eight-foot-tall rock. On some nights there are choirs singing carols on Straub Park's stage, and on others there are movies in the park. We began an annual movie series that shows the holiday classics outdoors in the park each Friday and Saturday night between Thanksgiving and Christmas.

I walked through Straub Park one night at Christmastime in 2009 and thought back to my Indianapolis childhood days at the Christmastime Circle. As I paused in St. Petersburg's waterfront park, I watched children climbing trees, sipping hot chocolate, ice skating, and talking to Santa. Some were sitting on blankets in the grass watching *Miracle on 34th Street* under the stars. I saw the buzz of activity on Beach Drive with shoppers and café customers talking and laughing, while passengers loaded up into a lighted Cinderella horse carriage. The background for the scene on one side was the growing skyline of a major downtown center, and on the other side were the blue waters of Tampa Bay, stretching out behind the Pier's five-story festive marketplace. The Pier was adorned with LED lights that changed colors at intervals, like a constantly evolving outdoor canvas.

I knew that St. Petersburg's children were making memories, much like those that I took from my childhood in Indianapolis. A pilot flame had been lit inside them that would never go out. It would always remind them that they were part of something special, a place where we all come together. The memories would give them affection for the town where they grew up, and it would enhance thoughts of their childhood life. The value of those thoughts cannot be overstated. It took decades for St. Petersburg's downtown to reach this point. I call it our twenty-five-year overnight success. Many contributed to the progress, and more work will need to be done to make it continue and grow, but the life-support equipment had been removed from the patient, and the prognosis was one that had been fought for by a generation of leaders: the city's heart was strong!

Chapter 6

Jobs

The Best Social Program

The key to everything we're trying to accomplish is jobs ... jobs, jobs and more jobs. Promises and programs, subsidies and studies, welfare and make-work have all been tried by well-meaning individuals. But any worker knows a job is the best social program there is.

—PRESIDENT RONALD REAGAN, 1981

My family loves North Carolina. Every summer we pack up the minivan with the dog and head north. There is something very peaceful and relaxing about the mountains, with the cool nights, trees, lakes, and seclusion. We always stay at Fontana Village, which is kind of a summer camp that the whole family gets to go on. It is near whitewater rafting and mountain lake boating. We stay in cabins in the valley surrounded by the mountains. In addition to rafting and boating, the diversions include swimming pools, mini golf, family volleyball and softball games, hiking, ultimate Frisbee, and waterfall swimming. At night the recreation center hosts country music, square dancing, karaoke, and bingo. We often share campfires and marshmallows.

Another nice thing about Fontana Village is the fact that, for most of the time my children were growing up, cell phones didn't work there. It is important every once in a while to disengage from electronics, especially cell phones. It is impossible to decompress when you know that, at any time, your hip may start to vibrate or ring with an urgent problem waiting to be solved.

For a mayor it is not a good idea to become completely disengaged, though, so my staff worked out an arrangement to find me through the village main office, and our police department had the contact information for the local sheriff. Also, I called in once a day from the pay phone that is located on a porch down the street outside an ice cream parlor, next to the country store. Of all our summers at Fontana, I can only recall one time when I agreed to interrupt my mountain routine and establish a scheduled time to make a work-related call. The call had to do with attracting jobs to the city.

Due to the importance of retaining and attracting jobs for our city, I made a rare Fontana call to an executive from ValPak one morning. As I walked down the valley road toward the pay phone, I mentally rehearsed my pitch. Bringing ValPak meant a lot to the city—over 1,100 jobs and a large new tax base. When I arrived at the porch a few minutes before the scheduled phone call, there was an elderly lady on the pay phone. I sat in a rocker looking at the list of flavors at the ice cream store and waited for the lady to finish her detailed conversation about hats and dinner plans. As the time for my appointed call came and went, I pictured myself explaining how I lost jobs for 1,100 people while listening to a debate about which sundress to wear for the upcoming mountain festival.

Finally I pulled myself out of the rocker, jogged a few blocks down the road to another porch, and made the call. The conversation and the follow-up negotiations went well, and we now have a beautiful half-million square foot building for ValPak, and jobs to support hundreds of families in our community. It was one of many successful efforts to facilitate the creation and expansion of jobs for people in our city.

Reagan Was Right

Ronald Reagan was right. Jobs are the best social program a community can provide to its residents. People who have good paying jobs with benefits do not need welfare or food stamps. They are less likely to commit crimes. They are more able to volunteer and contribute to charities and civic organizations. They can buy a house, own a car, and send their children to college or trade school.

As a city we can build great parks, libraries, and swimming pools, which we did and we should do. But our city will never move forward if we do not have enough jobs for the people who live here. Thus, the effort to attract and retain jobs for the city was a constant focus for our City Development Administration. It involved a multi-level effort:

(1) Improve the service within the building department in order to make doing business in the city a positive experience.

(2) Focus efforts on retaining existing businesses and attracting new businesses to the city, using personal contacts, economic incentive partnerships, and quality of life promotion. Also, respond to opportunities and concerns raised by existing businesses.

(3) Remember the importance of small businesses and provide services to help them in a city-sponsored Business Assistance Center.

(4) Adjust the approach to respond to the impacts of a changing economy, especially the sharp national economic downturn of 2008.

(1) Building Department

When I first ran for office, there were constant complaints about our building permitting department. It took a long time to respond to applications, the process was complex, and the staff interpretations were often inconsistent. A recurring theme was that we were the worst city in the region to do business in, at least with respect to the construction industry.

A surprising aspect of the criticism was the unanimity of the people who complained. It was not only the chamber and construction groups who were unhappy, although they certainly were vocal in their criticism. Criticism also came from people who gathered for coffee meetings held for me in homes throughout the city. It seemed that we were not only making it hard for people to build commercial developments or new homes. We were also making it difficult for the average homeowner to put an addition on their house or make a modification to the existing footprint. News reports calling our building permit department dysfunctional posed a serious problem for a city that needed to be redeveloped.

We approached the challenge from two directions. First, we focused on service. We set measurable goals for permit application response turnaround times: eight days for residential submits, twelve days for commercial submits, and five days for resubmissions. We charted the progress on our web-based City Scorecard. Our overall objective was to strike a better balance. It is important to enforce the city codes for public safety purposes, but we wanted the process to be helpful, encouraging and assisting with compliance by the building public, not a punitive system of roadblocks.

In order to maintain consistency, we set a base rule that required the same plans reviewer to comment on the original submission, as well as on resubmissions that came back in response to our department's comments. It is very frustrating for a contractor to respond with changes based on one set of comments from a city plans reviewer, only to receive a set of new, sometimes conflicting comments from a different reviewer.

I talked with employees from the entire building department on several occasions, emphasizing the need to provide good service so that people will want to build in our city. Finally, we held early morning meetings with contractors on a quarterly basis, inviting anyone who had complaints about the department, along with representatives from the building associations. I brought staff to the meetings. We addressed the issues presented and developed ways to make the department more customer-friendly. The process of moving to a customer-oriented service attitude was not easy or linear, but in the end it was critical to the success of attracting development to the city.

A second element of the permitting process that needed attention was the development code. I asked for our department to prepare a large chart showing the various paths that a proposed development project would take. The completed chart looked like a bowl of spaghetti, and it was visual proof of our need to revise the process. We proceeded with a multi-year process of revising our code, going to neighborhoods and business groups throughout the city for input. In the end we created a code that was universally supported, which fit our urban city environment, and which was much easier to maneuver through.

Fixing the building department took longer than I had hoped and required some staff changes. It also necessitated an overhaul of our development code. At times I felt I was battling an internal culture that was resistant to the concept of customer service, but in the end we prevailed. We responded to permit requests well within the response time goals, and we evolved into a department that was responsive to the building community and was widely seen as one of the best in the region.

More importantly, we were making it more likely that people would want to invest and develop in our city.

In a 2003 newspaper article, the developer who would build two of downtown's largest projects during the decade credited the efficiency of the city's planners for his decision to go forward: "The process was expedited," he said. "In many communities, even here in Florida, that isn't the case."

During the eight full fiscal years we served, the people who invested in our city helped St. Petersburg set five new construction value records, including FY 2007, which more than doubled the previous record set before we began. From 2001 through 2009 we saw $3.25 billion in construction within the city, a record amount with no close second place.

(2) Retention and Recruitment of Jobs

The effort to recruit new businesses to a community can be fiercely competitive. When a company relocates, it brings jobs, community corporate support, and new tax revenue for the local and state governments.

Businesses understand the value they bring, and they often request financial incentives before they commit to come. This applies both to companies who are somewhere else but looking to relocate to our city, and to companies who are already located in our city but are looking to grow. Our existing local companies also understand their value. When they decide they want to grow, we find ourselves in a defensive/offensive posture. We want them to expand their number of employees here, and we do not want them to take their existing jobs somewhere else.

There is no substitute for the mayor's personal involvement in the effort to attract and retain employers in the city. Expansion or relocation of a business is one of the most important decisions its leaders will make. The senior officers want to know that the top political leadership in the city is committed to helping them succeed. The mayor should display a sincere interest in learning about the companies' industry, employee bases, and needs, in addition to personally getting to know their leaders. The more the mayor knows about the employer, the better able he is to adjust strategy to meet the companies' needs and attract them to the city. I always tried to remember that my ultimate goal was to provide jobs for people who live in St. Petersburg so they can support their families. That thought is a great motivator to stay engaged in the process … even when on vacation in the mountains.

• • •

Often the effort to attract or retain a growing company involves a significant incentive program developed by a partnership of the economic development departments of the city, county, and state. From the city's perspective, the incentive can involve property tax credits, but we were careful to identify criteria that ensured the incentives worked for the taxpayer. These criteria include confirmation of new jobs created, new construction or development in the city, and a calculation of how long it will take the new city tax revenues generated by the development to pay back the property tax credits invested.

There are also economic drivers that do not pay taxes, such as public higher education institutions, cultural facilities, and non-profit research institutes. In many of these cases, the city has historically provided land for expansion with no expectation of a direct tax payback term. The rationale behind this approach is that the activity generated by the development will spur the economic vibrancy of the city. Using this approach over time has brought us creation and expansion of Eckerd College, St. Petersburg College, and the University of South Florida St. Petersburg, along with the critical cultural institutions like the Salvador Dali Museum, the Museum of Fine Arts, and others.

A similar approach, using city land along with county and state financial assistance, helped us recruit SRI International. SRI later helped us attract Draper Labs, which grew out of the Massachusetts Institute of Technology. In a short period of time, we had attracted two of the nation's great high technology research firms. Recruiting high tech institutes and manufacturers was consistent with a call by Florida Governor Jeb Bush to expand Florida's job base. While real estate development, tourism, military, and agriculture remain important industries for Florida, our state needs to develop additional industries in order to level the economic downturns. In St. Petersburg, attracting research organizations like SRI and Draper to supplement our established research focus in marine science helped us form the basis of technology-based industries where we can build jobs for the future.

State and local financial incentives were important in the effort to recruit a premier research firm like SRI to the city, but as it turned out they were not the determinative factor. Remember who we were dealing with. SRI is a Silicon Valley firm that is one of the country's great research and development groups. Among SRI's countless innovations are the computer mouse, bar codes, and speech recognition systems. My introduction to SRI was Curt Carlson, its CEO. Dr. Carlson's many accomplishments included publishing the powerful book *Innovation* and leading a team that set the United States standard for high definition television.

When you are attempting to attract one of the world's leading innovation research and development firms to your city, it takes more than the offer of a state incentive grant. They must believe that you are committed to excellence and that you are creating a city with a quality of life that will serve their employees. The best companies are constantly working to attract the brightest innovators to their organizations, and they know that these talented folks can live and work anywhere they want. If you want one of these companies to come to your city, you have to convince them that you are creating a place where their employees will want to live.

I started my first conversation with Curt Carlson with a bold statement: I told him that we had set out on a course of creating the best city in America, and I asked how he and SRI could help us accomplish our goal. I shared with him our approach to governance, as discussed in the chapters of this book, and I described our desire to build a seamless community with a quality of life second to none. We talked about dog parks, bike paths, schools, playgrounds, green city programs, downtown, and neighborhoods.

I gave Curt an unscripted tour of Midtown. He saw firsthand our commitment to the most underdeveloped part of our city. We visited the new Sweetbay grocery store, and Curt even got to meet a large group of kids at an after-school program in the Boys and Girls Club Royal Theater. Curt later confided to me that, by the time we sat down for dinner that night, he was convinced that we were serious about building a great city, and he wanted to be part of it. SRI St. Petersburg became an anchor in our city's growing assembly of high tech companies.

I could name several other examples where we worked with state and county officials to put together incentive plans to convince a company to come to, or expand in St. Petersburg. Despite these incentives, I believe that in almost every case, the factor that closed the deal was the desire of the senior officials to live and raise their families in our city. Companies know that their potential employees will be attracted to a place that has an outstanding quality of life, and leaders of these companies want to raise their own children in the same type of place. If a city focuses its efforts on improving that quality of life for its citizens, and communicates that commitment to potential employers, the commitment becomes a powerful recruitment tool.

Sometimes job recruitment means just listening. Our city's economic development staff put together a schedule for me to visit businesses throughout the city on a regular basis. The companies were always pleased to receive the mayor, and it was often the first time a mayor had come by to tour the operations. We would start by having the business leaders describe their business and industry. We would ask about their interactions with city departments, and whether there were areas where we could improve. Our constant theme was that we appreciated the fact that they were providing jobs for the people in our city, and we wanted to be of help to them in whatever way we could. I then toured the facilities and shook hands and talked with the employees, sometimes individually and sometimes as a group. In light of the fact that most new jobs that will come to any city during the next year will be generated by existing businesses, efforts to build good will with the city's existing employers are critical.

Once, after my son's little league baseball game, I offered a lift home to a volunteer who had locked his keys in the league office. During the drive home I learned he was with the National Oceanic and Atmospheric Administration's (NOAA) regional office. It turned out to be a great opportunity. I asked him why NOAA wasn't located downtown. They should be part of the significant marine science cluster that was forming around Bayboro Harbor. By the time we arrived at his home we had begun a dialogue that resulted in the group relocating downtown with 135 employees. NOAA became part of the St. Petersburg Ocean Team, our world class marine research center, described in chapter 5.

Listening can also result in keeping an important employer from slipping away. One day I received a call from Jim Koelsch, a close friend who is an appraiser in town. He had just talked with the owner of Euro-bake, a Midtown company that had decided to leave the city. They had already put a contract down on property in another county, and Jim suggested that I try to get involved.

Before the end of the day we called the company, and soon I was touring Eurobake with the owner and our economic development staff. As it turned out, the owner was looking to expand but was not having success at his current location in the Dome Industrial Park, so he made the decision to move. Our economic development team jumped in to assist Eurobake in assembling land within a block of their existing operations. The result was a new $8 million expanded facility in Midtown St. Petersburg, saving seventy-five existing jobs and adding seventy-five new jobs. A few years later when the company, later known as Unibake, needed to expand again, they contacted us first so we could help them grow again in our city.

(3) Small Businesses

While attracting and expanding large employers is desirable, it is important to remember that our core employers are the small businesses who provide jobs for many people in our city. Our Business Assistance Center, which the city operates, works with new businesses that are starting out along with existing small businesses that need a little help. City staff, along with retired business executives who volunteer their time, help employers navigate the governmental processes, develop business plans, and identify resources needed to start and grow. Our Chamber of Commerce offers an "Entrepreneurial Academy" for small businesses to learn about the many aspects of starting and operating a small business—insurance, marketing, accounting, legal, and many other topics. It is like a "mini MBA" for small businesses providing the practical information that can be hard to learn on your own.

Between our Business Assistance Center and Chamber of Commerce, small businesses in our city have a chance to receive advice and information that gives them a much better chance of success—especially through the tough early years. As a former business owner myself, I understood the challenges and stress of the difficult times. Although I received my Master of Business Administration from Florida State University, I always felt that my best business education came the first time my business had to make payroll when there was no money in the bank.

The difficulty of building a business during the early years deserves notice, so in addition to ribbon cuttings for new businesses, we also began the tradition of two- and three-year anniversary celebrations. Since there is a very high failure rate for new businesses during their first couple of years, it is appropriate to recognize small businesses that reach their three-year milestone. We sent out press releases, invited dignitaries, and televised the celebration on our city television's weekly show. The pride reflected on the faces of the small business men and women at their three-year celebration was a great confirmation of our efforts to support those who create jobs for the residents of our city.

(4) Adjusting Approach in Tough Times

During the boom of the early 2000s, our constant efforts at job expansion resulted in many new and expanded facilities in our city. Among them were major employers like Raymond James, Bright House, Progress Energy, Home Shopping Network, ValPak, and many others with less national names.

While we experienced several years of a growing employment base, the nation's 2008 financial collapse and the recession that followed triggered an increase in our city's unemployment rate toward the end of the twenty-first century's first decade—tracking increases in the Florida and national job loss rates. We responded to the economic downturn with several initiatives relating to job training, developing a market for foreclosed homes, stimulating energy-savings investment, and working with banks to help people reestablish a savings discipline, all under the umbrella of stpeterecovery.org. Most importantly, a difficult national economy made job expansion for a city an even greater priority, and we continued our focus on expanding, retaining, and recruiting businesses for our community.

Whether economic times are good or bad, cities must be actively engaged in the process of recruiting and retaining employers, because jobs are important. Employers add to the tax base and vibrancy of the community. More importantly, an adequate supply of jobs means that more people who live in the city can have the pride and self-respect that comes from going to work every day, earning a paycheck, making payments on a home mortgage, saving for their kids' college, and living the American dream.

Chapter 7

Inner Cities

The Power of Deciding

*The greatest truth must be recognition that in every man,
in every child, is the potential for greatness.*

—ROBERT F. KENNEDY

I t was Thursday, March 29, 2001. As I arrived at the police station a little before my noon appointment, it seemed odd that I had to stop at security and wait to be escorted into the building. Two days earlier I had been elected mayor of the city and in three days everyone in the building would be reporting to me. But at that moment I was still a civilian, so I chatted with the receptionist about the campaign and the excitement of the coming days.

After about a minute, Go Davis appeared with a big grin and a warm welcome. He seemed energized as he brought me in to the photo room so I could get my official city identification before heading up to his office for lunch. I didn't look my best after months of sleep deprivation during the campaign trail. As an officer snapped my picture, I glanced over at my old friend and thought of the path he had taken from a kid growing up in Methodist Town to becoming the first African American police chief of one of America's great cities.

Dr. Goliath Davis. The name Goliath was well chosen, for Chief Davis is a large man with an even larger presence. He was part of the second wave of African Americans to be selected to serve as police officers in our southern city. The first group, some of whom were dubbed the "Courageous Twelve," endured discrimination and worse in a department and city that, like the rest of America, was working its way through the difficult Civil Rights period. Those "Urban Buffalo Soldiers," like P. K. Killen, Horace Nero, Freddie Lee Crawford, and others, paved the way for Go Davis and his peers to move beyond the street and serve as leaders in the force. But many remnants of the past followed Go and others as they worked their way up the ladder in our recently integrated police department.

Go had the ability to walk comfortably in two places. He sat with the old men playing checkers under large oak trees in places called Pepper Town or Jordan Park, and he was equally comfortable serving as chair of our Chamber of Commerce's Leadership St. Pete program. As police chief he understood that the distrust of the police department by some in the African American community was rooted in history. He also embraced the importance of solid police work as a component in keeping the city safe for everyone.

During his four years as police chief, Go focused on reducing crime while demanding a high level of professionalism from his officers. The latter focus required strict officer discipline for inappropriate conduct. It also drew criticism from union officials and some neighborhood residents. The resulting conflict was fueled by the department's past. For instance, in one episode in 1992, a popular white police chief was fired by an African American acting city manager for alleged racial insensitivity. The resulting uproar in the neighborhoods triggered a successful charter petition drive to adopt the strong mayor form of government, and came within a couple percentage points of electing the fired police chief as mayor. Our history also included 1996 race riots triggered by a police shooting of an African American man at a traffic stop.

With this background, it is not surprising that a major part of my campaign included the police department, and specifically Chief Davis. My runoff opponent for mayor chose her words carefully, but it was clear that she had no interest in retaining Go Davis as police chief. I fully supported him and his approach. I had known Go for fifteen years and, as a private citizen, had endorsed prior decisions to promote him within the department.

It was in this context that I was about to have lunch with St. Petersburg's police chief to discuss the future. It was our first meeting since my election.

As we settled into the conference room to dine on sub sandwiches, Go's demeanor shifted a bit, and he looked weary. I could sense he was about to share news I would not like, and I stopped eating. Go began explaining his impressions of his four years as police chief, his positive view of the accomplishments of our police department, and his desire to move on. He held a Ph.D. in Criminology and had long desired to teach in a university. He now had the opportunity, and he had decided to accept it.

Go was retiring? I could not believe it. We had just spent months in a contentious election with one of the major issues being Go Davis and the police department. We won! But now, the police chief whom I supported was quitting.

I spent the rest of our time together trying to convince him to change his mind. I even suggested that he consider staying for a year or so to give me a chance to transition into the job, but he wouldn't budge.

As I walked out of the police station and drove back to City Hall, I felt a great sense of loss that I was not going to have my old friend with me as I started on the journey of rebuilding our city. The loss was especially significant because Go had an irreplaceable level of experience, history, and understanding of our city, particularly the most economically distressed area of our city, at the time referred to by city leaders as the "Challenge Area," which we would later call "Midtown."

Before I left my meeting with Go, he agreed not to talk about his retirement to anyone until I had the opportunity to think through my transition and the timing of an announcement. Actually, I had an idea that came to me while eating Go's sub sandwich, but I needed some time to sort it out a bit.

A week later, after I was sworn into office, I had another meeting with Go Davis at City Hall. As we sat in my office, I said that I had given up on the idea of convincing him to stay on as police chief. He had made it clear that his decision was final. I went on to say that, although his police career with the city was over, perhaps there was an opportunity to serve in a new way.

As someone who held a Ph.D. in criminology, Go understood the answer to crime and public safety is not just arresting people, although obviously that must be done. Many of our youth commit crimes because they grow up in conditions that lead them there. This is not an excuse for their actions. Criminal activity must be punished regardless of how someone arrives at the decision to commit a crime. But perhaps we could head off some of our youth from going in that direction.

What if he and I set out together to transform the poorest part of our community, to give these kids an environment in which it is less likely for them to go bad? What if we could make our entire city…*seamless*?

In order for a city is to reach its full potential, the whole community must be included in the progress. When a portion of the city is left behind, resentment follows, and the forward movement cannot be sustained. This is especially true of the most economically depressed portions of the city, areas that often have a high percentage of minority residents. A city can never declare success if children in some of its neighborhoods are growing up without hope, in urban decay and unsafe streets. It is not easy to turn around a part of the city that has seen little progress in decades, but it is important to do so, and I needed Go's help.

I don't recall ever having used the word *seamless* before, and I do not know why I blurted it out that day in my meeting with Go Davis, but it would define our efforts in Midtown and throughout St. Petersburg for the next nine years.

Interestingly, I didn't need to explain to Go what I meant by the term seamless. Having lived and worked throughout our city, he intuitively understood the term's powerful meaning, as a central focusing agent to build around. When I stopped talking, Go Davis remained non-committal. He said that he would give my idea some thought, but I could tell from the look on his face that, eventually, he was going to come along for the ride. In his heart he wanted to build communities as much as I did, and this was a rare opportunity to do just that. After a week or two Go Davis agreed to serve as my deputy mayor for Midtown economic development and, together with many others who would join us along the way, we set out to build a seamless city.

The Deuces

The African American community in St. Petersburg evolved in a manner similar to other places. Our city developed in the second half of the nineteenth century, and the biggest spark was the arrival of the railroad in 1888. Many African Americans came as laborers to construct the railroad. Many more came to help build the city in the development periods that followed, especially the 1920s boom. Like other southern cities, a segregated community grew, with the African Americans living in places called Pepper Town, Methodist Town, and Jordan Park.

Segregated institutions helped to define the community. They included schools (Gibbs High, Jordan Elementary, and others); movies (Royal and Harlem Theaters); a hospital (Mercy); a swimming pool (Jennie Hall); and many others. The main street of the area was a road nicknamed the "Deuces," called 22nd Street South on the city map, but the Deuces was more a place than a street.

One of the most important fixtures of the Deuces was Mercy Hospital. Before 1966, if you were black and born in St. Petersburg, you were either born at home with a midwife or born in Mercy Hospital, the city's segregated black hospital. The Royal Theater was also on 22nd Street, as were restaurants, barber shops, doctors' offices, and markets catering to the African American community. This area of town also included

Jordan Elementary, a segregated school for African American students. The Manhattan Casino on 22nd Street was a dance hall, but it was more than that. It was a special place with a second story wooden dance floor on which a generation of African Americans had danced, with live performances from legends like Count Basie, Ella Fitzgerald, and Duke Ellington.

The Deuces was a gathering place for people. They would meet friends there and socialize. It was a part of the community fabric, as much as front porches on summer nights and church on Sunday.

By 2001, the fabric of the Deuces, like that of much of the area we now call Midtown, had literally been torn apart. Mercy hospital had become an abandoned, caved-in building located on a five-acre site that doubled as an unauthorized dumping area. The Harlem Theater was torn down to make way for our baseball stadium, and the Royal Theater was a rusted, run-down building that had not shown a movie in decades. Jordan Elementary was collapsing and its basement was flooded. It had been scheduled for demolition by the school board. The road and sidewalks were in disrepair, and the bustle of the retail businesses had been replaced with the twin curses of drug sales and prostitution.

It's hard to pinpoint a single reason why Midtown had arrived at this point in 2001.

Many blamed the interstate. In the 1970s and 1980s, Interstate 275 was constructed through St. Petersburg. Since the city was largely built out at the time, the construction required that neighborhoods be split from the northern to the southern ends of the city, including the Midtown area. With two downtown interstate extensions, I-175 and I-375, Midtown was divided twice, since it sits on the south border of downtown. The Deuces was split in two, and neighborhoods were divided by large corridors with interstate traffic, making the nearby homes less desirable. Two separate sections of a neighborhood, totaling about forty acres, had been split apart by the interstate and were now de facto parts of the Dome Industrial Park. The resulting mixture of run-down homes, junk piles, environmental contamination, and shuttered industrial buildings com-prised the worst instance of blight in the city.

Another change in the Midtown area coincided with the progress of the Civil Rights era. Desegregation opened up access for African Americans to services and places that, in most cases, were in better condition than the facilities previously available, Midtown properties went unused and fell into disrepair. After Bayfront Medical Center began admitting black patients, there was no longer a need for the African American Mercy Hospital, and it closed in 1966. When large air conditioned theaters were integrated, the smaller, less impressive Royal and Harlem Theaters became less desirable and eventually closed. As shopping and dining opportunities expanded downtown and in Central Plaza, the retail establishments on the Deuces closed down, and in many cases were shuttered.

Finally, and more difficult to dissect, were the negative societal changes that took place in the last four decades across America. The increases in out-of-wedlock births and divorce rates, along with the growth of drug sales and use—especially crack cocaine—have acted like a cancer on our nation's urban cores. We can debate the causes of these changes, but the impacts are not arguable, and the solutions are difficult to identify and execute.

An area with urban blight, crime, and a loss of available services is not a place where people want to live. Many residents who could leave moved out—the population in the area we now call Midtown decreased by almost one-third from 1980 to 2000. By 2001, the area needed atten-tion, and I heard a lot about the problems during my first mayoral campaign.

The beauty of a campaign is that it tests the candidate and forces him or her out into the community to learn about the people who will be represented. When I ran for mayor, I held coffee meetings in people's homes throughout the city, walked door to door talking to residents in front of their homes, spoke at civic clubs and business groups, gave interviews to the press, and participated in thirty-four debates and forums with the other candidates.

Through this process I learned about many hopes and concerns. This was especially true of the talks I had with people who lived in our most economically depressed areas. The Midtown area, historically, had a large African American population, lower income levels, and higher crime rates than the remainder of the city. When I asked residents there about their desires for their community, I could feel a sense of resentment in their responses. It was more than a concern about crime, or the lack of services, or the condition of the streets and buildings, although these challenges were regularly discussed.

The residents of the Midtown area felt abandoned by the city.

After being elected, I resolved that we would launch a focused effort to change the conditions there, and replace the sense of abandonment with a feeling that this area was a "seamless" part of the city. Recognizing that many such promised efforts have gone unfulfilled in cities around America, I knew that we could not start something that was going to fail. If we began the effort, we had to succeed, and in order to succeed we needed a plan.

The Midtown Redevelopment Plan

The strategy to turn around the Midtown area would evolve according to the input we received and the lessons we learned along the way. Looking back, it contained the following elements:

(1) Making the case to the entire community that the redevelopment of Midtown was the right thing to do, and was in everyone's best interest.

(2) Identifying a leader for the effort who was respected throughout the city, and had the understanding, talent, and passion to make a difference for the people who lived in Midtown.

(3) Engaging the entire city government organization as the team to pursue the redevelopment.

(4) Adopting a positive identity and name for the area to be redeveloped.
(5) Working with the community to develop a plan for redevelopment that has buy-in from the residents within Midtown.
(6) Understanding the importance of schools, safety, and neighborhoods, and their relationship to redevelopment.
(7) Starting—Deciding you are going to succeed!
(8) Executing the Plan—Placing an emphasis on saving historic structures.
(9) Measuring success against the goals identified in the Midtown Plan.

(1) Make the Case

During my campaign, one of our four platform goals was economic development citywide, with an added emphasis on Downtown and the area we now call Midtown. Sometimes in elections, candidates will emphasize different elements of their platform in different parts of the city, but we did not do that in 2001. With respect to Midtown, we felt that in order to develop a community consensus for an economic initiative, we needed first to sell it citywide during the campaign. Since Midtown constituted less than 10 percent of the city's population, we would need support outside the area in order to succeed.

At first there was some resistance. In our city's recent past, there had been great resentment for the attempts to develop downtown, an effort that had not yet accomplished the desired turnaround. There was concern that we would spend huge amounts of money on the Midtown effort, causing an increase in taxes, which were already considered too high. In order to address the fiscal concerns, I emphasized that I did not intend to spend huge amounts of city money. The effort would cost some money, but my intent was to significantly leverage any city spending by partnering with federal and state government and with private businesses.

There were two reasons, I argued, for redeveloping Midtown.

First, it was the morally right thing to do. There were children in parts of our community who were growing up in conditions that most of us would never want our own children to experience. All of us, government, community, and business, have a responsibility to work toward changing these conditions.

Second, it was in the best interest of the rest of the community to turn Midtown around economically. When an area is economically depressed, the city must put a disproportionately large amount of money into social and public safety services for the area, and the city receives disproportionately less in tax revenues than it receives from other areas of the city. If the area turns around economically, the city receives more taxes from the area and spends less for services. In other words, the subsidy of the area by the other parts of the city is reduced, and the overall tax rates for everyone can be less.

This argument proved to be effective. By 2003, two and a half years into the Midtown initiative, the *St. Petersburg Times* performed a poll surveying the voters' view of the most important issues to be addressed by the city. In most cities across America, this poll would likely identify the top two issues as public safety and taxes. In the 2003 poll, as expected, the highest percentage (34 percent) named public safety as the top issue, but, significantly, the second highest percentage (23 percent) named redevelopment in Midtown as the top issue of the city.

We had made the case!

(2) Leading in Midtown

If we were going to succeed in the effort to redevelop Midtown, we would need a leader who understood the community, and who had the talent and character to relentlessly pursue success and strategically work through the many obstacles that would inevitably present themselves. Police Chief Goliath Davis was the only person I believed would make the effort succeed, for the reasons I described above. I was thankful that he had agreed to serve as deputy mayor for Midtown economic development.

(3) Build the Team

In order to make Midtown an organization-wide effort, we gathered all the managers, directors, and administrators of the city together for a discussion of our plan. Our new Deputy Mayor Go Davis summarized the results of the Midtown Report and described our mission. We then loaded the entire group on busses for a half-day tour of the Midtown area. It was important that every department understood the area and our goals, and that they committed to be an integral part of the Midtown effort.

To accomplish the second point, we told all the managers that we considered them each responsible for the success of Midtown. We did not build a new government bureaucracy for Midtown; rather, I told all existing staff that if Go Davis came to them to request help for a Midtown program, they should consider the request to come directly from me. Midtown was everyone's job! Its success was critical to the success of the entire city.

Another part of building the team was convincing the media to cover the good as well as the bad activities within Midtown. We gave dozens of tours of Midtown to newspaper reporters, editors, and senior executives, as well as to television reporters from the many stations in the St. Petersburg/Tampa market. At the end of the tours, we would ask the media people whether their impression of the area after the tour was more favorable than it had been prior to the tour. Almost all of them said that Midtown was in much better condition than they thought before they personally visited the entire area. We then tactfully asked them why they thought their uninformed impressions had not been as positive as reality. Several candidly acknowledged that the media could do a better job of looking at the good things going on.

We were successful with many of the television and radio stations covering our successes as they occurred: new businesses, a post office, Royal Theater, Mercy Hospital rehabilitation, Doorways scholarships, and many others. In the early years we also had great support from two *St. Petersburg Times* reporters—Sharon Bond and Jon Wilson—who were never hesitant to write about the problems, but who also understood the critical role they could play by sharing the Midtown successes with the entire city. In a very real way, these two reporters, along with others, helped us to gain support for the effort to improve the lives of the people who live in Midtown.

(4) Establish the Identity

I am a big believer in identity branding. In order to attract people to a cause, you must first establish a name around which you are uniting. In the city's neighborhood planning process, the first thing we do is reach agreement on the name and boundaries of the neighborhood. We then construct neighborhood entrance markers, put the neighborhood logo on street signs, and begin to develop neighborhood pride around the brand. You can tell you are succeeding when you see t-shirts with the name and stores along the nearby commercial corridors that adopt the neighborhood's identity.

We named the Dome Industrial Park in order to unite an effort around redeveloping an older industrial area that was deteriorating and losing businesses. We branded the "St. Pete Values," "CityTrails," "Play'n Close to Home," "St. Pete Arts," "St. Petersburg Ocean Team," and "Mayor's Mentors & More" programs described in other chapters of this book. Similarly, in order to build a united effort around redeveloping the most economically depressed part of our city, we needed to adopt a positive identity for the area.

In the past, the area that we now call Midtown had various names. It was often referred to as the "south side," although much of the city is south of Midtown, and Midtown comprises only a portion of the southern part of the city. The city began calling it "Challenge Area" in the late 1990s, but this reference was meant for government planning purposes. (The name "Challenge Area" is not one to develop a positive identity around.) Subparts of the community had their individual identification, and the neighborhood names continued in active use after the regional brand was established: Campbell Park, Harbordale, Palmetto Park, Highland Oaks, and several others.

In developing the name for the area, we felt it should be positive, descriptive, and geographic. The other regions of the city are defined by location, including the north, northeast, west, downtown, and others. Since the area we were focusing on is toward the middle of the city, both north-south and east-west, I decided to use the name "Midtown." The name has an upbeat feel, is geographic in nature, and gives an accurate description of the area's location. We communicated the new name by creating the position "Deputy Mayor for Midtown Economic Development."

The name was adopted both inside and outside Midtown. Businesses, apartments, and community groups have taken the name as their own, and the media uses it to describe happenings in the area. T-shirts boast the Midtown name, and the community has developed a renewed pride about living in Midtown. Once the name was established, we could begin the process of figuring out how to move the area forward.

(5) Develop a Plan

The mission of redeveloping Midtown was largely accepted by the community, the team was in place, and the name Midtown was established as the identity, so it was time to begin working on the initiative. Deputy Mayor Go Davis argued that we should start the process by hiring a consultant, seeking community input at a series of public meetings, and producing a written plan on how to redevelop Midtown. At first I considered the process Go described a waste of time and money. I had just completed eighteen months of careful study of city best practices and campaigning for mayor. I had listened to the community at neighborhood association meetings, coffee gatherings in people's living rooms, civic group luncheons, and discussions on the front porches of voters' homes. I knew what we needed to do and I was ready to get started!

Go Davis tactfully pointed out that he had served his whole career in the public arena, a venue that I had just entered, and that there were some benefits to seeking public input that I might be overlooking. First, you always learn something new when you receive public input on an issue, even though the process may sometimes be a bit painful. The input received helps build a better initiative, and therefore better advances our efforts to improve the city's quality of life.

Second, and perhaps even more importantly, the documentation of the public input process gives the effort greater credibility and helps insulate the effort from later attacks that the public will is not being served. No matter how great a program seems to be, there will always be those who attack the idea, either because of legitimate disagreement or because of a personal interest in an alternative direction. If you can point to documented results of a public input process, then you can legitimately claim that the plan is the community's plan, and therefore should be supported.

Ultimately I agreed with Goliath's approach, and we moved forward to develop a plan. The Midtown Strategic Planning Initiative Report (Midtown Report) was presented to the community in April 2002. It followed a state-funded, ten-month process of study and community input gathering. The analysis included a review of the twenty-five plans that had been previously developed for isolated parts of Midtown in order to take advantage of prior progress and present a comprehensive view for the future. Like our downtown redevelopment plan, we started with an inventory of the assets of Midtown: schools, historic structures, existing industrial areas, neighborhoods, and others. No matter how many challenges a community has, there are always strengths to build from.

In numerous community forums, the residents gave their opinion of what should be done in order to promote economic development, and how we would be able to recognize success when it comes. As might be expected, residents felt that the needs of Midtown were great. The Midtown Report outlined the main tenets of economic development as being in the areas of expansion/enhancement of existing businesses; opportunities for entrepreneurship; and employment opportunities that offer living wages and benefits.

The community expressed a desire to save and use historic buildings in order to preserve the character of Midtown. They also wanted to attract residents back to the community. They wanted less crime and less blight. There was a desire for better public facilities and infrastructure.

Residents also focused on a lack of services in Midtown that are available in other parts of the city, including retail centers, health care, social services, and restaurants. There was a recurring theme for four particular items that seemed to define whether a part of the community is being adequately served: residents wanted a grocery store, a post office, a bank, and a library. These are services that most of us take for granted, and it seemed reasonable that they should be obtained for Midtown.

The Midtown residents wanted what everyone wants: safe neighborhoods, good jobs, and nearby retail and public services that are available in other parts of the city. As we progressed through the coming years, we would find that these wants were not easy to realize, but we had to start if we were ever to achieve our goal of creating a seamless city.

If the Midtown plan was to succeed, we needed to track our progress. In my office, I maintained an aerial photo of the area and a color coded map, with planned and executed projects. A component of the Midtown effort was a focus on the major commercial corridors running through the area. If the corridors in an area are clean, vibrant, and attractive, then people will think positively about the area. If the commercial corridors are run down with blight, boarded-up buildings, and drug dealers on the corner, people are not going to want to visit or live there.

We started by identifying the major north-south and east-west corridors in Midtown. We established street landscaping plans for each corridor. It is amazing how much better a corridor will look if you add trees, landscape, upgraded sidewalks, mast arm traffic lights, and brick paver crosswalks. It makes people believe that change is coming, and it gives business owners an incentive to invest. We also inventoried the corridors' existing assets and identified sites that might become available for development. We reviewed the need list developed by the community in the Midtown Report and began the process of matching needs with locations. Always keeping one eye toward the community-identified goals, we set out to expand the services and retail amenities accessible to the Midtown residents, expand the opportunities for people to have good jobs, and assist in the development of existing and new business owners.

(6) Schools, Safety, and Neighborhoods

Among the discussion items of the Midtown Report were the importance of our public schools and the need to improve public safety. The city's public school support programs (discussed in chapter 8) apply city-wide, but they disproportionately help the Midtown residents since many are targeted at low income students.

One observation of the city's public safety effort (discussed in chapter 4) also deserves mention here. When I ran for office, I committed to establish a major economic renewal effort in the area we now call Midtown.

At some forums, members of the audience argued that we could not change the economics of the area until we got rid of crime. I agreed that crime was a major impediment to redevelopment, but I argued that we could not get rid of crime until we started to change the appearance and economics of the place. You have to passionately redevelop and aggressively go after crime at the same time. This was our approach, and we experienced great progress on both fronts. Importantly, the combined effort between 2001 and 2009 resulted in both urban renewal in Midtown and significant decreases in crime, especially violent crime, which dropped 26 percent in Midtown by 2009.

In addition to various neighborhood efforts (described in chapter 9), our city housing department has several programs to encourage home ownership and the redevelopment of some of the smaller apartment buildings that can often become crime and codes problems. We worked with neighborhood associations in the community to develop and execute neighborhood plans, respond to problems, and establish crime watch groups.

Our sanitation department hired one of our police detectives to investigate illegal dump sites on a regular basis, and our codes department worked hand in hand with neighborhoods to require people to take care of their properties. We also have a team in our codes department, funded through the sanitation department, which helps low-income elderly with minor home repairs and painting.

Jordan Park, a formerly crime-ridden, ugly, two-story federal housing project has been rebuilt under a Hope 6 grant. It is still federal housing, but it is now townhomes with porches, grass lawns, and a central play area. More importantly, after several years it is still in good shape and safe. Both Go Davis and I drove through regularly and called in reports to the housing authority of any sign of disrepair.

(7) Start—Decide to Succeed

When approaching a large challenge, it can be difficult to know when and where to begin. There is a tendency, especially in government, to want to continue to plan and study until all the questions are answered and the path is clear. I strongly believe in strategic planning, and incorporated the process into much of what we did. But at some point, even if the path is not completely clear, you just have to start.

Simple as it seems, if you don't start an effort, it can never be accomplished. In the case of Midtown, we had completed the Midtown Report, but there was so much to do that it was difficult to know how to proceed. We had to focus on something, so we decided to start with the post office.

During my campaign, and during the Midtown Report community input process, we heard a lot about the post office facility in Midtown. The facility had been constructed years before, but had never opened for retail business. It was purely a facility for mail carriers to pick up their mail for delivery. When Midtown residents received certified mail, they had to turn in their slip by standing outside and knocking on a window in the post office facility—an approach uncomfortably close to a part of the southern past we had moved beyond.

Midtown residents could not buy a stamp, mail a package, or get a post office box. Of the several post office facilities in the city, the Midtown site was the only one that refused to provide retail service. Many people in Midtown felt that the Post Office was discriminating against the area.

This was completely unacceptable if we were to succeed in building a seamless city. We decided we were going to have retail service at the Midtown Post Office.

When you decide that you are going to accomplish something, you are not saying that you will try … or do your best … or see if you can. You are *deciding*. Once the decision is made, the only remaining question becomes what resources will be required to accomplish the objective. Deciding is very powerful. When you commit to a direction and communicate that decision to the world, resources begin to flow to the effort.

To begin the process of obtaining retail post office service in Midtown, we met with the local postmaster, who advised that he did not have the capital budget to retrofit the existing facility for retail business. I responded by offering to pay the constructions costs for the improvements. I figured it couldn't cost that much to put in a new door and a service counter. The postmaster then advised that he didn't have the operating budget to fund the person behind the counter, although he agreed that it would be a busy branch.

My meeting with the local postmaster was the beginning of a three-year, frustrating process of attempted meetings, delays, and then multiple meetings with our local postmaster, the postmaster for Florida, and the vice president of area operations for the Southeast United States based in Memphis, Tennessee. The responses were consistent at each level, but the Memphis official at least provided us with his estimate of the cost of the improvements: $250,000.

At one point I became so frustrated with the Post Office's lack of response that I decided to hold a rally and picket the Post Office. I was certain that I could attract a large crowd, along with national media, to the event. As I discussed the idea in my Tuesday morning Cabinet meeting, our police chief became nervous. He did not like the prospect of the mayor organizing a large protest rally in the city. After some debate, I agreed to first go to the governor for help, but I kept the protest rally as an option in case the Post Office continued their opposition.

I met with Governor Jeb Bush in Tallahassee and sought his help. I told him Midtown's story, and showed him pictures of Midtown citizens standing outside the post office building, waiting for the window to open so they could conduct their business. The governor enthusiastically agreed to help. Later, I found myself in the Old Executive Office Building attached to the White House, meeting with the intergovernmental officer for President George W. Bush, for the purposes of getting stamps sold at an existing Post Office facility in Midtown.

The Post Office effort became an important symbol both inside and outside Midtown:

If you are willing to go to the White House to get stamps sold on 16th Street, then you have decided that you are going to have retail service at the Midtown Post Office, and you have decided that your city will be seamless!

After the meetings in Tallahassee and Washington, the Post Office contacted us to say that they would operate the retail post office if we agreed to pay the $250,000 construction costs. I agreed to cover the costs, and we contacted HUD, the United States Urban Development Authority, to request Community Development Block Grant funds to construct a post office expansion in the Midtown enterprise zone. They agreed. The post office expansion was built with federal funds and opened in late 2005. At the ribbon cutting, we announced to the large crowd, probably one of the largest ever for a post office opening, that the opening of the retail center was a strong signal from our national government. Essentially, the United States of America was confirming that Midtown is a seamless part of the city of St. Petersburg.

(8) Execute the Plan—Saving History

As discussed above, the Deuces (22nd Street) was the historic center of activity for St. Petersburg's African American community. It was the reflection of the health and vibrancy of the community. As 22nd Street deteriorated, it reflected despair and hopelessness, like someone had given up. In 2001, 22nd Street was the most blighted corridor in the entire city. We set out to change 22nd Street. We believed that if we turned around the worst corridor, people would start to think differently about Midtown, and the positive momentum would spread.

The community input described in the Midtown Report expressed a desire to save historic structures. I agreed. Preserving historic buildings maintains a link to the past and shows respect for the heritage and character of a community. We identified five historic structures that were along 22nd Street: Mercy Hospital, Royal Theater, Manhattan Casino, Jordan Elementary, and Seaboard Coast Line Railroad Station. Four of the five had been vacant for years, and all were in poor physical condition. Three were literally falling down.

The story of the redevelopment of these structures could each take its own chapter, or its own book. We worked either to secure control of the facility or partner with the owners. Our desire with each historic building was to find independent operators for the facilities. We did not want to create additional operational expenses for the city budget. In most cases we also sought a use that was similar to the original purpose of the historic structure.

We worked to develop plans, assess environmental issues, and secure funding, typically in multiple layers. We provided opportunities for neighborhood input and participation, and identified and negotiated with end users. After each project was completed, follow-up efforts were constantly required to ensure the continued success of the enterprise.

Mercy Hospital, the former segregated black hospital that had been closed for over thirty-five years, and was now falling down in the middle of a five-acre, blighted tract of land, became the Johnnie Ruth Clarke Health Clinic at the Historic Mercy Hospital site. The old building was saved and a new addition completed, resulting in a 26,000-square-foot medical facility. Construction funding came from a community development block grant and a federal grant procured by our congressman, Bill Young. Operating funds are supplemented by a grant from our county social services department. The completed facility included a clinic, dental offices, health education programs, and social services. At the opening many long-term residents were in tears, recalling the days when the hospital was active.

The Royal Theater and the Harlem Theater were the city's two formerly segregated black movie houses. The Harlem was torn down many years ago. The Royal Theater had stopped showing movies in the 1960s, and was in poor shape. As part of the Midtown Initiative, it was renovated and reopened as the Boys and Girls Club Royal Theater, a performing arts education center for Midtown youth. Bill Edwards, a local businessman who partnered with us in public school programs, holiday gifts for low income youth, and other efforts, contributed a significant amount of money to fund a recording studio for Midtown young people at the Royal Theater. Actress Angela Bassett also gave generously to the Royal. The support provided by Edwards, Bassett, and other business leaders was critical to the success of Midtown.

Jordan Elementary, the formerly segregated black elementary school, was completely rebuilt to its 1920s vintage as a LEED certified "green" building. It now houses a head start program for Midtown's pre-school children. The Manhattan Casino was completely rebuilt with the objective of attracting a restaurant downstairs and a banquet center upstairs on the historic dance floor. The funding for these projects came from a patchwork of federal grants, CDBG funds, privately raised money, state grants, and others.

The Seaboard Coast Line Railroad Station was the one project that required little city assistance other than encouragement, which often helps. The old brick station was rebuilt as one of the nation's largest clay and pottery co-ops. In 2005, my reelection victory party was held there— in Midtown!

Other improvements on 22nd Street include a St. Petersburg College campus, replacing a drug-infested apartment complex, and several smaller, new and improved businesses. The northern anchor for the 22nd Street corridor became the Dome Industrial Park, which I will discuss below. The southern anchor became Dell Holmes Park.

Dell Holmes Park was transformed from a rundown area on Lake Maggiore to one of the most splendid parks in the city with an exercise course, fishing pier, picnic shelters, golf chipping course, and, most importantly, a playground that I believe is the largest in Florida, complete with a water park and climbing nets. The area has become a beehive of activity on weekends, as people from throughout the city reserve the shelters for civic club picnics, birthday parties, and other celebrations. Importantly, Dell Holmes Park has been a magnet attracting people from outside the area into Midtown. Seamless!

One of the most important additions to 22nd Street South is at the 18th Avenue crossroads: Tangerine Plaza with its anchor Sweetbay supermarket. Like most Midtown projects, the Sweetbay story could be its own book. The effort to attract a national grocery store into the heart of an inner city is a difficult one. The work to help it succeed after it arrived was equally hard. We acquired three corners of an intersection that had previously housed a drug-infested apartment complex, a house converted to a pool hall, and an old gas station operating as a bar.

We learned about the grocery store business in an effort to identify potential stores to locate at the intersection. I sought and received Governor Jeb Bush's assistance in making introductions to the heads of the potential chains. We worked with a successful African American businessman who was not familiar with the grocery store business, but became paired with the Sembler Company, one of the southeast's largest grocery store developers, who helped us on a voluntary basis. A not-for-profit company owns the center that was financed with multiple layers of lending, some at subsidized rates under urban redevelopment programs.

One day Go Davis sat down with me in my office to pass along some bad news. The finance plan for the grocery store development was not working. The only way for the $11 million project to go forward was for the city to provide a $1.5 million interest-free loan. I was stunned. We had already agreed to lease the land for a nominal rent, land that cost $1 million to assemble. Knowing my philosophical leanings, Go understood that he was asking a lot.

I became a Republican after reading Milton Friedman's *Free to Choose*. I believe in balanced budgets, low taxes, and limited government involvement in private business. As a fiscally conservative person, I didn't know if I could swallow the additional loan. I knew that the investment would hopefully prime the pump, stimulating other private investment in the community, but I had trouble squaring it with my core fiscal values. I told Go that I would sleep on it.

I had a difficult time sleeping that night, and I talked through the dilemma with my wife, Joyce. She is a good sounding board for most of my difficult decisions. When the next day arrived, I went in to Go's office early in the morning with my decision: we could not—*not have* a grocery store! In reality it was the anchor of the Midtown effort, and we had to see it built. If we did not go forward with the grocery store, we were really deciding to abandon the Midtown effort. We would loan the money. We identified the source of the funds as a portion of the sale proceeds from a large tract of land that was sold for a major development in the north part of the city.

The grocery store opened in late 2005 and has been one of the chain's most successful new stores, although it took some effort from our team to assist the store in marketing to the Midtown residents. Many ministers in the Midtown community helped rally support in their congregations for the grocery store. They realized that the city had taken a bold step to help attract the store, and the community's successful turnaround was tied to Sweetbay's success. I enjoy dropping by the store often, not just for groceries, but for coffee and a sour cream donut.

The smaller stores in Tangerine Plaza include a locally owned suit store, beauty stores, and a dry cleaner, along with a Chinese restaurant and cell phone store that had ownership outside Midtown. One of the challenges of developing locally owned retail stores in an economically depressed area is the need to help the business owners write business plans, accomplish leasehold improvements, and obtain financing. The city's Business Assistance Center (discussed in chapter 6) worked with these and other entrepreneurs to help them build the capacity to successfully run their businesses.

The addition of the Tangerine Plaza and the Sweetbay grocery store gave others confidence in the positive movement of Midtown. Several new shopping centers followed to the under-retailed Midtown area, including Twin Brooks Common's dozen stores located on 34th Street; the Three Oaks Center with a large Family Dollar on 18th Avenue South; another Family Dollar on Fourth Street South; and the Sixteenth Street Plaza with about ten local retail stores. While the city worked with developers as they considered their sites, no significant financial subsidies were required for the projects.

Fast food restaurants also committed to Midtown. We started with McDonald's and added Checkers, Wendy's, Hungry Howies pizza, Gyros and Seafood Express, and Salem's Gyros and Subs. It is often a sign of progress in a redevelopment area when pizza restaurants feel comfortable enough to deliver throughout the community, so it was especially gratifying when Hungry Howies built their pizza restaurant in the heart of Midtown and provided delivery service. At times the city helped put these projects together, and at other times we played only a support role. I was always pleased when someone invested in Midtown without our significant involvement because it meant we were gaining momentum.

By 2009 Midtown boasted a new post office retail center, several new shopping areas, the Sweetbay grocery store, and a new Johnson Branch

Library that included extensive computer access for Midtown's residents. Additionally, the St. Petersburg Tennis Center was being rebuilt; several new public school buildings were complete; the new Davis-Bradley drug rehabilitation center was operating; St. Petersburg College was holding classes on 22nd Street; Mercy Hospital had been rebuilt as a medical clinic; the Royal Theater was an active cultural center; many parks and recreation centers had been added or upgraded; and there were countless other improvements throughout Midtown. But we lacked the final item on the list of desired services that residents had sought for the core of Midtown: a bank.

Several efforts were made to obtain banking services for the community. We came close on a couple of occasions, but the demographics of the area were such that it was a very hard objective to accomplish. Midtown did not fit neatly into the model most banks use when considering a new branch development. After the 2008 meltdown of the nation's financial system, it appeared unlikely that we would accomplish this final goal by the time I finished my terms in early January 2010. At the time of the national financial downturn, I placed a plaque in the Mayor's Reception Area as a reminder to everyone who visited that I still intended to bring financial services to Midtown. On the plaque was a slightly revised excerpt of Winston Churchill's 1941 speech at Harrow School: *Never, never, never give up!*

Fortunately, in April 2009, I had a conversation with Stephen Foster of GTE Federal Credit Union while we were both in the grandstands enjoying the Honda Grand Prix of St. Petersburg. As we talked about the financial needs of the residents of Midtown, our conversation turned to the possibility of GTE Federal Credit Union becoming part of the Tangerine Plaza center. The conversation quickly evolved into a proposal, negotiations, land site planning and development, permitting, construction, financing, and legal process, resulting in a ground breaking on August 31, 2009.

On December 22, 2009, a 3,800-square-foot GTE Federal Credit Union branch opened in the heart of Midtown, complete with a full service office and four drive-through tellers. It was located on 22nd Street across the street from Sweetbay and the Tangerine Plaza. The branch was built on the sight of a former gas station that had become a run-down bar. It was on one of the corners that the city had acquired a few years earlier. We provided the land for a nominal amount, and GTE Federal committed to operate a financial institution on the site for the long term.

In most areas of our city, a new bank or credit union branch would not be seen as a big deal, but in Midtown it represented the last major puzzle piece in a long list of amenities and services that had previously been denied to this part of our city, and were now in place. Six television cameras along with other media showed up for opening day.

Residents of Midtown could now buy groceries, go to a clinic, visit the post office, attend college classes, read at the library, play at upgraded swimming pools and recreation facilities, choose among many shopping centers, enjoy music lessons, perform on-stage, and make a deposit or take out a loan—all within their own neighborhood. It was a great feeling to cut the ribbon on the building that represented the completion of so many goals toward making Midtown a seamless part of St. Petersburg. Eleven days before I left office, at the ribbon cutting, my wife and I deposited $5,000 of our personal funds to become the first account member at the Midtown GTE Federal Credit Union branch. In the following year, it became a very successful branch under the leadership of its energetic leader, La'Shawn Hains.

The efforts for jobs in Midtown included both attracting employers and preparing people for jobs. Each of the retail centers and service providers described above need employees. The clinic needs nurses, the stores need managers and clerks, and the schools need teachers. One of the most visible evidences of both job creation and job training is the Dome Industrial Park.

The Dome Industrial Park (DIP) is a 120-acre industrial area on the north end of Midtown that had become blighted and unsafe, and was becoming vacant as businesses left on a regular basis. Theft of property at the businesses was common, and employees were afraid to walk to their cars after dark. Thieves would actually pull electric wire out of buildings in order to sell it to recycling outlets. The area was not well lighted; it flooded during rain storms and had roads that were in terrible disrepair. As small businesses grew to the point where they became profitable, they left for a better environment.

We started by establishing a brand name for the area. It had previously been an unnamed old industrial area. We called it the Dome Industrial Park, since it was near Tropicana Field, the domed home of our major league baseball team. We then constructed entry markers at multiple locations, upgraded the lighting and roads, and began assembling land for redevelopment. We initiated a focused code enforcement effort to rid the area of broken down automobiles, junk piles, and buildings that were in disrepair. If property owners worked with us to correct the problems, we tried to be patient with them as long as progress was being made. I did not want to chase employers away through the code enforcement process if I could avoid it. The expression we used was that we wanted to give businesses a reason to stay, before we gave them a reason to leave.

As businesses inside and outside the DIP area saw improvements being made, we were able to stop the exodus and recruit new employers to the area. Several new businesses came to the DIP, such as the St. Petersburg Clay Company, PetPal Rescue, Greenos Painting, JSI Sail manufacturing, Terra Construction, Sun-Guard Florida Solar Film, and many others. In the Dome Industrial Park, both the retained employers and new businesses provide needed jobs for the community. While every business is important to the area's success, in one case we got job training services along with new jobs.

Job Corps is a federal job training program under the United States Department of Labor. A few months after taking office in 2001, I visited a Job Corps Center in Jacksonville with U.S. Senator Bill Nelson. The Labor Department was considering creating a Central Florida Job Corps campus. Our county had shown an interest in the idea, and I wanted to learn more about the program. Fast forward to December 2009: the beautiful 15-acre Job Corps campus at the Dome Industrial Park in Midtown was complete, and its classes would begin in 2010.

The long, agonizing effort included our assembling and cleaning up the site. It was an incredible example of urban blight. We facilitated community buy-in, worked through the application, and navigated the bureaucracy of the federal government, but in the end a 15-acre campus was completed to train 300 people every six months for jobs that are in demand in our county. Among the planned skills to be taught were carpentry, electrical, plumbing, health fields, and automobile mechanics. The Center was intended to employ almost 100 new workers. It transformed a terribly blighted area into a beautiful campus. Our local congressman, Bill Young, was also of critical help in the success of the Job Corps Center, as he was for countless other redevelopment efforts in the city.

(9) Measure Success

The Midtown initiative was a very difficult, yet incredibly successful effort. The visible changes to the community, the decrease in violent crime, and the increase in commerce were proof that great progress had been made. It is easy to compare the list of needs set out in the Midtown Report against the programs and developments completed, as described above.

But one of the most important metrics of progress is a community's self image, and this is a factor that is hard to measure. One indication of our progress on this front came when I was giving a new reporter a tour of Midtown a few months after I left office. Herbert Murphy, the manager of Midtown's Boys and Girls Club, was walking us through the Royal Theater. "Murph" enthusiastically described Midtown's great progress during the previous nine years, and he listed change after change. Finally he stopped walking, turned to the reporter with a serious look, and summarized the Midtown community's new attitude: "We quit calling it the hood!"

Still, there is more work to be done. While the appearance of the community has changed remarkably for the better, the most important continuing mission is to convince children growing up in all parts of our city that their best opportunity for success is through achievement in school, hard work, and self-discipline. Opportunities for positive influence are now being provided through our public schools, churches, city recreation programs, St. Pete Values, Doorways Scholarships, mentoring and tutoring, Job Corps training, and others.

Ultimately it is a mission that must achieve success one child at a time. While the effort will continue, there is no doubt that we have advanced a long way toward the goal of making Midtown a more vibrant, safe, and prosperous part of St. Petersburg. The key to the achievements that have been made so far is the character of the people who live in Midtown, and the united spirit of a city that is committed to the goal of becoming seamless!

Chapter 8

Schools Belong
to Everyone

*A Bible and a newspaper in every house, a good school
in every district—all studied and appreciated as they
merit—are the principal support of virtue, morality, and
civil liberty.*

—Benjamin Franklin

One night, I was sitting in my captain's chair behind the home
plate fence watching my daughter Julann's softball game at the
Northeast Little League's Shorey complex. I like my captain's
chair. It is light-weight, folds up easily, and has a coffee cup holder. I
bought the chair on the night of Julann's first soccer practice—and I've
used it for all my kids' sporting events ever since.

The night of Julann's softball game, I had come straight from work
and I hadn't eaten dinner. I could smell the hamburgers grilling at the
concession stand so, in between innings, I got up from my captain's chair
and walked over to order dinner. The concession stands at our little
league fields are staffed by parents who volunteer. Actually, volunteering
may be a generous term. The league assigns each team days to work the

stand and, in turn, the coach or team mom works on getting parents to show up.

That night, my order was taken by a softball mom who seemed to be stressed and tired, either from the length of the day or from the busy pace of life. She took my hamburger order and glanced up at me. As she recognized me, the stressed lines of her face smoothed into a sweet, gentle smile. She touched the back of my hand, which was resting on the counter and said: "Mayor Baker, thank you for the wonderful things you do for our city."

Words like that are always nice to hear. I began to reply by thanking her and telling her that many people were helping in the effort, when she stopped me and continued: "You don't understand mayor. I am a single mom with two middle school daughters. A while ago they were going the wrong way and I didn't know what to do. Their grades weren't where they needed to be, and I was worried about the influences around them. I was in a panic. You gave them each a Doorways scholarship and now they are both doing well in school, and heading in the right direction. For the first time in two years, I am sleeping at night. Thank you!"

As I settled into my captain's chair with my burger in hand and soft drink safely in my cup holder, my eyes watered. The experience confirmed a belief for which I advocated five years earlier when I first campaigned for office:

Schools are everyone's responsibility!

During the campaign I had argued that our public schools should be one of the priorities of the city's mayor. The city should take an active role in supporting our public schools. With all the other challenges facing the city, helping the public schools had not been an effort undertaken by the city government in the past, and there was limited appetite among the other candidates to take it on now. Even members of my campaign team scoffed at the idea and sarcastically suggested that I needed a civics lesson: public schools were the responsibility of the School Board, elected countywide, and the Superintendent of Schools, selected by the School Board. Why would the mayor take on the political risk, and dedicate precious political capital, to address a challenge that was not even his responsibility, especially a challenge as difficult as the public schools?

My response to opponents and supporters was the same: public schools are important to the success of the city. If our schools are not doing well, we cannot attract businesses to our city. Companies want to know that they can employ a workforce that graduates from quality schools, and they want their employees' children to go to good schools. We also need good schools to attract people to our neighborhoods. One of the first questions potential home buyers ask real estate agents is what school their children will attend. If the schools are not good, people will not move into those neighborhoods.

In other words, if we want businesses in our city and people living in our neighborhoods, then we must have great public schools. City leaders cannot simply sit back and hope their public schools will improve. There is too much at stake. Schools must be everyone's job! If the mayor is to lead the city, he needs to step out front in support of the public schools—it is that simple.

Many voters agreed with this philosophy, and I won in 2001. After the election, I had to figure out how we could help the schools without getting in the way of, and generating resentment from, those who were charged with the job of running the schools. My pre-campaign review of other cities around the country failed to identify a model to work from, so we would need to clear a path on our own. Helen Levine, our city's first administrator for public school programs, branded the effort "Mayor's Mentors & More."

The Plan for Schools

The core principles underlying the effort were as follows: (a) help improve our public schools without using a lot of city taxpayer money; (b) seek partnerships in the form of advice, private contributions, and volunteer hours; (c) identify ways to tie the schools closer to the community; (d) always work in cooperation with the school board and superintendent; and (e) measure our success by reviewing student achievement. Over the years the program developed into a national model for city-school system partnerships. We frequently added new elements, consistent with the core principles. By the end of our two terms, the following activities were included within the program:

(1) Raising money and awarding "Doorways Scholarships" to low income children.
(2) Recruiting and training mentors for students who need role models and support.
(3) Recruiting and supporting Business Partners for every public school in the city to provide volunteers, financial help, and strategic planning advice—while developing a template for success.
(4) Developing an incentive program to reward the leaders of our schools that are succeeding.
(5) Creating incentives for teachers to teach in the urban public schools.
(6) Visiting the schools on a regular basis, meeting the students and talking with the administrators and teachers.
(7) Constantly challenging city staff to seek out new ways of improving.
(8) Measuring success using the State system of school grading, which is based on student achievement test scores. This includes communicating the progress to our residents in simple graphs published in the city's online "City Scorecard."

We started our effort with a scholarship program that had already been developed by the Pinellas County Education Foundation, a group of businesses established to help schools in our county. Since it opened doors for students' education, it was named Doorways.

(1) Doorways Scholarships

*The child furiously worked to save the starfish—scores of them had
washed along the beach as far as he could see—the boy was trying to put
them back into the water before they died. But a man who was watching
told him that it was a futile effort—he could not save them all in time.
The little boy paused for a moment, picked up a starfish, showed it to
the man and said: "Maybe not, but I can save this one!" He then gently
returned the starfish to the sea.*

—Adapted from the Starfish Story

The Doorways program involves a promise. It tells a low-income
child (in the case of our version of the program, a sixth grade student in
a free or reduced lunch program) that if through twelfth grade the student: (1) maintains at least a "C" average; (2) stays free of crime and
drugs; and (3) maintains good conduct and attendance, then upon high
school graduation the student will be awarded a four-year college scholarship in a state college or university. I refer to the Doorways Scholarships as an incentive for a child to stay good for six years.

The statistics are impressive. In the 2002 school year, when we started
the city's Doorways scholarships, about 64 percent of Florida's students
graduated from high school with a general diploma. Although the statistics are difficult to segregate for students in free or reduced lunch
programs, it is a fair assumption that the percentage of graduates from
the low-income population would be significantly less than the general
population average of 64 percent.

Our Doorways students performed incredibly. Of the sixth grade
students who received Doorways scholarships in our first two years, 93
percent graduated with a diploma from high school by the end of twelfth
grade. *Ninety-three percent!* The college scholarship provided students
with a strong incentive to stay on track from sixth through twelfth grade.

As our program evolved, we discovered that an unacceptable number
of our students were losing their scholarships because they slipped on

one or more of the established criteria, as described above. Lori Matway, a former middle school principal who served as our school programs administrator during my second term, concluded that we needed to be more active in helping students regain their footing, not just allow them to be removed from the program after a problem was identified. We designated a staff person, funded by the Pinellas County Education Foundation, to act as an advocate for our Doorways students. When students were identified as being at risk of losing their scholarships, we contacted the students' parents and attempted to get the students back on track. Our objective was to help the students succeed, not wait for them to fail.

We used multiple levels of funding leverage for the Mayor's Doorways Scholarships. We started with the Florida pre-paid tuition program that allows the purchase of four-year college scholarships in advance, in our case when a student is in sixth grade. As an example, in 2009, the cost of a four-year, pre-paid college scholarship for a sixth grader was about $12,000. Under Florida's "STARS" program, the state paid one-half of the cost of the pre-paid tuition costs for children who fall below certain income levels, leaving $6,000 to raise. Shortly after I took office, we received a commitment from our Pinellas County Education Foundation to match any money I raised, leaving us $3,000 more to find. One generous businessman agreed to match one-half of this amount, leaving $1,500. Thus, our sales pitch to businesses, individuals, and civic organizations was that for $1,500 (in 2009), they could send a low-income child to college, and change a life.

It worked. During almost nine years in office, we gave four-year college scholarships to over 1,000 low-income sixth graders. By the time we completed two terms, the sixth graders from our early years were in college. The number of students who received scholarships was limited by the amount of funds that we obtained, but since 93 percent of our original Doorways students graduated, our Doorways students set examples for other students as they worked their way through middle and high school. The program had a cumulatively profound impact on St. Petersburg's schools.

(2) Mentors

The Doorways program matches students with mentors who regularly visit the student at school, providing a role model and advisor who can expose the student to ideas and information. We have no idea how much we know about things that our students need to know. It is remarkably helpful to have a caring adult with whom the student can discuss problems and make plans for their future.

In order to increase the number of mentors for our students, the city launched three efforts: providing training to mentors; recruiting mentors from businesses and the general public; and providing mentoring incentives to city employees. We allowed city employees one hour per week paid time to mentor a child in the public schools. We averaged between 150 to 200 city employees as mentors each year of the program. We also recruited and trained over 1,200 mentors for our public schools. Each mentor was helping to direct a child toward success!

(3) Business Partners

One morning I was touring one of our elementary schools with its principal and I noticed that the grass was overgrown in an area where the children were playing. When I asked why the grass was so high, the principal replied that the school system only cuts the grass every few weeks. In times when there is a lot or rain, the grass gets long. She said that she had someone who could cut the grass but she couldn't afford a lawn mower for the school.

A lawn mower?

It started me thinking. How many things are public schools missing, such as art supplies, computers, software, or backpacks, which are impeding their progress? Having come from the business world, I was certain that any one of a dozen companies that came to my mind would jump at the opportunity to buy a lawn mower for a school if they knew that one was needed.

Our schools are often isolated from many parts of our community. They are filled with hard-working, dedicated administrators and teachers, but they may lack contacts with the businesses that would be willing to provide help. The schools and businesses need someone to bridge the gap by making an introduction. We found that businesses are generally willing to help our public schools when we ask, but they also want to know that their help is having an impact. They like to see where their money and efforts are going.

My search for a lawn mower became the beginning of our Business Partner program. The program matched each of the forty-six public schools that we supported with a business in our community. The business had input in the selection process and, when possible, we matched a business with a school nearby. We also tried to match larger businesses with high schools and middle schools, leaving our elementary schools for smaller businesses, although there were exceptions.

When we first started, we debated whether or not to identify specific requirements that a Business Partner must meet, but we decided against that direction. Instead we simply matched the business and school together with the understanding that either could choose to discontinue the partnership at any time. As long as the business and school were both happy with the arrangement, they were free to shape the elements of the partnership in whatever manner they chose.

Most Business Partners helped in three ways. First, they provided mentors and tutors from their employee base for the schools. I always requested that the CEO become a mentor, and many did. I let them know that I was a mentor also. It is a powerful statement to an employee if their top boss is a mentor, especially if that boss adopts the city program of giving their employees an hour paid time a week to mentor a student. Our Business Partner program was responsible for most of the mentors and tutors that we recruited.

A second way that Business Partners helped was with money. The amounts spent were typically not great, but they were often important. Examples of support given included the purchase of computers, software, classroom supplies, teacher business cards, student agenda planners, food for parent nights, art supplies, and many others. Often the Business Partner provided a conduit to another business that provided the help. What seems like a small contribution by the business is generally a huge benefit for the school.

The third way that the business helped was strategic planning. The business leader and principal will often get together to review the school plan and student achievement scores, and discuss methods of improvement. In twelve of our schools, this was done through a grant and business-funded, three-year strategic planning program targeted at low performing schools—led by Florida's Council for Education Change, and its energetic leader Elaine Lifton.

The first of these schools, Mt. Vernon Elementary, started their plan before we developed the Business Partner program, and they later became part of our program. Mt. Vernon was fortunate that its partner, Raymond James Financial, which is based in St. Petersburg, had selected senior executive Elliot Stern to lead the plan from the business side. Stern and the school's principal, Valerie White, working with teachers and staff, developed a plan that included incentives for parent involvement, teacher and staff bonuses, mentors and tutors, and data analysis that resulted in a remarkable turnaround.

Mt. Vernon and their Business Partner approached their effort strategically. They studied the test data to determine which students were having problems and identify core subject areas that needed improvement. They directed their volunteer mentors and financial resources to the students and areas that needed improvement the most. In order to improve parent involvement, they rethought the regular group meetings of parents. In order to increase attendance, they began catering the meetings with donated food from quality, local restaurants, charging a minimum amount to the attendees. They also held a raffle for all attendees who stayed to the end, giving out prizes. In between the dinner and raffle, they had their business meeting where they shared with the parents various ideas on how to help their children succeed in school. The result was a full house at the parent meetings, and significant increase in the parent's participation.

Before their partnership with Raymond James, Mt. Vernon had a 73 percent free/reduced lunch population, one of the oldest buildings in the school district, and three consecutive years of being a "D" school on the state's formula, which is based on student achievement scores. During the three years of the plan, the school's grade increased to C, then B, then A. As of 2009, the school had been an A school for six years in a row, the later years under a new principal, Peggy Pearson. The school's facility and student mix have not changed appreciably, but its approach and success is life-changing for the students who are achieving.

After the results of Mt. Vernon, we reverse-engineered their strategic plan, put it online, and gave it to the other schools involved in the strategic planning process. We found that the keys to success are the commitment and capability of both the Business Partner and the principal, and the development of the plan as a school "team" receiving input and buy-in of teachers, school staff, and others involved.

With Mt. Vernon in mind, we actively recruited other Business Partners and encouraged them to assist their partner schools in similar ways. By the end of 2009, we had 100 Business Partners for our public schools, enough that every school had one or more. The partners were providing mentors, financial support, and strategic planning help. It is impossible to adequately measure the remarkable cumulative impact that these businesses had on our schools. Among many other benefits, they have sent a message to the school leadership and teachers that the community cares about them and wants to be part of the effort to help them succeed.

We decided to fix the number of Business Partners at 100 and not increase beyond that point. For us, it was a number we could manage and, by having a limit, it put pressure on the businesses to perform so they would not be dropped from the program. Business Partners are not the complete solution to the needs of our schools, but they are a very important start.

(4) Top Apple

A few years after we started our public school programs, I was flying home from Washington, D.C., and began to review the latest state grades for our schools. The results were impressive. Our schools, the urban center schools, had made great progress based on our student achievement scores. With all the criticisms our school systems receive, it seemed to me that this was a cause for celebration. Under the leadership of our second school programs administrator, Sarah Lind, the Mayor's Top Apple program began.

A school becomes a Top Apple school if, based on the state's grade system, it either increases a letter grade (e.g., D to C, C to B, etc.) over the course of a year, or maintains a letter A grade. The program was designed to reward principals and assistant principals of the school. Leadership drives success, and it is important to reward successful leadership, but there are few public school programs that have the resources to reward successful principals. It frustrates me at times when we move a highly successful principal to school administration. While it is helpful to have experienced principals in the administration, it would often be better to find a way to reward the success of good principals and keep them in their schools.

Under Florida's A+ program, when public schools increase the level of their state grade based on student achievement tests, they receive additional cash that is often used for teacher and staff bonuses. Top Apple supplements the state program by providing direct rewards to the principal. The in-kind and cash incentives for Top Apple came from private businesses and individuals. The program was administratively supported by our Pinellas County Education Foundation.

The Mayor's Top Apple ceremony was held at a televised meeting of City Council. Other attendees include the superintendent, members of our state legislative delegation and school board, along with the principals, assistant principals, and Business Partners of the Top Apple schools. At the ceremony the principals, assistant principals, and Business Partners are brought up, one school at a time, and presented with recognition of their success.

For example, in 2009, each principal received a red marble apple with their name and date engraved; an eight foot tall Top Apple banner with the year and their school name to hang in front of the school, in their cafeteria, or in another prominent location; season passes to the local theater; dinner for two at the famous Columbia restaurant at the Pier downtown; a weekend stay at the Tradewinds resort on St. Pete Beach; and a $2,500 cash bonus. After the ceremony, a stand-up dinner reception was held in City Hall and an apple juice toast was given. The Business Partners received a plaque, and the assistant principals received a marble apple and a smaller cash bonus.

The Top Apple Ceremony has the aura of the Academy Awards on a local level. It accomplishes the objective of rewarding success and demonstrating to our school leaders that our community honors and appreciates them. I am also certain that it provided an incentive for great leaders to stay in, or come to, our urban schools. One principal gave us proof of that incentive by withdrawing her transfer application within a week after she received a Top Apple award.

(5) Teacher Incentives—A+ Housing

It is important to retain good teachers in our schools. Teachers tell me that the discipline and academic issues of students in the urban center are more difficult than those in the suburbs, so teachers with seniority often elect to relocate. Fortunately, we have a dedicated core of talented teachers who see their service to the urban students as an honorable calling, and I am thankful for them. In order to provide an additional motivation for a teacher considering coming to our schools, or staying here, we created the Teacher A+ Housing program.

The A+ program, in 2009, provided a teacher in a public school in our city with a $20,000 interest-free loan, to use as a down payment when he or she buys a house in the city. If the teacher stays in the St. Petersburg schools for ten years, he or she never has to pay the loan back. Since we use state housing assistance money to fund the loans, the teacher's income cannot exceed state maximum levels. I have been told by some teachers that they came to our schools because of the loans, and I have been told by others that they turned down positions in other districts because of the loans. It is fundamental that we have great teachers to make our schools great, and the A+ program provided one tool toward achieving that end.

(6) School Visits

I will never forget the handshake I received on the blacktop outside Pinecrest Elementary School in Miami. I was in sixth grade, and the handshake came from Congressman Dante B. Fascell. The congressman's son went to Pinecrest, so he came by to visit us. I had never met anyone who had been elected before, so it made a big impression on me. I felt important and somehow more connected to the state and country.

I remembered that handshake thirty-two years later when I became mayor of St. Petersburg, and I decided that I wanted to visit the kids in our schools. My hope was that a visit from the mayor would help the students feel more connected, take more pride in the place where they live, and take more pride in themselves. The gesture may even make it a little more likely that our children will want to raise their own children here. In any case, over the course of my term, I visited all of our public schools many times. I also visited most of our private schools.

For elementary schools, I met each class; shook hands with every student after reminding them to look into my eyes when they speak and tell me their name clearly; encouraged all of them to read every night; inquired as to what books they were reading; and told them all how great their teacher and school were. I then asked them to recite, and sometimes sing (inventing their own tunes), my theme expression: "It's another great day in St. Petersburg!" I learned to keep a marker handy so I could sign casts of any injured students, and I kept hand sanitizer nearby to avoid catching or spreading germs of the 600 or so hands I shook at each elementary school.

Before leaving I gave every child a card talking about the importance of reading, and containing a word search game on the back, with the search words being the various responsibilities of the mayor. For middle school the cards were a bit larger and had a crossword puzzle with similar words. The cards were always a big hit!

I also visited the middle and high schools. I will never forget one of my visits to Lakewood High School. I was there around lunch time so I headed to the cafeteria. I decided to eat with some of the students. The school staff was a little nervous as I went through the line and picked a group of young men to sit down with: High school students can be a little unpredictable in the lunch room.

To my delight, the group of guys I sat down with seemed to be the same group I used to eat lunch with thirty years earlier at Palmetto High School in Miami. As we talked, I could almost identify my classmates'

personalities in each of the students sitting with me: the class cut-up, the
varsity player, the guy with the cool car, the one who wore striped pants
and a plaid shirt, and the fast talker. (I won't say which one I was in the
1970s.) We had a great talk about a lot of things, more fun than philo-
sophical.

It occurred to me on that day that it is important to look beyond the
statistics and challenges of the school system, and view things from the
eyes of the young people who are living the school experience today. It
is also probably a good idea for the students to see their mayor as a
regular person, not as someone they only see on television. The only way
for the exchange to occur is to go into the schools and meet the students.

It can take two or three hours at a school to talk to children and shake
their hands, but it is worth the effort, and it was one of my favorite ways
to spend time. I love kids! I know that my visits taught me a lot, and that
I became a better mayor by meeting the students in our city. My hope is
that my visits also helped the students to become better citizens, and made
them feel that they were an important part of our city, because they are.

(7) Ongoing Improvement

Once a connection is made between the city and public schools,
opportunities for additional benefits seem to present themselves. We now
have dozens of shared facility arrangements with our schools, a very
efficient way of using taxpayer money, including many joint use playgrounds and athletic fields. Students take field trips to visit their school's
Business Partner and make bulletin boards describing employers in our
city. They learn about different fields and different professions when the
business representatives visit the schools.

Our recreation department provided student before and after care
programs, as well as summer play camp, at recreation centers throughout
the city. We paid the school system to transport the students to and from
our centers, covering our costs through fees and grants for low-income
children. The city also supplies part time crossing guards for streets near
our elementary and middle schools. The mostly retirement-age guards
were scheduled for the hours around the start and end of the school day.

Sometimes the school partnerships can be personal. Once, after a police officer was shot, elementary students at multiple elementary schools prepared hand-made thank you cards saying "Thank you for protecting us" and "Get better soon." Since the officer was undercover, the children could not meet him. The pleased look on his face, and his wife's face, was priceless when my daughter Julann and I delivered three boxes of cards, made by over 1,200 individuals, to his hospital room.

With each new program we followed a simple rule. First, I presented the idea to the superintendent of schools, Julie Janssen. If she did not want to do it, we didn't do it. It was my desire to work with the school leadership, not to compete, and they responded with enthusiastic support.

(8) Progress

During the more than eight years of our Mayor's Mentors & More, the forty-two graded public schools that our programs supported improved significantly. While the city helped, the primary credit for the success goes to the school administration, principals, and other school-based leaders, dedicated teachers, Business Partners, parents, and students who joined together to make our schools better.

As a community working together, we saw the number of our urban center's "A" and "B" schools, measured by the state using student achievement scores, increase by 260 percent: that's more than two and a half times as many St. Petersburg schools where our student achievement scores were significantly higher. Out of a total of twenty-seven elementary schools, we went from having zero "A" schools in 2001 to sixteen "A" elementary schools at the end of 2009. These numbers were not just statistics. They represented students who were achieving, learning, and becoming better prepared for life. Importantly, these gains came during a period when the state raised the bar for reading, writing, and math achievement, and added a science component to the measurement. Both moves made it harder to reach "A" and "B."

Although our elementary and middle schools made remarkable improvement, there is still a great deal of work to be done. High school performance is a challenge nationally. There is a directed focus, in partnership with the Pinellas County school system, to improve high school performance in St. Petersburg. Graduation rates for St. Petersburg's public high schools increased significantly, from 53 percent in the school year 2001–2002 to 81 percent in 2008–2009. Our urban schools went from graduating at a rate 11 percent below the state graduation rate, to 5 percent above the state rate.

By January 2010, the high schools' state grades had not yet reflected the same progress as the lower-grade students, but progress will continue as our achieving pre-high school students move up, and as the community responds to the challenge of moving our high school students forward.

As time advances, and standards and measurement systems evolve, the measured progress of schools will ebb and flow. This is how it should be. If increased standards of measurement reveal weaknesses in schools or a system, then it allows adjustments to be made to make the learning process better. As problems are revealed, such as when a school receives a bad grade, then it should be looked at as an opportunity, not a failure. It would be a failure only if there was no accountability system, and the low performance was never revealed. It is much better for the students if problems are identified, improvements are made, and a foundation for future success is built. But cities need to be part of the solution.

The partnership of cities with public schools provides an incalculable benefit. It reverses a decades-old trend of separating public schools from the rest of us, and takes a step at weaving our schools back into the fabric of our communities. Businesses, community groups, and residents should embrace public schools as being everyone's responsibility. If we keep tightening this weave, we will have better schools, and our children and country will have a more promising future!

Chapter 9

Neighborhoods

Make Memories for Kids

---

*The impersonal hand of government can never
replace the helping hand of a neighbor.*

—Hubert H. Humphrey

During my first campaign, we seemed to have a debate or forum every other night. Typically the mayoral candidates would square off for about forty-five minutes, followed by a debate of the city council candidates. Since the debates were so frequent, the nine mayoral candidates and the dozen candidates in the five different city council races all got to hear from each other a great deal. The questions raised at the events were common city issues: jobs, redevelopment, infrastructure, taxes, and crime.

One night after a forum in a church fellowship hall, John Bryan walked me to my car. He was a candidate for city council from the north part of the city. We had only just met during the campaign, so I was kind of surprised when he leaned against his pickup truck and said that he wanted to help my effort. He told me that he had come across an idea that would help me a great deal in my race, and he strongly urged me to learn more about the concept. He even had a web site (still a fairly new concept at that time) for me to look up: "Dogwalkpark.com."

Dog parks?

This was going to help me become mayor of the fourth largest city in Florida? We had just finished a debate discussing violent crime, poverty, and failing schools, but the solution being offered was a park for dogs.

I listened half-heartedly to John's argument until he came to his closing point. He said that many people in the city wanted to let their dogs run loose somewhere, but when they did the city's response was to give them a $25 fine. Instead of fining them, why don't we give the dog owners a fenced-in park area where their dogs can run around without a leash? We could put in some benches, a water spout, and a painted fire hydrant for character. It's good for the community, and it is a good idea politically. After all, half the people in the city owned dogs.

Half of the city's population! That was an argument and a statistic that caught my attention, so I decided to look up the web site. It didn't take long to convince me after that. Dog parks would provide an inexpensive and enjoyable way to build community within our neighborhoods. It would also give people the space they needed to let their dogs run loose and get needed exercise. After the elections, we set about opening dog parks. Our city lawyers had concerns about liability issues, dogs biting people, and dogs biting dogs, but we decided to give it a go. We started cautiously, but the idea quickly caught on.

I will never forget two days in September 2001, when I became convinced of the value of dog parks. On the first day, we broke ground on the construction of a new library that would cost about *$3 million* to build. It was a nice event attended by city staff, along with a small group of people from the neighborhood.

The next day we cut the ribbon on a new dog park at Crescent Lake, which cost *$9 thousand* to build. About two hundred people showed up, along with hundreds of dogs! The park was so overcrowded that the grass was quickly worn out, and neighbors complained about the overuse of the park. I began to announce, only half jokingly, that dog parks are cheap, everybody loves them, and I want to get reelected, so we were going to build as many as we could! By 2009, the city had dog parks located throughout the community. If we received the support of the local neighborhood association, we built the dogs' area in portions of existing parks. Once we created a new community asset in the Kenwood neighborhood by building a dog park on a three-acre site under the interstate. We had to receive approval from the State Department of Transportation. The end result was the conversion of a blighted area into an active, attractive park used by our residents and their dogs.

What we came to learn was that dog parks were not just for the dogs. They became a place where neighbors get to know each other. They were sub-communities of the city. Most people who use the parks are regulars, and groups get to know each other based on the time and day when they generally show up. These parks are heavily used. Although we never did a survey, there is no doubt in my mind that dog parks are more used, on a per-square-foot-per-person basis, than any other park in the city. We even formed a dog park community advisory group to deal with the issues that arose, and to provide ideas for improvement.

There is something interesting that occurs at dog parks. If you go to most parks and see people milling around, you are not generally inclined to walk up to a complete stranger and try to strike up a conversation. Doing so tends to generate suspicion. A dog park is different. All you have to do is walk up to anyone there and ask them which dog belongs to them, and you have instantly made a new friend. Before long, everyone nearby has gathered around to talk about their dogs, discuss what is going on in the city, and maybe even complain about the mayor! It becomes an informal community get-together, and it is a delightful experience.

As an expansion of our dog friendliness, St. Petersburg became the first Florida city to enact a dog friendly sidewalk café ordinance. We now have cafés and shops all over downtown that have dog biscuits next to their cash registers and water dishes by the sidewalk umbrella tables. We also supported an annual dog walk with hundreds of dogs called Pets on

Parade, and we started an annual dog swim where we turn one city pool over to the dogs on the last day of the summer pool season. Since we have to completely clean the pools before the next year, we might as well let the dogs cool off for a day. Their owners love it! Our dog parks became a symbol of the city doing something that makes sense, which addresses a very specific need of the community. They became shorthand for the city's commitment to improving the quality of life for its citizens. People love their dogs, and they love a city that understands the need for an urban dog to run loose for a while without its owner getting fined.

The Plan for the Neighborhoods

With the lessons of dog parks in mind, we set out to develop programs that advanced the mission of constantly improving the quality of life for the people who live in our neighborhoods. Neighborhoods are where most residents spend the majority of their time. They are host to the city's libraries, swimming pools, recreation centers, parks, and playgrounds. People feel a special bond to their neighborhood. If a city is to become the best in America, then it must have very special neighborhoods.

The effort to make neighborhoods better involves a team of elected leaders, neighborhood leaders, crime watch volunteers, city staff in multiple departments, and other community leaders. In association with these partners, we focused on multiple strategies in an effort to make our city's neighborhoods even greater places:

(1) Working with our organized neighborhood association leaders to develop plans for improvement and address problems and opportunities as they arise.

(2) Adding amenities that provide more opportunities to enjoy the outdoor life, especially playgrounds.

(3) Aggressively working to become one of America's most pedestrian friendly cities, with safe sidewalks, and the Southeast's largest bike path system.

(4) Supporting strong recreational programs and libraries, and develop a component within each recreation program that strengthens the character of our youth while improving athletic abilities.

(5) Focusing efforts on keeping the community clean by aggressively pursuing illegal dumping and graffiti.

(6) Planting trees throughout the city and establish a flowering tree program to enhance beauty, shade, and the environment.

(7) Becoming a national leader in developing green programs that advance the quality of life and environment in our city.

(1) Working with the Neighbors

My predecessor, Mayor Dave Fischer, initiated a national-model neighborhood department to coordinate with and support volunteer neighborhood groups throughout the city. It was a way of supporting what Hubert Humphrey called "the helping hand of a neighbor." They worked together to make our neighborhoods better, and are a key to our neighborhoods' success. When I served as chair of the Chamber's Leadership St. Pete program in the early 1990s, I teamed up with the Council of Neighborhood Associations (CONA) to start a training program for existing and potential neighborhood leaders. The CONA Neighborhood Leadership Program provides seminars on the city's history, code enforcement, public safety efforts, and a number of other topics related to making the neighborhoods better. It also introduces participants to the leaders in our community, including elected and appointed city officials and leaders in other neighborhoods.

Upon taking office, we continued the neighborhood efforts, and by 2010 we had over 100 formed neighborhood associations located throughout the city. They partnered with city staff to develop and execute individual neighborhood plans and identify challenges and opportunities as they arose. Among the many issues that we worked on together were crime, speeding, codes enforcement, beautification, and parks.

Neighborhood associations sent out newsletters to their residents to inform them of ongoing issues and activities. The groups also planned annual events like chili cook-offs, yard sales, founder's day picnics, pot luck suppers, tours of homes, mini-parades for the 4th of July, and Easter egg hunts. The city set aside budget money each year to fund neighborhood grants for projects developed by the neighborhood associations addressing beautification, traffic, safety, or other needs.

St. Petersburg's progress in its neighborhoods was greatly aided by the work of very dedicated neighborhood leaders. We recognized their efforts by holding a neighborhoods awards ceremony each year to highlight the neighborhoods and individual leaders for their accomplishments in making the city better. In order to continue the dialogue with the grassroots leadership, staff from codes, police, and neighborhood departments regularly attended neighborhood meetings.

We held regular morning coffee meetings in my office, with five to ten neighborhood association presidents at a time, to discuss current issues and identify ways that the city government could help. It was a great opportunity to learn what was going on in the neighborhoods, communicate the programs and efforts we were working on, and share ideas on how to make the city's neighborhoods even better. I learned constantly from the volunteer leadership in our neighborhoods.

(2) St. Pete Outside

St. Petersburg is located on a peninsula on the Gulf of Mexico in central Florida. It has been historically known as the Sunshine City for good reason: the city still holds the Guinness Book of World Records for the most consecutive days of sunshine. It only makes sense that, in improving the quality of life for the people who live in the city, a high priority should be given to programs that get people out to enjoy the sun. "St. Pete Outside" was created to consolidate the many efforts to enhance the outdoor facilities of the city. Parks, golf courses, sidewalks, beaches, skate parks, pools, kayak trails, and other amenities were added or improved.

Many of our neighborhood outdoor programs were small like our dog parks, not big, expensive, flashy programs like stadiums or amphitheaters. They were projects that fit our budget and resonated with the community's desire to constantly advance our quality of life. The St. Pete Outside additions helped our residents enjoy the beautiful Florida weather and environment by biking, jogging, kayaking, swimming, or competing in other sports.

We improved golf and tennis facilities while opening these sports to low-income kids through our versions of the national First Tee and First Serve programs. We also developed a kayak and canoe trail system branded "BlueWay Trails" around the perimeter of our peninsular city. We found that by building two waterslides at each of our city's swimming pools, our summer attendance at the pools went up by 40 percent.

Finally, we added to the ample outdoor fields throughout the city for team sports, and we also built parks for skateboarding kids, many of whom are not attracted to soccer, baseball, or basketball. Each of these outdoor programs enhanced the lives of adults and children within our city, but my favorite involved the playground policy.

It began one afternoon while I was walking my children to Coffeepot Bayou playground, about six blocks from my house. Julann was five and Jacob was four. As Joyce and I talked with some of the neighbors, we watched the dozen or so children chase each other around the playground equipment, glide on the swings, and attempt to cross the monkey bars.

I believe that we feel differently about a place when we can travel there without getting in our car. We have a fresh market stand, an ice cream shop, and a pizza parlor within a few blocks of my house. Somehow we feel that they are more personally ours because we get to them by foot. We get to know the people who work at these shops and we all feel like they are part of the neighborhood.

The same is true for playgrounds. When someone can step out of their home with their young child and take a short walk to a playground, they feel differently about their neighborhood. Parents and children get to know each other better because they gather at the playground down the street. It seems like a small thing, but it is a big idea.

That evening at Coffeepot Park I had a thought. Every child in our city should be able to walk to the playground. This will help every neighborhood feel a little closer, and will give every child more chances to exercise, have fun, and meet new friends. We established Play'n Close to Home, a commitment to build a playground within a safe, half-mile walk of every child in St. Petersburg. I set up a chart in my office—I love charts! This one has dots where each public playground in the city is located. We drew a half-mile radius circle around each dot. Our challenge became to fill in the blank spaces where there are no playgrounds. If a child has to cross a six-lane highway to reach the playground, it is not considered close enough. A *safe* walk is required.

Many of our playgrounds were built at existing parks, but not all. Since land is tight, we built several "joint-use" playgrounds at elementary schools, churches, and privately owned properties that allowed access to the public. The school joint-use playgrounds are closed to the public during school hours and closed off from the school after school and on weekends. One playground was donated to the city by Kool-Aid. We completed a community-build playground that was sponsored by a great national group called KaBOOM!, which is dedicated to spreading playgrounds around America. We also built what may be the largest playground in Florida at Dell Holmes Park—a playground that is also predominantly disabled accessible and includes a water park. It is wildly popular.

The playground circle chart in my office filled in like a Pac Man game, thanks to the great work of Suzie Ajoc, a passionately pro-playground member of the city's Neighborhood Department. By the end of 2009, we had built or planned thirty-seven new playgrounds. Upon completion of the playgrounds scheduled for 2010, 78 percent of our children (based on residential parcel data) would be able to take a short walk to a playground. That is up from 46 percent in 2001, a great improvement. But as playground access expanded, we realized that we also had to pay attention to the safety of adults and children as they walked or rode their bikes to the playground, and throughout the city.

(3) Becoming Pedestrian Friendly

On June 26, 2000, about nine months before I took office, our local newspaper announced that the Mean Streets 2000 report had named us the most dangerous large metro area in the country. They had included St. Petersburg and Tampa together as a metro area. The list of Mean Streets cities was published by the Surface Transportation Policy Partnership. Local officials quoted in the article acknowledged the pedestrian death numbers and the need for sidewalks, but there were no solutions proposed. In a word, as far as pedestrian travel was concerned, we had been cited as having the most dangerous streets in the country, and we had no plan to fix the problem.

In line with my stated objective to make St. Petersburg the best city in America, we set about creating a solution to this problem. We sought and received a grant to do a comprehensive study of our pedestrian safety system, including roads, crosswalks, sidewalks and bike paths, along with statistics on accidents, safety, and enforcement. The study took about a year to complete. At first I objected to the timetable, but I was convinced to proceed. Our transportation system had evolved to the point where it was primarily geared to moving cars quickly, with little thought to bicycles and pedestrians. If we were going to make changes, such as adding bicycle lanes where an auto lane previously existed, we first had to study the capacity and existing volume of our road system. Otherwise we could inadvertently mess up our vehicle traffic flow while trying to make our streets safer for pedestrians and bicycles.

Our study, completed in 2003, concluded that we had work to do, but that we could make great progress if we focused our efforts. We branded the initiative "CityTrails," and set out to completely transform our city's streets. We wanted to attract bicycles, joggers, and those who enjoy the urban feel and scale of a walkable place.

CityTrails had five components.

First, we set out to improve our sidewalks. As I describe later in this book, we had a backlog of broken sidewalks in the city that resulted in residents enduring a thirty-month wait for repairs. We set a goal of bringing the backlog to zero and expanding our sidewalk system by 100 miles, with locations to be prioritized according to our study's safety needs assessment.

Second, we set a goal of developing the largest bicycle path system in the Southeast United States, as measured by bicycle lane miles as a percentage of vehicle lane miles. Although "CityTrails" includes the entire five-point program, we coined the name primarily for the bike path system. It was intended to apply to both on-street lanes and off-street paths. In some cases we dropped auto lanes and added on-street bicycle lanes. In others, we expanded existing sidewalks to meet bike trail standards. Along our new downtown trail, we took up a railroad feeder line that was purchased from the railroad company. The result was a dedicated bike path running through an active industrial park.

Using these and other methods, by early late 2009, we created twelve major bike trails and routes reaching all parts of St. Petersburg, along with many miles of other road bike lanes. We created a CityTrails map, color coded and patterned after metro/subway maps with routes and trails named after the ending destinations. We built new bicycle parking areas, including many downtown. Most of our trail improvements were financed by state and federal grants—one called the Congestion Mitigation and Air Quality (CMAQ) program, designed to reduce auto emissions and promote alternative forms of transportation. Ironically, after we had developed many miles of trails, we lost access to CMAQ funds because our air quality became too good for us to continue to be eligible for the funding.

Third, we implemented crosswalk safety. Our study identified sixty-one crosswalks in the city that were the highest volume with the least safe condition. All targeted crosswalks received signage and painted line upgrades, and eighteen received electronic crossing light upgrades. Our traffic department, in conjunction with a local business man, developed a new, fast-blinking yellow flasher light crosswalk system that very effectively alerts the motorist to stop when a pedestrian is crossing, and allows traffic to continue after the pedestrian crosses without having to wait for a red light to change. The system has since received Federal Highway Administration approval and is now being implemented around the country.

The fourth and fifth CityTrail components focused on pedestrian safety education for motorists, cyclists, and pedestrians, as well as enforcement measures. In each case we developed and executed a plan to meet the objective.

The results of these efforts is that, in a relatively short period of time, St. Petersburg has become a hot bed of bicycle activity and a place recognized as one of America's great cities for pedestrians. In 2006 our city was named a Bicycle Friendly City by the League of American Bicyclists; and in 2008, *Prevention* Magazine named St. Petersburg the most walkable city in Florida and the 35th most walkable city in the United States.

Perhaps even more impressive, the Surface Transportation Policy Partnership, the same group that gave us the #1 Mean Streets designation in 2000, invited me to be the opening speaker for their 2008 national conference where the organization's president called St. Petersburg *"one of the best safety turnaround cities in America."*

While it is nice to receive national recognition for turning mean streets into a walkable community, the most important point is that people who live here are safer. Between 2003 and 2009 we experienced a 50 percent decrease in pedestrian-related accidents in the city. Our citizens have less chance of being injured.

(4) Supporting Recreation Programs and Libraries

Among the basic elements of strong neighborhoods are good libraries, where the entire community can gather to learn, read, and research. Strong neighborhoods also need a variety of recreation programs where adults and children can enjoy exercise and fellowship. In addition to the adults served, our city's recreation programs touch the lives of over 18,000 children and teens each year. The activities include athletics, before/after school care, and summer programs.

The team and individual sports programs were very popular: soccer, baseball, basketball, football, swimming, tennis, golf, and many others. Generally the sports programs were organized and run by private groups, and held at city recreational fields, pools, courts, golf courses, and gymnasiums. I did not create the city's great recreation programs: they were strong when I took office, and since they were the backbone of the city's efforts to help direct youth in a positive direction, we supported their continuation and expansion.

We built, renovated, and replaced adult and recreation centers and swimming pools throughout the city. These amenities, along with the St. Pete Outside projects described above, were partially paid for with a one cent local sales tax passed in our county by a voter referendum: the "Penny for Pinellas." Every ten years the governments of Pinellas County put together a list of the types of projects to be initiated, and let the voters decide whether or not they want to continue the sales tax. We found that when we were faithful regarding how the money was spent, the voters approved the program, which has now passed three consecutive voter referenda.

We built four new libraries and upgraded others, significantly increasing the number of computers for access by children and the general public. We even added a coffee shop element to the traditional library experience. Getting city staff to support allowing Starbucks drinkers in the library was no easy task. After much debate I finally asked them whether we allowed people to check out books and take them home. Did we think that readers sometimes sit at the kitchen table and drink coffee while enjoying their book? Did we have a problem with books being returned with coffee stains? The opposition faded. After a pilot coffee test at the main branch was successful, we expanded coffee service, and it was a big hit.

In order to ensure that we help build the character as well as the body of a child, we developed *St. Pete Values*. Under this initiative, each program within our recreation department was required to demonstrate that it advanced the character of the children involved in the core value areas of self-discipline, teamwork, achievement, honesty, respect, and responsibility. Children at play received regular reminders that honesty is important, that achievement comes through hard work, and that it is best to respect each other and play as a team.

While values are best taught at home, it is also a good thing for the values to be reinforced whenever possible. There are few things we can do that would have as great an impact on our city's future as a successful effort to instill these positive values in our children.

(5) Keeping Clean

If we want our neighborhoods to attract people, they must be clean. It requires a focused effort on graffiti removal, a strong sanitation department, a parks department that keeps the parks and road medians clean, and a codes enforcement effort to ensure that property owners are maintaining their sites. We developed a set of ordinances that allowed us to pursue judicial fines against people who refused to move old cars out of their front yards, or who placed small "snipe" advertising signs illegally in the rights of way throughout the city. Sanitation department employees were responsible for quickly painting over graffiti as it appeared. A team that included police, sanitation, and neighborhood department staff worked together to identify and prosecute those responsible for the graffiti.

Part of the effort also required an aggressive policy against illegal dumping. As of 2001 we had parts of our city, especially in Midtown, where people regularly dumped their old appliances, construction debris, and other trash in vacant lots and alleys. One of the most offensive practices occurs when building contractors drive into our city from other cities to use our neighborhoods as a trash pile so they can avoid having to pay the dumping fee at the county's landfill.

At first, we simply aggressively cleaned up the mess hoping that the cleaner atmosphere would make it less likely that people would dump their trash. But the regular clean ups didn't stop the dumping, so we decided to try another approach. We assigned one of our police detectives to the sanitation department with instructions to go through the dumped trash to identify the violator. We had laws that allowed us both to arrest violators and seize their vehicles.

For a contractor, this is a severe penalty, so I decided to broadcast to the region that we were serious. We held a press conference at a vacant lot where trash had been dumped. The television stations showed me operating a front-end loader and putting trash into a garbage truck. After

I picked up a part of the pile, I announced to the cameras that we had assigned a police detective to illegal dumping, and that we would identify those who were putting their trash in our neighborhoods. I described it as an outrageous offense to the community for people to use our neighborhoods as a garbage dump, and I assured everyone that we were serious.

Evidently one contractor didn't believe me. Within days he took a load of building material from a house outside our city and dumped the trash on the same lot where I held the press conference. After our detective identified the contractor, we seized his truck, arrested and fined him, and sent out another press release. The message eventually got out. Between 2003 and 2009, our instances of reported illegal dumping in Midtown dropped by over 86 percent, and the annual amount of trash picked up from Midtown's lots and alleys dropped from 348 to 19 tons, a reduction of 94 percent.

(6) Trees

April is a beautiful time of year in St. Petersburg. It is still cool much of the time and everything is in bloom: Oleander, Crape Myrtle, Magnolia, Royal Poinciana, and especially the purple Jacaranda trees. The Jacaranda are large trees, some as big as oaks. In the spring the entire tree becomes filled with beautiful bright purple blooms. Although I have never been able to confirm it, I believe that St. Petersburg's women's garden club planted the trees along the major corridors in the city when they worked on the city's last flowering tree program in the 1960s. When my family goes to church on Sundays in April, we try to count how many Jacaranda trees we can spot during the five-mile drive along 38th Avenue North. Typically, we count about forty along the way. On the way home we sometimes travel different routes just so we can see how many more Jacaranda trees we can count! It became a special memory for my young children growing up.

After taking office, I decided that it was time again for the city to implement a flowering tree program. It had been forty years since the last one. We completed an inventory of different types of flowering trees that would grow in our city, along with an identification of the times of year when they bloom. We then worked with our neighborhood associations, and gave them the opportunity to pick flowering trees for their local parks. Each type of the flowering trees described above was planted throughout the city, especially the magnificent Royal Poinciana and the Yellow Poinciana: over one thousand are now clustered in parks throughout St. Petersburg.

We also set out to plant flowering trees along our interstate corridor that runs from the north end of the city at the Howard Frankland Bridge (connecting to Tampa) to the south at the Sunshine Skyway Bridge (connecting to Bradenton). We distributed the trees along the highway according to the time of year when the flowers come out. We included trees all along the road that bloom during each of the seasons. Our intention was that, when the trees mature into full growth, visitors and locals will experience trees in bloom from one end of the corridor to the other during every time of year. It will take several years to see the full impact, but it will be magnificent when the trees mature.

During almost nine years in office, we planted about 6,000 flowering trees and over 20,000 total trees, many oaks and pines. The original name of our city was the Spanish term *Punta del Pinal*: Point of the Pines. At my request, many of our road corridor oak tree plantings were coordinated by former Mayor Dave Fischer, who had also aggressively worked to plant trees throughout the city during his terms of office. St. Petersburg's trees will provide beauty, shade, and comfort for many generations to come. Without a doubt they have enhanced the quality of life for people who live in our city. The trees were also one of the elements that helped to make St. Petersburg Florida's first designated Green City.

(7) Florida's First Green City

A critical factor in evaluating a city's quality of life is its commitment to improving the environment where its citizens reside. Breathable air, living estuaries, clean beaches, parks, abundant trees, and good water are all indicators of a community's environmental health. As a tourist destination, St. Petersburg historically had a continuous need to evaluate the beauty of its outdoor environment, and was well along the way in that commitment when I took office.

During my second term in office, a program developed by the Florida Green Building Coalition (FGBC) provided a mechanism for consolidating our environmental programs and establishing performance objectives. It was first introduced to me by Jamie Bennett, a member of our City Council, along with Karl Nurse, a neighborhood leader who would later serve on City Council. FGBC's program evaluates the environmental and energy progress of a city much in the way the LEED program certifies buildings. They require completion of an application that includes over two hundred criteria and results in a point accumulation. If a city demonstrates a sufficient number of points, FGBC awards them the Florida Green City designation.

On December 1, 2006, St. Petersburg became Florida's first designated Green City as a result of the city's commitment in the following areas:

1. *Electric energy.* This includes both conservation programs and the use and reuse of alternative energies such as solar, waste to energy, and bio-fuels. We partnered with Progress Energy and the University of South Florida to develop a Solar Park program, started at Albert Whitted Park downtown, with a plan to use solar energy and on-sight battery storage to generate the energy used to power the park's lights and other electric use. After completing the pilot, we were awarded a federal grant to develop twenty-four additional solar parks. One of the significant energy uses and costs of governments throughout the country is for street light electricity; St. Petersburg's annual cost approaches $2 million. We piloted a program on three streets where we compared the electricity use and installation/maintenance costs of street lights using LED, induction, and our traditional sodium light technologies.

2. *Transportation.* This includes fuel conservation through fleet reduction, maintenance, and traffic signal synchronization saving countless idling hours; alternative fuels such as biodiesel and ethanol; vehicles such as electric, hybrids, and plug-in hybrids; and transit and multimodal programs such as general transit, bus rapid transit, and bike paths.

3. *Parks, preserves, and estuaries.* This involved the expansion of active parks and athletic fields; maintenance and expansion of our three major environmental preserves; storm water treatment programs to protect our bays and estuaries; the planting of over 20,000 trees; and restrictions on the types of chemicals and fertilizers we use at city parks. Among other projects, we worked for over ten years on one of the state's largest lake clean-up efforts pre-treating the stormwater runoff entering Lake Maggiore, and dredging four feet of nutrient-rich muck from the lake's bottom. The result was a substantial decrease in the lake's phosphorous and nitrogen level and a sharp increase in water clarity. The lake became a favorite fishing spot once again.

4. *Water conservation and supply.* Through numerous conservation programs, in 2009 the city used less water collectively and per capita than it used thirty years earlier. It has one of the country's larger sanitary sewer water reuse programs that significantly aids in the conservation. City parks, golf courses, and homes use the "reclaimed water." We also worked with our regional water authority partner, Tampa Bay Water, to develop the western hemisphere's largest desalination plant with a planned capacity of 25 million gallons per day.

5. *Other programs.* Among our other environmental efforts, we developed environmental purchasing programs; drop-off recycling for consumers, along with

recycling of construction debris, yard waste, and waste-
water sludge; and land development plans.

In approaching potential green initiatives, we reviewed the environmental, energy, and economic impacts. For energy savings programs, we
evaluated how long it would take for the savings to pay back the cost of
the new program. We spent $450,000 to switch out our traffic signals
to LED, and we saved $150,000 per year on electric costs—a three-year
payback that translates to a 33 percent annual return on investment. We
committed $730,000 to change 1,800 parking lot and decorative street
lights to induction lighting, and our annual energy savings was estimated
at $150,000—a five-year payback for a 20 percent annual return. After
performing energy audits for our city buildings, we planned a $2.8 mil-
lion investment in building improvements designed to increase water and
energy efficiency. The estimated $382,000 annual building operating
savings represented a less than eight-year average payback on the costs
and an annual return of about 13 percent.

We estimated that the additional cost for our hybrid fleet would be
paid back in fuel savings over an eight-year period. Our conversion to
bio-diesel for our trucks and partial ethanol for the rest of our fleet
reduced pollution at no significant cost change. Other green initiatives,
like bike paths, tree plantings, and nature preserve expansions, had no
economic return to the city government, but they had the dual benefits
of environmental enhancement and the addition of quality of life amenities for our residents.

I asked Mike Connors, one of our senior administrators, to serve as
quarterback for our "Green St. Petersburg" initiatives. In addition to
having a great depth of knowledge of the city infrastructure, which is a
critical component of all of our green programs, Mike was an engineer.
All proposed energy and environmental programs received critical review
to establish that they will work financially and technically. Farfetched
ideas that have little hope of accomplishing the environmental, energy,
financial, or quality of life objectives of the city were discarded quickly.
Someone of Mike's background has the ability to enforce accountability
in the process.

I was first sworn into office on April 1, 2001. My former boss, Florida Supreme Court Justice Ben Overton, swore me in after my reelection on January 2, 2006, while my family—Julann, Jacob, and Joyce—stood by me.

By the end of 2009, Downtown St. Petersburg's skyline boasted ten new condominium towers, new townhome developments, new and renovated hotels, and the new Progress Energy Florida center. The area is now filled with shops, museums, theaters, and restaurants, setting Downtown St. Petersburg apart as one of the nation's emerging activity centers.

Public safety is the city government's number one responsibility, and the men and women who serve on the police department have the toughest job in the city—it is important to have an adequately sized, well-equipped, well-trained force.

Our city hosted the November 2007 YouTube Republican Presidential Debate at St. Petersburg's Progress Energy Center for the Arts.

Bringing the Rays Major League baseball franchise Downtown capped a 20-year effort of city leaders. The 2008 World Series brought great excitement to the city, along with a visit from General David Petraeus, who served as Commander of Central Command across the bay at Mac-Dill Air Force Base.

One of the keys to the revitalization of a downtown is the effort to bring more annual events. We brought the first Honda Grand Prix of St. Petersburg in 2005. Left, Indy 500 winner Dario Franchitti is skeptical about the chances of fitting my 6'7" frame into the open wheel race car.

Development of the arts and culture is another key to bringing vitality downtown and enhancing our quality of life. For St. Petersburg, our Downtown arts anchors included the Progress Energy Center for the Arts with the stunning new Dali Museum (above left) and a newly renovated Mahaffey Theater (above right).

Beach Drive became another downtown gathering place for our city. Here at Cassis American Brasserie, Chef Jeremy Duclut talks with diners. Owner Philippe Berriot calls Beach Drive his American reminder of Paris' Avenue des Champs-Élysées.

The Saturday Morning Market in Downtown St. Petersburg is a weekly event that became a gathering place for our community. Mark Johnson, director of the market, chats with folks enjoying a sunny Florida January morning—a few of about 10,000 visitors who dropped by.

Local musician Sam Stone and I often played classic rock and roll at the Saturday Morning Market—he was good and I was the mayor.

In St. Petersburg, our public school support programs included providing incentive cash bonuses, beach weekends, dinner out, and engraved marble apples—all with privately raised funds—for principals who achieved success at "Top Apple" schools.

Gathering places are a key to the city's quality of life, for both adults and children. A favorite initiative was "Play 'n Close to Home," my commitment to build a playground within a half-hour walk of every child in the city.

Dog parks were another popular gathering place, and were a particular favorite of my daughter Julann, and our dog Comet—St. Petersburg's Pier is in the background.

Family-oriented events can be the center of a downtown's rebirth. By 2009, St. Petersburg had about 400 events along the Downtown waterfront parks each year. To celebrate the winter in Florida we created a snowy toboggan course. Here I was racing my son Jacob (I lost).

The Albert Whitted Airport terminal building was financed in part by a gift and interest-free loan from philanthropists John and Rosemary Galbraith, pictured here with me and city council members at the dedication.

In our Midtown redevelopment efforts, we worked to preserve historic structures and return them to a use similar to the past. The Royal Theater—a segregated African American movie theater that stopped showing movies in the 1960s—was renovated and reopened as a Boys and Girls Club arts center.

Redeveloping the most economically depressed parts of a city requires partner-ships with charities, businesses, individuals, and all levels of government. The administrations of both President George W. Bush and Governor Jeb Bush were extremely supportive of our efforts to improve the lives of our city's residents, especially in the economically depressed areas.

Green St. Petersburg was more than a demonstration of our city's environmental commitment. Clean estuaries and beaches, adequate water and energy supplies, open parks and clean air improve the quality of life for all of us. They helped us to become part of America's effort to make our nation more energy independent, improve the air we breathe, and seize the emerging opportunities of the alternative energy industries.

Our neighborhood programs are all about quality of life. Developing playgrounds, bike paths, libraries, green programs, and recreation centers and combining them with a downtown full of family-oriented events and neighborhoods that are safe for play creates a place where children will grow up with happy memories for life. You even wind up with a town that is "going to the dogs." In St. Pete, that is considered to be a good thing!

Chapter 10

Improve Government Operations

Filling the Potholes

I know we've got some mayors here....
Thank you all for coming. I'm honored you're here.
My only advice is to fill the potholes.

—President George W. Bush

One Thursday afternoon in March 2003, at about 5:00 p.m., our Water Department Director Patty Anderson came by to see me. She came without an appointment, and it was late in the day, so I figured that we had a pretty big problem. One thing I've learned is that most of the problems that arrive at the mayor's office are big ones. With an organization of almost 3,000 employees and 34 departments, the small problems, or the ones that are easily solved, typically are dealt with before ever bubbling up to the mayor's desk. Patty's problem was a good example.

The water main had broken.

When I first heard the news, I was not overly alarmed. We have two water mains coming down the east and west sides of the city from our water plant thirty miles to the northeast. When we do maintenance or have a problem with one of the lines, our pumping stations can direct water to the city from either main line.

Unfortunately, Patty was talking about a different main line: the large, seven-foot diameter line that comes into our water plant from the north, bringing the regional system's water for treatment. In the late 1990s, the city entered into a partnership to establish Tampa Bay Water, a regional water authority. We now have no water sources of our own—we purchase all our water from the authority and treat it before sending it to our customers.

The break in the seven-foot main put our ability to supply our customers at risk. It would take an estimated three to five days to fix the main. Our city demand was about 28 million gallons per day. We had 30 million gallons in storage, and could pump another 34 million gallons per day from the wells on our side of the seven-foot main, so we were not in danger of running out of water for our citizens while the repairs were taking place.

Unfortunately, Pinellas County was also served by the same main line, and they were already out of water. They had requested that we send them 22 million gallons per day in order to prevent an imminent failure of their system. This would dry up our water supply before the time projected to fix the main line. Not sharing our reserves would cause much of Pinellas County outside St. Petersburg to run dry right away. Hospitals and residents would be without water, and their system would lose pressure, leaving water to sit still in their pipes, a condition that would allow bacteria to grow in their water system.

Patty said that while there were additional old wells that the system could attempt to tap into, we didn't know if we could get enough water from the wells to serve our needs (and if we could, how long it would take to tap into the old wells), and we didn't know if the Florida Department of Environmental Protection would approve using the water, or even if they could respond in time.

Her final point: I had about ten minutes to decide whether or not to allow Pinellas County to share our reserves.

It was a dilemma. Whether we shared our water or not, a water outage would impact hospitals, businesses dependent on its availability, and residents living their daily lives. It would also result in bacteria growth in the systems, requiring a major, costly recovery effort.

It was one of those moments when I did not have all of the information I needed, but I had to make the decision anyway. There was no time to do further research or complain about the situation. I simply had to make a decision knowing that, either way, the consequences could be tragic and the political fallout immense. A decision with negative results would be second guessed by those in the media and elsewhere who would have the twin benefits of time to analyze the options at length and 20/20 hindsight.

Keeping the City Running

The water main incident was a tangible example of President Bush's advice for mayors to fill the potholes, a metaphor for keeping the infrastructure of the city sound and the operations running smoothly. A city government supports many efforts, from economic development, to arts, to sports enterprises. But elected leaders must never forget that they are responsible for many of the basic services that people in the community depend on every day.

A city maintains roads, sidewalks, traffic lights, sanitation services, water, sewer, storm water, and reclaimed pipes, in addition to pumping stations and treatment plants. The community doesn't think much about this infrastructure unless something goes wrong. But those responsible for their upkeep need to keep it in mind every day.

By the mid 1990s our city's sanitary sewer pipes had deteriorated to the point that in the rainy seasons the rise in the water table would result in storm water filling up the sanitary sewer pipes through the leaky structures, and placing an increased demand on the treatment plants. Finally, one day heavy rains overloaded the system, and large quantities of untreated sewage were discharged into bay waters, a result known as a "sanitary sewer overflow." The city's alternative to discharging into the bay would have been to allow the untreated sewage to back up in the homes and businesses of the city—not a good option.

After the bay discharge, the city spent over ten years replacing pipe and upgrading treatment plants, at a cost of tens of millions of dollars, in order to bring our treatment infrastructure to an appropriate level and reduce the number of sanitary sewer overflows. It was a responsible approach, and one that was necessary from a regulatory perspective, but it did not garner positive headlines. The media discussion was reserved for the water rate increases needed to fund the improvements.

During my terms, the issue that generated the single largest number of complaints came in 2002 during a drought. In times of low rainfall, residents use more water for their lawns, especially those residents who are connected to our reclaimed water system. Reclaimed water is treated sewer water that is used for irrigation in parks, golf courses, and many residential homes. Since, during droughts, less water infiltrates the sewer system from the underground water table, we produce less reclaimed water at a time when there is a greater demand for the water for lawns.

The result in 2002 was an over-use of the system and a drop in pressure. As homeowners who were hooked up to reclaimed water turned their irrigation pumps on, nothing came out of the sprinklers. The combination of dry lawns and no reclaimed water for the grass resulted in 5,000 complaints working their way to City Hall. In response, over the next few years, we added large reclaimed water storage facilities and worked out a better scheduling of usage by the large consumers, such as parks and golf courses. The combination of these approaches resulted in better pressure during dry periods, and a significant reduction of the number of emails, calls, and letters we received relating to reclaimed water pressure. The ongoing number of reclaimed water complaints was tracked on the City Scorecard.

In addition to the sanitary sewer and reclaimed water system improvements, we spent millions of dollars upgrading our storm water drainage system to reduce street and home flooding during major storms. We also invested significantly in our water distribution and treatment systems. We replaced fire stations and equipment, eliminated the backlog in sidewalk repair, and followed master plans for road and bridge upgrades.

Our pothole repair time dropped from eighty-seven days to three days; President Bush would have approved. Our number of traffic signal trouble calls was reduced by over 40 percent, bringing the traffic signal response times to about seventeen minutes. These results were partially due to our traffic light conversion to LED lights, which use less electricity and last much longer than the incandescent bulbs that we previously used. The progress on these and other infrastructure items was tracked and reported to the public on our City Scorecard as well.

We also upgraded most of the computer systems in the city, an effort costing both money and management focus, but the investment paid off. The result of the technology upgrade was better service and information available to the community. The upgrades also enabled us to achieve staff reductions and operational savings. On the web, our residents can now access substantial amounts of city data and file complaints about issues relating to city operations. Reported issues may include code enforcement, road and sidewalk repair, park and recreation issues, or others. Residents can also use our site to pay their water and sanitation bills or access status information on building permits.

Taxes and Fees

Part of "filling the potholes" is running the operations of the city in a way that maintains the fiscal soundness of the enterprise. This includes charging fees and taxes at the lowest possible levels, providing the government only those funds needed to give quality services to the public. No one likes to pay taxes, and it is no fun being the one to charge taxes, but government needs money to operate.

In Florida, the city tax that is most felt by the residents is the property tax. Property tax is calculated by applying the millage tax rate charged by a city against the value of the taxed property, with the property values being assessed by a property appraiser elected county-wide. One mill is one-thousandth, or one-tenth of one percent. In St. Petersburg, the city charge is less than one-third of a property owner's property taxes; the other large components are school board taxes and county taxes, and there are other minor taxing districts as well.

For a variety of reasons, the city total millage rate had climbed to 9.632 by 1990, among the highest in Florida. There was widespread unhappiness among the residents, as reflected by two failed efforts: one to recall the mayor and entire city council in 1988, and another by western neighborhoods to secede from the city in 1989.

In the 1990s, a new one cent county sales tax went into effect that provided the city with millions of dollars annually for capital improvements such as roads, recreation centers, libraries, fire stations and others. The sales tax had been approved by a county-wide vote. Revenues from the new sales tax, along with an administration focused on millage reduction, enabled the city to provide property tax rate relief during the 1990s. By 2000, the city's total millage rate had dropped to slightly under 8 mills, but it was still substantially higher than most other major Florida cities, including Orlando, Ft. Lauderdale, and Tampa.

After taking office in 2001, our team set out to reduce property tax rates in order to become more competitive with other jurisdictions. The effort was made more difficult by two economic downturns, the first after September 11, and the second being the great national recession that began in 2008 and continued through the end of my second term. Another challenge was a state constitutional amendment passed by referendum, which doubled the homestead exemption, taking millions of dollars of property tax value off the rolls. On the other hand, the decade's record-setting amount of new construction in the city added significantly to the tax rolls, as did substantial increases in values of real estate associated with the mid-decade economic boom, although the latter trend was reversed by the end of the decade.

If tax rates are to be lowered, the most important focus must be on fiscal discipline. There is constant pressure from inside and outside the organization to increase the costs of doing business. There are elements and constituencies within the public that demand increased services and funds for countless worthwhile reasons such as bigger libraries, more police officers, more code enforcement, more public pools, cultural grants for museums, and increased social service funding. The list goes on.

The public unions also play a role. Our city had four unions and six bargaining units; they all involved themselves in political campaigns for Council and mayor. Unions fight relentlessly for more pay, pension, and benefits for the city employees they represent: police, fire, and blue and white collar. The increasing costs for employee pay and benefits are the largest cause of fiscal challenges in a city.

At the beginning of the decade, our city was regularly losing police officers to nearby jurisdictions that paid more, and our on-the-street strength was significantly less than our authorized strength level. The union was always quick to point these facts out while pushing for higher pay. In order to address this issue, the greatest single operational increase to our budget during the decade was increases in compensation for public safety personnel. By the end of the decade, our increased competitiveness, focused retention and recruitment efforts by our police chief, along with the national recession that resulted in public safety lay-offs in other jurisdictions, resulted in the city having the greatest number of police officers on the street in its history; but the increased costs made the budgets significantly harder.

We faced the difficult budget times by establishing a set of ground rules. First, we would only eliminate uniform police officers as a last resort. This never became necessary. Second, we would use every effort not to close facilities such as libraries and recreation centers. We never had to close these centers. Third, we would plan the budget on a multi-year basis so as not to make one-year fixes that jeopardize the long term fiscal soundness of the next year's operations. Fourth, we would always seek to minimize the impact that cuts had on the services provided to our residents.

My personal goal was to show a significant reduction in the real estate tax rates and increase reserves. Fortunately, I had many allies on City Council who shared this objective. Among them was Bill Foster, the chair of the Budget Committee, who would become my successor as mayor of St. Petersburg; and Jim Kennedy, who led the effort to establish higher reserve targets and chaired the Budget Committee during the difficult times of the deep recession that began in 2008.

Upon leaving office, after nine budgets, we had *lowered property tax millage rates five years* and left them flat the other four years. The property tax rate reductions totaled almost 20 percent, with the 2010 city property tax millage rate falling from 7.29 in 2001 to 5.9125 in 2010. We also reduced the city business tax for small employers. After nine years, we had cut about 300 full-time budgeted positions, 10 percent of the city's staff. About half of the eliminated positions were management, supervisory, and professional. At the same time we increased uniformed police staffing.

● ● ●

In the midst of significant staff reductions, we increased the number of swimming pools, recreation centers, parks, libraries, and overall services to the public. This was difficult to accomplish, but it worked because we had people working for the city who were committed to efficiency, and who were passionate about constantly improving the quality of life for the people who live in St. Petersburg.

With respect to fees for services, there is a built-in pressure to increase fees. Costs of operations increase due to inflation, while there is typically no automatic inflation adjustment for fee revenue increases in departments like water, sanitation, and storm water.

There is a particular irony in the water fee analysis. When the community does a good job conserving water, the water department sells less water and receives fewer dollars. Since a large component of the water department's expenses is fixed costs, it becomes necessary to find money to compensate for the successful conservation efforts. When the high costs of new alternative supplies, like a desalination plant, are factored into the equation, the result is that better environmental stewardship typically drives water rates up.

Nevertheless, efforts at cost cutting should be implemented to mitigate the need for increases. In the early years of my terms, our water rates were increased to pay for huge regional authority water projects (a desal plant, water treatment plant, and a reservoir, among others), which the city committed to in the 1990s, along with dramatic increases in costs for infrastructure required to fix our aging water and sewer system. Otherwise our objective with respect to the sanitation, water, sewer, and

storm water departments was to keep fee increases at or below the inflation rates and competitive with nearby jurisdictions.

Fiscal

Evaluating the financial strength of a city is much different than I was
accustomed to in the private business world. Instead of income statements
and financial position statements, we monitored fund balances in our
city's general fund, internal funds, and enterprise funds. Each has a minimum target balance that the auditors and rating services review carefully.

While all funds are important, the budget and fund which tends to
get the most attention is the general fund. It is the fund which receives
real estate taxes, sales taxes, utility taxes, and other revenues, and pays
for the police, fire, parks, recreation, libraries, roads, traffic, and many
other operations of the city. Although we absorbed significant increases
in public safety compensation and benefit costs during this period, the
average increase in the general fund operating budget from 2002 (first
budget) to 2010 (last budget) was 3.28 percent per year. The 2010 general
fund budget was actually less than the budgets for the prior three years.

Within the general fund, we established and funded an Economic
Stability Fund in the boom years of the mid 2000s in order to provide
the city with contingent resources in the case of natural disaster or financial difficulties. Even after the national recession arrived in 2008, the
undesignated (emergency) reserves within our general fund, including
the Economic Stability Fund, had increased by 370 percent from $9.6
million in 2001 to $36.83 million at the end of 2009.

Perhaps the greatest challenge to the fiscal integrity of governments
in America is the high costs of long-term medical and pension costs for
employees. While we made progress in this area in some ways, we lost
ground in others. It is an issue that must be addressed on a state-wide
level, as the state pension requirements often impact the process.

● ● ●

Recall the water main break dilemma discussed above. Should we
send our reserve water to Pinellas County, hope we can tap new supplies,

and risk running out of water for the city residents? When confronted with a set of bad choices, we decided to send the requested water to Pinellas County. This was the only option that provided us with the possibility that *no one* would run out of water.

After making the decision, I talked that night with the secretary of the Department of Environmental Protection, who was at home. We were able to secure permission to pump from the old wells. Thankfully, there was enough water in the old wells for both St. Petersburg and Pinellas County to use for a while (though the estimated time frame for fixing the main line was wrong—it took about eleven days), and our collective staffs did an incredible job of tapping into them.

If you were to ask most people in our community about the incident, they would have no idea what you were talking about. The tough decision got virtually no media attention, and the great work of our public employees in keeping the water running was quickly forgotten. Had it gone a different way, we would be debating the decision for years to come in newspaper columns and blogs.

The water main break is a great example of the importance of maintaining the smooth operations of a major city as challenges arise. The garbage must be collected and sewer systems need to work properly. Traffic lights, street lights, and roads must function smoothly. Children must be protected at recreation centers, libraries, and swimming pools. Employees must be hired, bills must be paid, and countless legal issues must be addressed. Budgets need to balance and investments must be protected.

When there are problems in delivering the city's services, they receive great publicity later—hindsight is, after all, 20/20. If things run smoothly, no one talks about the calm—*but calm is hard work!* It may seem unfair that the attention only comes when things don't work as planned, but that is the nature of public service, and that is okay. After all, it is the city's job to fill the potholes.

Chapter 11

Homelessness

Hard to Solve, Important to Manage

The poor you will always have with you.

—Jesus Christ, Matthew 26:11

I try to take time off around Christmas in order to be with my kids. They were four and five years old when I took office. I knew that if I was going to enjoy their growing up, I would have to set aside time for them while I was mayor, especially during the holidays. At Christmas, our house is decorated inside and out. We get pleasure from long mornings with holiday movies and fires in the fireplace. It is one of the most enjoyable and relaxing times of the year for me ... with some exceptions.

During one morning of the Christmas break in December 2006, when my children were ten and eleven years old, I picked up the newspaper at the end of my driveway, got my coffee, and started to read. The daily routine of reading the newspaper changes after becoming mayor. Instead of reading to learn about what is going on, it becomes partly a defensive exercise.

How are the editors portraying the things you are doing, or that the city is doing? Editors generally reflect their view on a story by the topics selected, the headlines, the location in the paper (such as the top of the front page versus the bottom of the back page), the emphasis of the parties selected to be quoted in the story, and the pictures chosen for publication. Columnists and editorial writers often follow in succession to the news view. Normally, if something bad is coming you have a pretty good idea ahead of time, but not always.

That morning's newspaper came with a surprise. There was an article with a picture about a transition homeless center on 16th Street, toward the west side of downtown. Over the course of several weeks, some of the area's homeless had taken to pitching tents in the right of way next to the center. At some point, the 16th Street center's leadership decided to invite the homeless to bring their tents into a partially fenced-in area of their property next to their building. In a very short period of time, a make-shift tent city had formed.

I was annoyed. Before running for office, I had read a great deal about homeless efforts around the country. I reviewed the successes and failures of other cities' homeless programs, and I was determined not to repeat the mistakes of others. After taking office I used the lessons learned to develop and distribute the City of St. Petersburg's Six Homeless Principles:

(1) *Children.* No St. Petersburg child should be homeless.
(2) *Financial Downturn.* Efforts should be made to provide St. Petersburg residents who are temporarily homeless due to unemployment or financial stress with access to temporary shelter, as long as they continue to take steps to transition back to self-sufficiency.
(3) *Drugs and Alcohol.* Efforts should be made to provide St. Petersburg residents whose homelessness results from alcohol or drug addictions with access to treatment and shelter, so long as they take meaningful steps to change their behavior and return to self sufficiency.

(4) *Mental Illness.* Efforts should be made to provide St. Petersburg residents whose homelessness results from mental illness with access to treatment and shelter with an effort to make them as self-sufficient as possible.

(5) *Attractor.* While addressing the homeless status of St. Petersburg residents, our city should not become a community that attracts homeless individuals from outside the city.

(6) *Negative Impacts.* In St. Petersburg, homelessness should not be used as an excuse for allowing public behavior that is detrimental to our community.

The first four homeless principles deal with the community's commitment to help the homeless in our city. In the summary we listed the providers in our city that worked to help the community reach the goals by providing residential and social services. There were literally dozens of them.

Consistent with these objectives, we developed a card handout entitled "Want to help the Homeless? Give a Hand Up. Not a Hand Out." The card contained contact information about fourteen of the major homeless shelters and food providers in the community. The message was for people not to give money to panhandlers, even though it may make the giver feel better. If they truly want to help, they should donate to the homeless service providers, and give the panhandler the card informing them where they can get food and shelter. This approach makes it less likely that money will go toward beer, and more likely that the homeless person will get help working toward independence.

The last two homeless principles dealt with the need for the community not to become a magnet for homeless people from other places, and not to allow some in the homeless community to do harm to our neighborhoods and business community. At times this requires ordinances dealing with panhandling, tents, and other issues. The values of charity and compassion must be joined with the concepts of respect and responsibility.

St. Petersburg is a sunny Florida city with a downtown renowned for its beautiful parks and pedestrian friendly atmosphere. These qualities also make the city a natural destination for homeless people from the north, especially during the winter months. When you add to that atmosphere the large numbers of near-downtown social service organizations that feed and house the homeless, you run the risk of becoming an attractor for the homeless to come from other places: both those nearby in our own region, and those from outside our area.

The worst thing you can add to our "natural attractor" status is a homeless center with no rules! Thus, the makeshift tent city established by the 16th Street center was exactly the wrong approach to dealing with the homeless. The objective for any homeless effort should be to help people work toward independence. In order to accomplish that objective, it is necessary to have rules of conduct. When you open the doors to anyone who wants to come for a free meal and bed with no rules, you quickly become a magnet for people who want to be taken care of without having any responsibility for their conduct.

In our new tent city's case, the area became overrun by those who had heard through the network about the no-rules tent city located by downtown, next to a center with free food. A school crossing guard along the Fourth Street corridor on the far north side of the city told me he had spoken to a number of homeless individuals travelling into the city to stay at St. Petersburg's new tent city. They weren't alone.

Over the course of the next week, the lot overflowed and was spilling over into the surrounding neighborhoods. We had criminal activity going on both inside and outside the tent city. Police advised me that a homeless person was assigned to provide security for the tent city by the self-proclaimed tent city "mayor." Unfortunately, the new security person had recently been released from prison. The downtown was being overrun by the influx of homeless from other places, and the neighborhoods around the center were full of furious people.

After consulting with our legal department I decided to send the 16th Street center a notice of code violation. Typically, a notice of code violation can take months or years to enforce if the violation recipient decides to stall or fight the citation. In this case, those who ran the center chose a different approach. Word spread that the mayor was shutting down the tent city, and the center's management proceeded to prepare to send folks off the property. Our city and county social services staff set up a station on site to get information from the people leaving, and work toward placing folks at shelter facilities. Many of the homeless who did not want to follow the rules of the other shelters simply moved across the street under an interstate overpass.

The city received a lot of negative media coverage for removing the homeless from the illegal, makeshift tent city. The self-proclaimed homeless "advocates" were very effective in portraying their cause as David versus Goliath. Little attention was given to our efforts to place people in shelters, and even less coverage was given to the unsanitary, unsafe, dismal condition of the makeshift tent city. There was great publicity when the "advocates" picketed my church on Sunday morning. Off camera the "advocates" swore at my young children as we left the church parking lot.

Public Opinion

Most of the emails and letters to the city and newspaper were critical of the city's position in closing the illegal tent city. The neighborhoods around the 16th Street center were pleased with the closing but concerned that the more hard core homeless had simply moved across the street. As the tents migrated closer to the interstate exits, I started receiving reports from the police describing near accidents when cars exiting the interstate almost struck the homeless who had chosen to stay under the overpass.

The police decided to order those in the tents to move away from the road, but some refused. Television cameras hovered around the tented area, often responding to cell phone calls sent by those living under the overpass or claiming to represent the homeless. The police were faced with the unhappy prospect of going into the tents and arresting those who refused to leave, dragging them out of the tents in handcuffs, and doing it all on the evening news. The media commentary would certainly have portrayed the police actions in a negative manner.

Conversely, the police could have left the tents in harm's way and taken the risk that a motorist would strike someone, with the resulting criticisms of the police for not responding to an unsafe condition. Faced with a no-win situation, the police chose a third alternative that may have seemed like a good idea at the time, but turned out to be a mistake. They cut the bottoms from the tents and lifted the tops away in order to remove them from the area. Video of the police actions was carried on the local news with reporters characterizing the event as the police "slashing" the tents.

The police conduct was heavily criticized by the media and by the bulk of emails, calls, and letters to city hall. We were portrayed as being unsympathetic to the plight of the homeless. After all, our police had "slashed" tents. Some of the remaining tents moved to the right of way adjacent to a heavily trafficked corridor, while some stayed under the overpass. A power struggle developed between two groups of "advocates" claiming to represent two competing homeless groups.

After a few days of the two expanding makeshift tent cities, the complaining emails to the city flipped. Fewer emails were expressing sympathy for the plight of the tent dwellers. While it is likely that most of our citizens still disagreed with the police action of cutting tents, the public was now demanding that the city do something to move the tents out and stop the associated activity in the surrounding area.

In sum, we had an expanding homeless population attracted to the illegal tent city that the 16th Street homeless center had created; growing tent city populations on the west side of downtown in visible locations; anger from nearby businesses and residents who were feeling the negative impacts from the population, including crime reports, panhandling, and serious sanitary issues; anger from some in the community who felt that the city should not have closed down the illegal tent city; fierce criticism of the cutting of the tents by the police; and a news media that had become transfixed on the issue, doing television and print stories daily.

We were not managing the situation very well.

From Crisis to Opportunity

I have come to believe that almost every crisis presents an opportunity. The opportunity develops due to the enhanced public attention. Intense media focus on a problem, combined with the public's desire for conditions to change, gives the mayor the opportunity to recruit help and marshal resources that would not be forthcoming in the absence of crisis. On an airplane flight from Washington, D.C., back to St. Petersburg, I developed a plan for seizing the opportunity, and reaching out to the community for help.

In late January 2007, about a month after reading the Christmastime news story, I had traveled to Washington to attend the annual meeting of the U.S. Conference of Mayors. After I arrived, I discovered that one of the presentations at the conference dealt with the homeless challenge. With the homeless issues swirling at home, I jumped at the opportunity to get some advice from people focused on the national homeless problem, which touched most American cities.

The speaker was Phil Mangano, President Bush's director of the U.S. Interagency Council on Homelessness. After his presentation, I had a chance to talk with Phil about the homeless issues in our city. He provided his thoughts on the situation. It was helpful to be out of town for a couple of days, and to learn about the similar challenges other cities were facing. Thinking through the issue, I put together an outline of steps we should take to regain control of the situation and move the city forward. While driving across Tampa Bay's Howard Frankland Bridge, I summarized my plan on a cell phone call with City Council member Jamie Bennett, who was also chair of the county's Homeless Leadership Network. Jamie agreed to help.

A few days later, on January 30, a large group assembled at a City Hall press conference to lay out a five-point initiative to address near-term and long-term objectives for St. Petersburg's homeless situation. At the podium with me were people who constituted a broad representation of our community: the chair of the County Commission, the chair of the county's Homeless Leadership Network, the president of Catholic Charities, the

president of the Council of Neighborhood Associations, the Downtown
Partnership president, the HUD field director, the president of Progress
Energy Florida (our power company), the president of St. Petersburg Col-
lege, and several City Council members.

I started by acknowledging that we had challenges to face, but that
with a united community I was confident we could overcome any obstacles and make progress. Over the course of the coming weeks I would
reiterate my belief that we have a duty to help those who are willing to
work their way out of homelessness, and that we must also ensure that
the homeless population does not adversely impact those in our city who
have invested their life savings in their homes and businesses.

At the press conference, we outlined our multi-item approach:

(1) Work with the U.S. Interagency Council on Homelessness,
and coordinate our effort with the county's established
10-Year Plan to End Homelessness.

(2) Increase Voucher Funding/Housing Availability. This
involved a commitment to quickly identify short term
housing during the winter months.

(3) Hold a Neighborhood and Business Summit on Homelessness. We committed to hold this summit soon to address
the concerns of the neighborhoods and businesses around
our present homeless provider facilities.

(4) Develop a Project Homeless Connect Program. Introduced
around the country by the U.S. Interagency Council, Project Homeless Connect involves a periodic "Service and
Job Fair" where those who are homeless receive housing
and job referrals, along with medical exams, haircuts,
clothes, identification cards, and other items. Computer
access is provided to help homeless contact their families.

(5) Identify Additional Transition Beds and Services. We
announced a partnership to develop a 150-200 bed transition facility for homeless in the county. Twenty minutes
before the press conference, I was able to confirm a $500,000

contribution from Harry Stonecipher, a private businessman who had committed to help fund a portion of the facility development. We announced the gift to the media.

The post-Washington press conference was the tipping point in us transitioning from constant crisis-response mode to driving the process. We had a plan and a united group of community leaders focused on a set of objectives. While we knew that the problem was not going to be solved quickly, we felt we were on the right path. We also realized that we needed to do a better job of letting the community know what we were trying to do, and how it was progressing.

I made multiple efforts to communicate to the public the rationale for our approach and the ongoing efforts being made to help those in need. In addition to the press releases, interviews, and press conferences, I wrote two separate, lengthy columns for the newspaper. A newspaper column is often the only realistic way of accurately setting out a mayor's views on a complex issue. Among other information, the columns described the many organizations within our community who provided homeless services.

With the mission defined and communicated to the public, we set out to execute on the plan:

(1) U.S. Interagency Council on Homelessness

Throughout the remaining time I was in office, we maintained ongoing dialogue with the Council, and specifically with Phil Mangano, its director. Phil and his group provided a national perspective on the homeless challenge around America and ongoing advice on the Pinellas 10-Year Plan to End Homelessness. The Council was especially helpful in the development of the Project Homeless Connect.

(2) Voucher Funding/Housing Availability

A joint effort of the city, county, and Catholic Charities became focused on identifying immediate funding for short term housing to get through the winter months.

(3) Neighborhood and Business Summit on Homelessness

A few weeks after the City Hall press conference, a large community summit was held at downtown's University of South Florida St. Petersburg. The gathering included everyone in the region who had an interest in the homeless issue: social service agencies, government officials, businesses, residents surrounding the tent cities, advocates, and homeless individuals. We used a "charrette" format, which I typically prefer, with the large gathering being broken up into groups of five to ten people to discuss the various issues. A representative of each group then reported the suggestions of the break-out group back to the large gathering. This process allows for more constructive dialogue and less grandstanding and speech-making than a typical public forum.

At the summit, the break-out group spokespersons reported the concerns of each group. Homeless advocates who attended the forum asked us to allow the tents to reassemble at the homeless center. Neighbors and businesses voiced their concerns about the impacts the make-shift tent cities were having on the surrounding areas. The impacted areas requested stronger ordinances to limit the tents and to require better control of the areas surrounding the homeless provider centers. After the summit, we held another press conference to announce our progress. We allowed the tents back into the 16th Street center's parking area for a 90-day period—this time supervised by the city with rules of conduct. Although I resisted even a temporary restart of the tent city due to fears that we could once again find ourselves with an attractor, the move was necessary in order to buy us some breathing room to get people out of the street-side tent cities, pass necessary ordinances, and place those homeless willing to leave with appropriate providers. Eventually most who wanted shelter were placed, and the interim parking lot tent city was closed. Much of the shelter obtained was provided through the county vouchers that we announced at the post-Washington press conference.

At the summit press conference we also agreed to pursue new ordinances that address tents and sleeping in the right of way. City Council would pass ordinances dealing with panhandling and other issues relating to the impacts of homelessness on the community. The ordinances, which had been requested by the surrounding property owners, were not a simple task to take on. There is a large body of constitutional case law that analyzes ordinances dealing with panhandling, sleeping on sidewalks, piles of belongings, feeding in public places, and other homeless issues.

It is necessary and appropriate for each new ordinance to be reviewed against the case law in order to ensure that we are protecting individuals' rights while also protecting the health and safety of the general community. Our legal team, led by city attorneys John Wolfe and Mark Winn, were cautious, bright lawyers who were talented at balancing the needs of the city and the need to protect the rights of our citizens. At any given time there are many ongoing lawsuits instituted around the nation by civil liberties law firms against cities that pass ordinances that impact the homeless population. Our city is no exception, and many of our ordinances have been challenged in court, requiring a commitment to defend as well as prepare the laws.

As ordinances were passed, City Council carefully considered the important legal and social balance. They passed an ordinance prohibiting people from storing large piles of belongings on the sidewalk or other right of way, but the city also provided a trailer storage facility near the 16th Street center for those who wanted a safe place for their things. Council passed an ordinance prohibiting the use of temporary shelters, such as tents, on public property unless a permit is obtained. At the same time, the city took steps to find alternative places for the homeless people in our city to go. The public safety and sanitary issues that adversely impact the surrounding neighborhoods were addressed, and new shelter was developed.

(4) Project Homeless Connect

We held our first Project Homeless Connect about seven months after the post-Washington press conference, and held them annually thereafter. They are staffed by dozens of volunteers and are attended by hundreds of homeless individuals in our community. They provide individuals with needed services of the kind that I described above, although obviously this is only a temporary solution.

(5) Additional Transition Beds and Services

The most difficult challenge we faced was developing a center to take people off the streets, stabilize them, evaluate their needs, and decide the next steps needed to move them toward independence. I call it a homeless triage center. We had many providers focused on subsets of the homeless population: mental illness, alcohol and drug dependency, veterans, mothers with children, etc. Still, we lacked a large center to take people in and start them on the path to independence. The team of civic leaders that assembled for our post-Washington press conference began to search for sites and assemble resources such as portable buildings, contractors, volunteers, and money.

I felt that the new center should be far removed from downtown. The existence of several homeless shelters and feeding places, and the availability of parks and pedestrian targets for panhandling, had already made downtown an attractor for homeless individuals to come from other places in our county, state, and nation. The warm weather of central Florida adds to the impact, as homeless people travel from northern states during the winter.

If we could build a homeless triage center in a secluded location away from downtown then services could be provided to those who were willing to help themselves, but it would be less likely to attract people from other places. Ultimately it would help us secure community support for resources to help the homeless.

After multiple efforts to find a homeless triage center site, I asked Neighborhood Deputy Mayor Dave Metz to contact Frank Murphy, CEO of Catholic Charities in St. Petersburg. Frank had been very helpful in the days following the closing of the initial 16th Street tent city. He was a very successful businessman before taking on his job at Catholic Charities. I believe he saw the organization's mission of helping people in need as a calling. Since the Catholic Church owns a lot of land in the county, we asked him if he had any ideas.

After many discussions, our team presented to me Frank's idea to create a homeless center on wooded land owned by the Catholic Church in the center of the county. Catholic Charities would operate the center. We would use portable buildings donated by St. Petersburg College for offices, food staging areas, and social services. City crews would help clear and mulch the land. Contractors, some discounting their services, would prepare the site establishing running water and electric lines, and fencing in the area.

The partnership would acquire large portable restroom, laundry, and shower facilities and would construct large covered areas for dining and assembly. Harry Stonecipher's contribution would be used to fund the capital expenses. We would seek funds from Pinellas County, St. Petersburg, and other cities to operate the center for four months, from December through March. This would get us through the winter influx of northern homeless visitors and then the center would close down. The idea was to buy enough time to put together a plan for a more permanent facility. The consensus was to call the center "Pinellas Hope." I liked the plan, but it was unclear to me where the homeless would sleep. "In tents" I was told.

After all we had gone through to get past our tent city issues downtown, I was amazed to hear that Frank Murphy's plan was to create a new one in the woods. My response was quite negative. Frank argued that the plan could be quickly implemented, and would involve a low cost for construction of the facility, permit Catholic Charities to run the center at a much lower operational cost than more permanent facilities and, perhaps most importantly, enable us to start right away. It was this last point that swayed me.

I have come to believe that there is great value in starting. Often, especially in government, there is a tempting inclination to plan and plan and plan. Studies take place, forums are held, and working groups meet, but at times it seems like nothing is really happening. Planning is an important exercise, but at some point, especially in times of crisis, you simply have to do something. After you begin you can always add, reduce, or adjust the effort, but you are on your way. In the case of our homeless challenge, we did not have time to spend two or three years to find a site, raise money, and construct a concrete homeless center. We needed to start!

Pinellas Hope opened by December 2007, several months after my post-Washington press conference. It served about 200 people who lived in tents in a fenced wooded area, had bathroom and shower facilities, had access to computers and telephones, provided assistance with on-site social services caseworkers, and gave meals that were donated by churches, civic groups, and other organizations from throughout Pinellas County. The center was in a remote, wooded area so it would not act as an attractor for homeless people from outside our area. Residents were admitted by one of our county's three sets of "homeless outreach teams," consisting of a police officer and social worker located in different parts of the county. One of the outreach teams is based downtown. Busses shuttle residents to employment.

Although Pinellas Hope was supposed to close after four months, Bishop Robert Lynch of the St. Petersburg Diocese consented to my request to keep it open. My appeal was given along with an offer by me to help raise private funds to operate the facility until the new fiscal year for the cities and county. We would then seek ongoing government funding. We succeeded in obtaining both the short-term private funds and the long-term government financial support.

Pinellas Hope, which started as a temporary fix to our homeless problem, evolved into a multi-level triage and transitions center for on-street homeless individuals in our county, led by Catholic Charities' Sheila Lopez, an incredibly passionate, energetic, and capable servant of God. About two hundred residents were in tents while others stayed in dozens of small sheds called "casitas" (Spanish for small house). By the end of 2009, construction was underway to build eighty permanent housing units, restrooms, and dining areas, which opened in September 2010.

Catholic Charities' staff used the progression of accommodations as a reward to those who were willing to work toward independence. The center gave homeless individuals a chance to stabilize and move forward. Some were reunited with family members, others found employment and a place to live, and others were placed with another provider to deal with their specific challenges such as alcohol, mental illness, and drugs.

Catholic Charities statistics demonstrated that about half of those who enter reached the next level of independence either with family, transition shelter programs, or independent housing. They limit the length of time residents can stay so there is pressure to work toward independence. It is not intended to be a long-term living facility, and there are strict rules that residents must follow. Pinellas Hope operates at a fraction of the cost of similar transition centers in other cities. The tents are much less costly to maintain and keep secure. The residents are separated from each other with their belongings. Residents are screened with background checks and are evicted for violations of rules.

The existence of Pinellas Hope had a positive impact on the neighborhoods downtown—our weekly downtown homeless count had reached 186 just before the opening, but dropped significantly within a few months after the opening, and stayed well below the higher level on an ongoing basis. After the 2008 U.S. financial market meltdown, followed by the extended recession, our county unemployment rates and homeless count increased significantly, but our average downtown on-street homeless count stabilized through the end of 2009. Without Pinellas Hope, our downtown homeless count would certainly have increased sharply as the unemployment rates tripled.

The model of providing effective homeless services quickly, at a low per person cost, has drawn national attention. Phil Mangano, the former director of the President's U.S. Interagency Council on Homelessness, called Pinellas Hope a partnership that is "a model for the country … one which is solution-oriented and cost effective," although Phil expressed his preference for the housing units being constructed, as opposed to the tent dwellings.

More importantly, Pinellas Hope lived up to its name. It provided people with a chance, with hope. It is hard to describe how hard it is for someone to rise up once they have fallen into homelessness. On the street they carry their life's belongings with them wherever they go and fear robbery or worse when they go to sleep. After a short while their appearance, state of mind, and homeless condition make them virtually cut off from any chance of employment or forward movement.

For those who choose not to help themselves, there is little that can be done. But for those who are willing to work themselves back to independence, Pinellas Hope offered an opportunity. I have talked to many formerly homeless individuals who have found a way off the street because of the center. Some are amazing stories of gut determination to overcome great obstacles. They are proof of the powerful force of a human spirit that has been given the gift of hope.

Chapter 12

Promote the City

We have a saying here that "It's another great day in St. Pete"...It doesn't get much better than this.

—MAYOR RICK BAKER, ANNOUNCING GRAND PRIX RACING SERIES

Beginning in the mid-1980s, I spent many years in various volunteer positions within the Chamber of Commerce. I like the Chamber. People who get involved with Chamber work are generally those who care about the city and want to help make things better. The collective work of our St. Pete Chamber during the 1980s and 1990s had a big impact later on in the great renaissance that our city experienced during the first decade of the twenty-first century.

At the Chamber, during those building years, we used an expression to summarize a purpose of our efforts: "We're building a great city so our children, when they grow up, will want to raise their own children here." This was not the case in the mid 1980s. My older friends at that time complained that their children, upon graduating from college, had no interest in returning to St. Pete. They tended to start their working lives in Atlanta or Charlotte, or in an up and coming northern city.

Young people did not want to return to the city where they grew up because the city had little to attract them. There was a limit in the types of jobs for them, and there wasn't much to do in the city. Most of all, they just did not feel good about the future of St. Petersburg.

Young people starting out in life are investing a portion of their future in the town where they choose to live. They want it to be a good investment. They certainly do not want to waste their time building a career in a place where they do not enjoy living. They want to believe that they are part of a great place and that their city has a great future. "A city with a great future" is not how most observers would have described St. Petersburg in the mid-1980s.

Let's fast forward to 2009. Downtown St. Pete became the hub for nightlife—from events in the parks, to movies at BayWalk, to theaters, to Beach Drive cafes. Outdoor concerts at Jannus Landing became a regular for those in their twenties, and teens lined up at the State Theater for music. From the Saturday Morning Market to the First Friday night street parties on Central Avenue, St. Petersburg had become "cool."

A popular Facebook website named "You know you're from the 'burg' when" was born for young people. It was a favorite for college students and had over 4,000 members, with hundreds of pictures and slogans describing their hometown. A downtown twitter site "I love the 'burg'" became popular, quickly jumping to over 17,000 supporters. St. Petersburg had transformed its self image. It had become a town whose residents believed it was the best city in America.

Taxi drivers bragged about the town, and young people from other places moved here to be near the excitement. The change started with the turnaround downtown, and the creation of activities that drew young people: Major League Baseball, Grand Prix IndyCar racing, a college bowl game, bike paths, dog parks, music festivals, marathons and triathlons, arts festivals, farmers markets, and street parties.

For young children there were playgrounds everywhere, a children's hands-on science museum, skateboard parks, water slides at swimming pools, and family-oriented festivals along the waterfront. The public schools were moving in the right direction. In short, the city became a place with something for people of all ages, and something else happened: a change in attitude.

We started to assume we were going to succeed at whatever we set out to achieve. We aggressively recruited employers and they came. We began calling ourselves the cultural center of Florida, and then made it a reality by landing new museums, galleries, and performing arts. We didn't just decide to build bike paths. We set out to build the largest bike path system in the Southeastern United States. Rather than be satisfied with a few environmental programs, we became the first designated Green City in Florida; we then wrote the Green City Action Accord that was adopted by the National League of Cities.

We wanted great schools, so we built a national model of city-supported public school programs. We decided that we would turn around the most economically depressed part of our city and we did, to a degree that few cities in America have achieved. When we set out to make more playgrounds available for our kids we set big goals: To have a playground within a short walk of every child, and to build the largest playground in Florida.

Pride in the city is part of its quality of life. When people feel good about their city, they feel good about themselves. They are likely to recommend the city to others, and others will sense the enthusiasm and want to be part of the city. Cities like Chicago and Charleston have it, but it is not easy to create when it is missing.

When you decide to build the best city in America, you have to set big goals. You then must develop and execute a plan to achieve them, and you must believe that you will succeed. We constantly described the time we were living in as the greatest renaissance in St. Petersburg's history, and our community willed it into existence.

As success after success came our way, I began using the phrase, "*It's another great day in St. Petersburg,*" which became the symbol of our self-confidence and success. The phrase was repeated daily by people throughout the city, from members of Congress, to the media, to school children.

We also fought for our brand, naming our new race the "Grand Prix of St. Petersburg." Regional post office marks added St. Petersburg to the stamp. Florida's Coast Guard west coast headquarters was renamed "Sector St. Petersburg." We constantly worked to promote our city's image. We knew that we had made progress when ESPN elected to name their new college football bowl game "The St. Petersburg Bowl." Clearly ESPN and others concluded that our city's image had progressed to the point where it would be an asset to brand the nationally televised game with the city's name.

We engaged in a multi-year effort with the State transportation officials that ultimately resulted in St. Petersburg destination signage on interstates throughout Florida. From newspaper weather maps to airport route signs, we relentlessly promoted our city brand. Some make the odd claim that advocating for your city is not being a "regional" thinker, but is parochial. The claim has no merit. If the mayor doesn't fight for his city then who will? At the end of the effort, St. Petersburg became a city that was proud of itself. People who lived here loved their city!

I have always believed that the self-image of a city is reflected in the comments you hear from waitresses, store clerks, and taxi drivers. When I travel, I make a point of asking the taxi driver how his city is doing. The responses are sometimes colorful and always interesting. By the time I am dropped off at my destination, my view of the town I am visiting has either been enhanced or reduced by the conversation. The spectrum of responses ranges from a recital of problems to an enthusiastic promotion, and everything in between.

One day it struck me that the taxi drivers in our city were the first encounter for many of our visitors, so I decided to be proactive. We set up a series of coffees for taxi drivers in the city. I met each of the drivers who attended, and we introduced them to representatives of our marketing department and the county's visitor bureau to talk about the many things to do in the city. We provided them with lists of events and handouts to provide their customers. Those who attended were very pleased that the city would take such efforts to reach out to them, and I believe it helped.

Florida Governor Charlie Crist was married in the city, his hometown, in 2008. At the reception, the governor's chief of staff made a point of introducing me to his wife. The chief's wife smiled and said that she had been looking forward to meeting me. Evidently the taxi driver who brought them from the airport went to great lengths to tell them what a great city St. Petersburg had become, and went on to extol our various assets. He even bragged about the mayor! She was very impressed by his enthusiasm for the city, and I was pleased that we had passed the "taxi driver test."

Each year during St. Petersburg's spring festival, the Festival of States, we hold the Coronation Ball at the Coliseum. The Coliseum is a large 1924 Quonset hut-shaped dance hall that holds over 1,200 people for dinner and dance events. Its entire floor is wooden, and it has a rounded ceiling with heavy wood beams, beautifully decorated with draping lights. My inaugural ball was held there, and it is home to many of our city's great events.

At the 2008 Festival of States Coronation ball, I welcomed the crowd, then sat back to enjoy the show, which culminates in the selection of the festival sun goddess. The sun goddess court consists of college age ladies who are introduced to the audience as they walk from the back of the room to the stage in the front of the room, typically with a military escort. That particular year I recall listening to the description of a member of the court who was about to be presented. The speaker listed her college, her sorority affiliation, and her volunteer activities. As she approached the front of the room the announcer finished his introduction by saying that upon completion of college the young lady wanted to return to St. Petersburg to pursue a career in telecommunications. She wanted to come home!

The words made me catch my breath. I listened closely as another sun goddess court member was introduced. The announcer ended by saying that upon graduation she intended to return to St. Petersburg to work as a speech therapist in a local hospital; another wanted to come back to St. Pete and become a nurse anesthetist. One by one the speaker introduced the ladies, and one by one he spoke of their desire to return home to St. Petersburg after college.

I felt silly, but I became misty-eyed as each new name was announced. I am quite sure that most people that night didn't focus on the "return home" portion of the contestants' resume, but to me it marked a milestone in our city's history. The goal set at the informal gatherings of Chamber of Commerce members two decades earlier had been achieved. We had become a city whose children, as they grew up, wanted to come home so they could raise their own children here.

It was another great day in St. Petersburg!

Chapter 13

Measure Progress

Data matter. Measuring matters.
It you don't measure, you don't care.

—FLORIDA GOVERNOR JEB BUSH

A fter being in office for a few months, I developed the uneasy feeling that I was not actually driving the ship.

Before I became mayor, I was president of a medium-size law firm. People often do not think of a law firm as a business, but lawyers experience many of the same business challenges faced by the companies they represent. In order to keep track of the status of our firm, I received a five-page "Tuesday Report" every Tuesday morning, which I reviewed with the firm administrator. I found it both helpful and comforting to have a detailed summary of employee matters, financials, sales, collections, caseload, cash flow, and other information summarizing the status of the organization for which I had assumed responsibility. It gave me a chance to react to problems quickly and seize opportunities from time to time.

With the Tuesday Report as my frame of reference, it seemed odd to me that I did not receive many reports after I became mayor of a major city. I now had responsibility for a much larger organization that included 34 departments, about 3,000 employees, and a budget over $500 million. Yet after three months in office, the only regular reports I had received were the crime statistics and regional rainfall levels. Intuitively, I knew that I needed more facts if I was going to pursue an agenda. You cannot tell where you are going if you don't know where you are, but I also understood that government is different than business.

In business, the indicators may change from industry to industry, but the core measurements are pretty uniform: sales, profit and loss, collections, balance sheets, stock value, and others. Government can be harder to measure. How do I know if the parks department is doing a good job? How can I tell if our police, fire, roads, or water departments are improving or operating efficiently?

I decided to start with sidewalks.

Of all the important issues and challenges facing a city, it may seem odd to start with sidewalks. Certainly, improving public safety, providing reliable utilities, and reinvigorating the urban core are arguably among the most important jobs to face up front. But developing a performance measure for sidewalks was the natural result of an assignment that I gave when I first took office. I asked Mike Dove, our original Deputy Mayor for Neighborhoods, to provide me with a list of the top complaints received by the Mayor's office, whether by telephone, email, or letter. As it turned out, the largest number of unresolved complaints received were for sidewalk repair.

Sidewalk repair?

This seemed odd to me. Of all of the issues, from drug sales to speeding, sidewalk repair would not have been the first issue I would have picked for citizen concern. So I asked Mike to dig a little deeper to find out why. How long did it take us to repair a sidewalk? What is our backlog? It took Mike a little while to answer this question because we weren't keeping statistics on turnaround time for sidewalk repair. The look on Mike's face as he walked into my office with his answer some time later was a mixture of amusement and disbelief.

Thirty months ... it took two and a half years to fix a sidewalk. *Two and a half years!*

Well, at least I now understood why sidewalk repair was the number one complaint to the Mayor's office. Fixing this particular problem was the easy part. We shifted capital money into sidewalk repairs in order to take care of the backlog, set aside a "sidewalk repair strike team" within our traffic and engineering department, and started measuring our progress.

The tougher part was what I didn't know. In what other areas were we failing to meet our customers' (the voters') expectations? More importantly: how could we know if we were succeeding in our goals for the city?

Measure

Keeping in mind our goals for the city, we decided to develop a set of performance measures for every department in the city, and tie the measures to the four core areas of our plan: Public Safety, Neighborhoods, Economic Development, and Public Schools. We later added Improving Government Operations as a fifth category to highlight our efforts to reduce property taxes, improve maintenance turnaround times, streamline staffing, and make other improvements to the job of running the city.

We decided early on that the performance measures should be made available to the general public by putting them on the city's website home page, and we branded them the "City Scorecard." By putting the City Scorecard online, we provided a public check on the organization. I felt that future administrations could not abandon the measures if we developed a public constituency for their maintenance and review.

We started the development of our list by reviewing performance measures in place within other major cities in the country. It is much easier to copy a successful practice than it is to create a new one. Unfortunately, none of the examples that we reviewed had all the attributes we were seeking for our system, although we did borrow some ideas.

To prepare the City Scorecard, we gathered the leadership of each of the city's departments in my office, and asked each person some very basic questions. For instance: Is the fire department serving the residents of the city better today than a year ago? How can we measure the improvement in a way that is clear to the public? What measures are relevant? We looked at response times for a fire call, comparing the current year to the past. The length of time it takes for a fire engine to show up is extremely important, especially if you are the one whose house is on fire. Likewise, there are thousands of statistics gathered by the various city departments each year. Knowing that most people don't have time to sift through countless statistics, we had to narrow significantly the number of measurements we included in the City Scorecard, giving only the relevant items.

The Big Picture

In developing the general performance measures for the city, the key is to isolate those that are important to charting the broad course of the city. Similarly, the number of performance measures should be limited. Some of the other cities whose measures we reviewed had several hundred measurements. If we expect leadership and the public to focus on the measurements, then the number of statistics must be such as to allow a fairly quick review. My goal was to keep the number at about 150. We decided early on that the measurements should be in graphs, and that the formats for all the graphs should be the same. A graph can present a tremendous amount of information in a manner that can be easily and quickly reviewed. It also provides the best method of comparing the present to the past.

Accomplishing this objective turned out to be more complicated than I first anticipated, because the various departments were using different software, and had different preferences for format. Eventually we decided on the format we wanted for the graphs, and sent instructions to the departments to adopt the standard format for the general performance measures submitted. It remained the individual department's responsibility to prepare and submit the periodic updates to the person with overall responsibility for the City Scorecard.

We also established a policy for the city's internal audit department to review selected measurements on a regular basis, and test the accuracy of the data. In most cases the measurements are compared to the past in order to provide context and reveal trends. In some cases we compared the data to other major cities in Florida, also to provide context. In a few cases we established minimum goals to be met, but for most measurements the goal is simply to improve.

Input versus Output

In developing the City Scorecard, we tried to measure "outputs" whenever possible. "Input" activity without result is of little value to the organization or the community. Our public school programs are an example of where we measured both the actions taken to improve our public schools—the "inputs"—along with "output" items such as graduation rates and the state grades of our schools based on student achievement test results.

While input measurements are helpful, output measurements are very important. The input versus output discussion is relevant in all our efforts. As an example, it is helpful to know how many college scholarships we have awarded to sixth graders, but it is important to know whether the standardized test scores of the children in our middle schools have been improving. The former measures our effort, while the latter measures the progress of our core mission: improving the education gains of the children in our schools.

Because input measures are helpful in measuring our efforts, we included many of them in the City Scorecard in order to inform the public about the steps we are taking to make the community better. But it is important to keep output the significant focus in order to ensure that we are accomplishing the core objectives that we have set out to achieve.

Tie the Measures to Goals

We categorized all performance measures within the five strategic goal categories of the city. Upon completion of our initial City Scorecard, we put about 160 performance measures online for public observation. They were all in graph form, similar formats, and most provided historical data. They were updated quarterly, semiannually, or annually and, importantly, were subject to internal audit review.

The public can go to www.stpete.org and see the city's crime rates, response times for priority one police 911 calls, the length of time it takes to repair a pothole or traffic light, the grades our public schools are getting based on student test scores, how much graffiti is being reported, how many arsons we have, our latest unemployment statistics, and the turnaround time for obtaining a building permit.

Our City Scorecard was periodically reviewed at our Cabinet meetings, and was continuously checked by the city's top administrators and me. When the trend lines go in the wrong direction it gives us the opportunity to make tactical corrections. In most cases the trend lines were positive. Just by measuring an item, we tag it as being important, and all who are involved adopt a mission of improvement.

Of course it's tempting only to measure areas where you are confident of continued improvements, but that would be a mistake. One of the greatest values the measurements provide is their highlighting problem areas so the organization will feel the pressure to improve.

As a result of the recession in 2008, our city's unemployment rates spiked significantly following the Florida and national unemployment rate increases. Although it is not pleasant to watch unemployment rates rise, it is important to track them closely because they become a leading indicator of other measurements that are impacted when people start to lose their jobs: the number of boarded-up homes due to foreclosures; the number of homeless on the streets; and the number of burglaries, larcenies, and other property crimes.

In each of these areas we developed policies and programs to respond to the challenges. This included participation in the national Neighborhood Stabilization Program, which stimulated the turnover of vacant homes; expansion of the Pinellas Hope homeless center; and numerous police and neighborhood strategies to counter the property crime increases.

When our number of graffiti complaints rose, the media picked up on the increase by reading our City Scorecard online. Newspaper reports followed, along with public discussion of efforts needed to reduce graffiti. City staff in our neighborhood department responded by assembling a team from police, sanitation, and codes to develop and execute a plan to reverse the trend. They put resources into painting over graffiti quickly after it appeared; investigating the trends represented by the graffiti symbols in order to identify those who caused the vandalism; and arresting those responsible, sometimes gang-related and sometimes individual "artists." That is exactly how the measurement program should work!

During my two terms we regularly updated and revised the Scorecard as we thought of new ways to measure our progress. The measurements became a way of ensuring that we were advancing our vision for the city, not just responding to challenges as they popped up. The system worked so well that, upon taking office, Florida Governor Charlie Crist asked that we present the City Scorecard to his Cabinet in order to assist them in the development of performance measurements for our state.

Among other measures, we now track sidewalk repair turnaround. As in the case of many of our measurements, we first had to research our records in order to develop historic data for comparative purposes. We then were able to compare the current results of our efforts to the past. The average length of time it takes to fix a sidewalk dropped from thirty months to less than two weeks, and it stayed that way for seven years. The mayor's office received very few sidewalk repair complaints after the turnaround time was reduced!

Chapter 14

Run the Business; Handle Crisis; Advance the Vision

Being the Mayor of New York City sure isn't easy.
Every day I go home with a headache!

—Brooklyn grammar school student,
imagining the life of the mayor

B eing a mayor is complicated, and often headache-inducing, but it is also an incredibly rewarding way to spend a portion of your life. During the mornings when I was mayor of St. Petersburg, I could not wait to get out of bed and drive to City Hall to begin the day. Each day had its share of struggles, but there were also great opportunities and exciting challenges. I can think of few better jobs.

As the leader and chief administrator of city government, the mayor often does not get to choose his battles. While pursuing an agenda, there are daily tasks to be accomplished and unforeseen challenges that spring up. Over the course of almost nine years in office, I came to view the mayor's job as having three distinct parts: (1) running the business of the city; (2) dealing with the crises that present themselves; and (3) advancing a vision for the future of the city.

(1) Run the Business

In a "strong mayor" form of government, the mayor is the top administrator and has the responsibility of running the business of the government. Like any large public organization, our city has budgets, legal and financial issues, employee matters, union contracts, taxes, infrastructure, maintenance requirements—all the issues associated with keeping the engine running in an organization with almost 3,000 employees and 34 departments.

Problems with any aspect of the operations of the city can disrupt the efforts to move the city forward. It may be a budget difficulty, a union impasse, or an infrastructure collapse. Having talented professional leaders "running the train" is critical to the organization's success. Our main train engineer was First Deputy Mayor Tish Elston, an ethical, hardworking, talented professional who spent her career in civil service. Finally, a big part of running the business of the city is the ongoing need to maintain and improve government operations by "filling the potholes," as I discussed in chapter 10.

(2) Handle Crises

Calm is hard work. When a city appears to be moving forward smoothly, there is typically a lot of effort going on behind the scenes to work through the challenges that find their way to City Hall without letting them distract from the primary mission of advancing the quality of life of the community. Every mayor will have to deal with crises of all sizes that fall across his or her desk on a frequent basis, from both anticipated and unexpected sources. These crises differ in type, but the major ones typically have similar stages.

The beginning phase is chaos. The mayor will receive lots of information at this point—most of which is wrong. The mayor must be cautious about making decisions based on facts as they are presented. In this stage, he must gather data, question all information, and trust his instincts. At times he will have to make decisions, even though he is not fully informed.

The next stage of a crisis arrives after the facts and information are fairly clear, and a plan can be developed for working through the challenge. The plan is then executed upon and is constantly reevaluated for progress. Typically, since crises often have multiple layers, a mayor will find himself moving back and forth between the first two stages, reassessing and redeploying resources to address the challenges as new information arrives.

The final stage of a crisis is the assessment of responsibility, and adjustments in policy to prevent the recurrence of the problem. This stage progresses under the scrutiny of, and is sometimes driven by, the media, who will search for fault—either associated with the crisis itself, or the response to the crisis—once the immediacy of the crisis passes. Most leaders tend to focus on solving the problem and then relax a bit after the danger passes. Not being engaged during the assessment process is a mistake. Until the crisis is clearly in the distant rear view mirror: stay engaged.

And remember: crises almost always present you with an opportunity. Budget problems give a city the opportunity to rethink priorities and become more efficient. The risk of a business moving out of town presents the possibility of the company expanding in the city. Homeless difficulties present the chance to rethink service delivery methods and assemble support and resources to better address the problem. Even public safety incidents can unite a community around the need to reject and oppose criminal activity. The public recognition of a major crisis presents leadership with the opportunity to rally support that might not respond in the calm of day. Crisis presents opportunity!

(3) Advance the Vision

The third part of the job of the mayor is to advance his vision for the city. My vision was summarized by the Baker Plan, described earlier in chapter 3 of this book: Improving Public Safety; Building Strong Neighborhoods; Promoting Economic Development, especially Downtown and Midtown; Supporting Public Schools; and Improving Government Operations. Advancing the vision requires an enormous effort of developing ideas that promote the objective, creating programs that implement the ideas, gathering resources needed, selling the public on each program, and executing on the plan.

A key to advancing the vision is to build and maintain momentum. In 1994, I sat in Doak Campbell Stadium, home field for Florida State University, watching FSU play the University of Florida in football. For three quarters FSU could do nothing right, and the scoreboard in the early fourth quarter reflected the Seminole's lack of progress: FSU 3, UF 31. Then, all of a sudden, "momentum shifted" as sportscasters like to say. Florida State scored four consecutive touchdowns in the closing minutes of the game in what had to be one of the most unlikely and largest comebacks in college football history. For the Gators it became known as the "Choke at Doak." What happened?

Momentum shifts in politics are legendary, from the 1960 Nixon-Kennedy debate to the famous picture of Harry Truman holding the 1948 *Chicago Daily Tribune* headline incorrectly proclaiming "Dewey Defeats Truman." Sometimes during a campaign, everything is going right for a candidate until an event, a revelation, or something undetected causes the tide to turn. Momentum shifts may be hard to describe or quantify, but they are real.

Just as in sports and politics, momentum is critically important in developing cities. In order to succeed, the leaders of the city's efforts need support and partners. People must believe that the city is going in the right direction. They must feel that they are part of the effort, and they need to feel the positive forward movement. Success should be publicized. Both the strategic planning and marketing efforts of the city should be focused on accomplishing goals that advance the city vision and communicating the progress to the public.

A mayor runs the risk of becoming diverted by a problem or crisis and then failing to continue to advance the vision. Of course, challenges must receive the attention necessary to become resolved. At the same time, the organization must have the focus, discipline, and processes in place to ensure that it constantly keeps its eye on advancing the established vision for improving the quality of life for the people who call the city home. Maintaining positive, forward momentum should always be in the minds of those who lead the city, regardless of problems and challenges that arise.

There are no degree programs that can adequately prepare someone to become the mayor of a major city. I described the process of my first year on the job as climbing a "vertical learning curve." I came in very early every day in order to study the departments, budgets, and other aspects of the organization. It was on-the-job learning.

While each city and mayor's job is unique, over the course of nine years I came to believe that there are certain core principles that should be embraced by anyone taking on the job of leading a city. Some are personal in nature, and that is appropriate. As mayor, the line between personal life and city life becomes blurred, if not completely wiped out. Many of the principles could apply to most professions, while some are unique to public life. Still others have more focus on the home than the office. For me, the first to be considered are those that are the most important in my life: faith and family, which I will discuss in the next two chapters.

Chapter 15

Faith and a Public Life

My concern is not whether God is on our side;
my greatest concern is to be on God's side,
for God is always right.

—ABRAHAM LINCOLN

olitical campaigns are exhausting. During my 2001 race for mayor, we had thirty-four debates, countless coffees, speaking engagements, and strategy/planning meetings. We raised money, dealt with media, studied the opposition, learned about the city, developed and evolved positions, planned advertisements, and performed countless other tasks.

On the Sunday morning before the primary election, a campaign supporter picked me up for a church visit. In some churches, mostly in the African American community, the congregations allow candidates to come by and speak for a couple minutes to give their qualifications and reasons for running. The pastor will generally take a few minutes' break from the service for those candidates who visit. It is a good idea for the candidate to be brief and respectful, remembering that he is in a church.

The congregation usually responds with a polite welcome, while the pastor is careful not to endorse from the pulpit.

The process can be complicated because there are a large number of potential churches to visit, and only a couple hours when services are occurring on Sunday mornings. Since the pastors understandably do not want to interrupt the service right away when a candidate arrives, the candidate typically spends some time at each church, and it is difficult to visit more than a few churches on a Sunday morning campaign day. This particular Sunday morning we only had one church to visit, and we were scheduled to come by at the end of the service, a little after noon. As we drove to the church I reflected on the challenges of the campaign, and particularly the past twenty-four hours. It had been a rough day.

On the Saturday morning before the primary, I experienced something that many people who enter politics know they will endure at some point, but it still comes as an unpleasant surprise when it arrives. Although there were nine remaining candidates in the race by the time of the primary, I was considered the frontrunner, and therefore the target. For whatever reason, one of my primary opponents—he is now a friend of mine—decided to send an attack direct mail piece against me that arrived in the city voters' mailboxes on the Saturday morning before the election.

The direct mail piece was not all that terrible, as I view it in the nine-year rear view mirror of columnists' opinions, news reports, blogs, and emails. But until that point, I had never had anyone do a mass publication to thousands of people for the purpose of portraying me as someone unworthy of receiving a vote.

The experience reminded me of a movie I once saw where the lead character, a non-public person, was being drawn into a public controversy. He picked up the newspaper one morning and, standing in his bathrobe on the front lawn, began to read an article portraying him in a scandalous manner. Horrified, he began to run down his street picking up the newspapers in front of all the other houses, as if he could somehow stop the media onslaught that was underway. That feeling, in many ways, is what any candidate and elected official at some time will experience, probably on a regular basis.

Knowing that I could not pull this particular mail piece out of the mailboxes throughout the city, I elected instead to focus on the three remaining days before the primary. As I was going through my emails Saturday night, I received a call from Carl Kuttler, a good friend.

"I read the direct mail piece today," he said.

"So did the rest of the city," I replied, in a voice that betrayed how sorry I was feeling for myself.

Carl asked me to look up a Bible verse—Isaiah 54:17—and read it out loud. I read: "*No weapon formed against you shall prosper.*" Carl pressed: "Does it say no weapon except nasty direct mail pieces?" "No," I confessed. "It says no weapon will prosper."

Once he was convinced that I had gotten the point, Carl exacted a promise from me that I would memorize both the verse and the citation before I went to sleep that night. I wrote "Isaiah 54:17" on a yellow post-it note and stuck it on my wife's dresser mirror. The note would stay on the mirror for the next nine years. Before I drifted to sleep that night I had both the citation and the verse memorized: *No weapon formed against me shall prosper.*

The next morning was my pre-primary church visit. The church parking lot was empty when we arrived—the service was over and everyone had gone home. We had obviously gotten our time wrong. We were all frustrated, since it was the only church we had scheduled that day, and it was now after noon. We discussed our options and concluded that our best chance was to go to New Life, a charismatic church on U.S. Highway 19, which would probably still have its services underway. Maybe they would let me speak.

We arrived at the church, located in a converted two-story office building on a busy highway. The parking lot was full, so I was dropped off by the staircase and raced up to the second floor sanctuary. I stepped into the back of the church, relieved that the service was not yet over. They were singing the final praise hymn. I leaned against the back wall and caught the eye of the pastor, Chico Dials. He smiled and nodded, indicating that he would give me an opportunity to speak when the song was done.

At that moment a series of bizarre circumstances collided that would define my next nine years, and in many ways the rest of my life.

As I leaned against the wall and began to gather my thoughts, I saw a familiar figure in the front pew. It was my opponent who had sent out the negative direct mail piece. My blood pressure began to rise, and I noticed my opponent's campaign supporter standing against the wall next to me. He took the opportunity to lean over to me and make an unpleasant comment about me not caring about poor people.

I was furious. Exhausted by a difficult campaign and insulted in church, I now had to wait my turn to speak after the fellow who had trashed me in a letter to thousands of people just one day before. I tried to calm down by focusing on the final praise hymn that the congregation was singing. I had never heard it before, but it had a great spirit and rhythm, a good diversion for my attitude. As I listened to the words of the chorus, a chill ran through my body. I asked my campaign supporter whether he recognized the words they were singing in the chorus.

"Yes," he said. "No weapon formed against me shall prosper."

At that moment I felt like I was the only person in the room. I started to think of the odds that this series of events could occur by happenstance. The letter the day before, the call from Carl last night, the verse and cite he urged me to memorize, the missed church service, randomly picking New Life out of a hundred churches, my opponent who sent the letter being at the church, his supporter's insult and, finally, the verse I memorized the night before being sung by this congregation before which I was about to speak.

It was not coincidence. I will always believe that God took the time that Sunday to assure me that He would be standing with me if I stood close to Him.

After my opponent spoke, I made my way to the front of the church. I was very much feeling God's presence, and I paused for several moments while I collected my thoughts. Finally I looked up at the congregation, then over to the choir. "New Life," I said, "I love that song." Those in the pews looked a little amused, but then I added, "Isaiah 54:17." At that point jaws dropped. Everyone in the room became intent on what I said.

"No weapon," I began, and the entire gathering repeated in unison: "No weapon ... formed against me ... shall prosper."

I assured the audience that weapons had been formed against me in my campaign, but that they would not prosper, because I had put my faith in God. At the conclusion of my talk the entire group encircled me with hugs and support. I knew everything was going to turn out just fine because God was in control

The Isaiah 54:17 experience reinforced a lesson I learned many years ago: in life's greatest challenges, stay close to God. Being a mayor of a major city is a big job. Although you prepare by doing a lot of things in life, you are never really prepared. Most days are great, an exciting process of meeting people, facing issues, and learning many things. You learn a lot about the person you see in the mirror every day.

There are also tough days: the unexpected crises, the personal attacks, the nasty media reports, the disappointments when plans don't go as hoped. A mayor—and any leader—needs to turn to God both in the good and the bad days.

During my first race, we had a campaign hot dog cookout in Campbell Park, which is now part of Midtown. We had a good crowd. When we finished, a homeless man, clean and well dressed who looked to be in his mid-thirties, offered to help pick up the plates and food. As we were carrying supplies and posters back to my car, he stopped for a moment. With a very serious expression, he said that God had given him a message for me that he felt compelled to share.

When a homeless man says he has a message to you from God, the tendency is to be dubious. But on the other hand, I thought, if he is telling the truth it would not be a good idea to refuse to listen. I decided to hear him out.

He said that God told him that I would be elected mayor, but that God wanted to remind me of something. Often, when people seek positions of great responsibility, they ask for God's help to succeed, but after they succeed they turn the glory back to themselves. His message to me was that after I was elected, God wanted me to turn the glory back to Him.

Whether this encounter was an indirect word from God, or just a piece of advice from a homeless man who had enjoyed my hot dogs, I don't know. Either way, the message is the same one found in 1 Samuel 2:30, and I believe it to be correct: "*Those who honor me I will honor.*" I made a decision at that moment that I would do my best to turn honor to God while serving, and that I would seek his honor and blessings for our city.

I should be clear that I know myself to be far from perfect. I do stupid, sinful things at times. My faith sometimes falters and I need a constant reminder to keep God in my life. Acknowledging my own weaknesses and flaws, there are some things that, I think, move us in God's direction.

First, we should publicly thank God on a regular basis for the success in our life and for the success of our city. God returns the honor. Some will use professions of thanks or faith as an opportunity to draw public officials into religious debate, especially in relation to social issues. The line of questioning starts with an attempt to get the official to acknowledge that certain political positions are based on one's faith or belief in the Bible; then the effort is made to discredit unrelated faith-based beliefs in order to undermine the political position. Once a reporter asked me if I interpreted the accounts of the Old Testament to mean that man and dinosaurs lived at the same time. My response to him was that I believe in God; that I believe that He created everything, including me; that I believe the Bible is God's word; and that I believe that Jesus Christ died so that I can be forgiven of my sins and go to Heaven. Beyond that, I refused to enter into a debate on the specifics of the Bible. I didn't get quoted for the story.

Second, we should ask God for his blessings and protection. During my first few years in office, my family spent almost every other Sunday attending services at churches throughout our community, and soliciting their members to pray for our family and for our city's success. Likewise, through the YMCA we initiated a Mayor's Prayer Breakfast so that people from throughout the community can gather each year to commend our city to God's grace. Again, I believe that God hears the corporate and individual prayers of the city and responds to those prayers.

Finally, our city, state, and federal leaders should take Lincoln's advice by striving to be "on God's side" by staying humble in personal prayer. The Lord's Prayer (Matthew 6:9–13) is of special importance to those of us who believe in Jesus Christ and His gift of sacrifice and life. Another prayer was given by Jabez (1 Chronicles 4:10), and it helps organize thoughts. Among other points of the Jabez prayer, it asks God to "expand my territory." I admit that during the vertical learning curve of my first year of office, I started to skip that part. I didn't need any more territory to try to figure out. But I have come to learn that God expands His grace as He expands your responsibility, so—most of the time—I go back to the full Jabez prayer.

Under our nation's constitution we must not use public resources to promote or prevent the exercise of religion. Our leaders should show respect to all faiths. This was at the core of the foundation of America, and it is a principle that has made us a stronger nation. Still, that principle does not mean that our leaders are prohibited from seeking God's guidance and blessings on our people. In fact, I believe that seeking God is critical to our success. My personal prayer, especially during my time as mayor, but certainly throughout my life, is for God to grant me the wisdom to know His will in my life, and the strength to do it no matter what challenges and attacks present themselves.

The concept that leaders should turn to God for wisdom, direction, and help is not a new idea. Abraham Lincoln, perhaps our greatest president, regularly reminded the nation of the importance of seeking God's guidance during America's most difficult trial. As our sixteenth president vigorously pursued a horrible war to save the nation, he contemplated God's purpose in a September 1862 private memo entitled "Meditation on the Divine Will":

> *The will of God prevails....In the present civil war it is quite possible that God's purpose is something different from the purpose of either party...I am almost ready to say that this is probably true; that God wills this contest, and wills that it shall not end yet.*

On March 4, 1865, after four years of civil war and hundreds of thousands of casualties, Lincoln delivered his Second Inaugural Address, one of the most amazing speeches of all time, and one which is now chiseled on the wall of the Lincoln Monument in Washington, D.C. The speech was given at a time when the nation was about to transition to another difficult period. The next month, on April 3, the Confederate capital of Richmond would fall to the Federal troops, and President Lincoln would visit the fallen city the next day, on April 4. On April 14, Good Friday, Lincoln himself would be shot down at Ford's Theatre.

One can only imagine the emotions the president experienced as he prepared to deliver that famous address. He had led a country through an indescribably difficult period and had felt the heavy weight of the cause for four long years. As he looked both backward and forward, he chose again to turn to God for direction. His speech was less than 700 words, one of the shortest inaugural addresses in American history, and one-fifth the length of his First Inaugural Address. Yet in this address he invoked his faith constantly, quoting King David and Jesus Christ in passages from the Psalms and the New Testament books of Luke and Matthew. Lincoln summed up his belief and faith that God's purpose was being carried out through the great contest:

> *Fondly we hope, fervently do we pray, that this mighty scourge of war may speedily pass away. Yet, if God wills that it continue until all the wealth piled by the bondsman's two hundred and fifty years of unrequited toil shall be sunk, and until every drop of blood drawn by the lash shall be paid by another drawn with the sword, as was said three thousand years ago, so it must be said "the judgments of the Lord are true and righteous altogether."*

Lincoln's words are among a constant stream of examples of the faith of America's leadership. On the Liberty Bell, the words "Proclaim Liberty throughout all the land" come from Leviticus 25:10. The cap of the Washington Monument includes the inscription "Laus Deo," Latin for

"Praise be to God." For almost one hundred and fifty years our nation's currency has proclaimed "In God We Trust."

Thomas Jefferson, who authored Virginia's Statute of Religious Freedom, also asserted that "God who gave us life gave us liberty." George W. Bush turned squarely to God after September 11. Barack Obama, moments before being sworn into office, had the Lord's Prayer read on the steps of the United States Capitol. They were the same words given by Jesus Christ in his sermon on the mountain. Each of these men understood that we have a creator who loves us, and who hears our prayers. Each understood that somehow America's prosperity is tied to its moral soundness and its search for the will of God in our lives. And I believe they all would have agreed with the advice that I received from the homeless young man at my hot dog cookout, to turn the glory back to God.

Chapter 16

Family

Raising the Mayor's Children

You have to love your children unselfishly.
That is hard. But it is the only way.

—BARBARA BUSH

I t is important for parents to attend their children's events. Whether the child is involved in sports, music, ballet, or horseback riding, they need mom and dad's attention and approval.

I can remember one night sitting for two hours at a Christmas program listening to children I did not know singing solos and chorus music. At times the notes hit the mark. Other times the children created new sounds necessitating what my wife calls "loving ears" to appreciate. My thoughts began to drift to the many things I needed to do, and what I could accomplish with the two hours I was spending sitting there.

Finally, my son Jacob's sixth grade class was called up to perform. The boys, some in clip-on ties, all wore oversized shirts that had come un-tucked in the game of tag they played before the concert. The girls wore new Christmas dresses, freshly pressed, and beautifully combed hair with red and white ribbons. The class shuffled their way toward the front of the church and gathered together. The two fairly straight lines of nervous performers assembled in front of hundreds of parents and grandparents.

I stretched my body up to try to get a glimpse of Jacob as the piano started to play. My son looked nervous as he peered out over the large crowd. I could tell he was searching for his Mom and me, so I stretched up a little more and waved a bit. Jacob's eyes caught mine for a moment. He gave me a slight smile and his face relaxed into an expression of relief.

The look on Jacob's face for that instant made the two hours of sitting in the pews completely worthwhile. It is for that moment that parents need to be there.

For my family, the moment was often when Julann stepped up to the plate at a softball game. I can remember many times when she would look back over her shoulder toward the stands where we were sitting. Once, the moment came right after Jacob scored his third consecutive three-point shot in the championship basketball game. As he ran across the court to get back on defense he looked over to the bleachers to make sure I'd seen the shot.

It happened after Julann hit a mid-field goal in soccer. As long as I live I will never forget the surprised and delighted look on her face when her eyes caught ours, as we sat on the sidelines in our captain's chairs. In each of these cases, and many others, it was very important to our children that the pews, grandstands, and sidelines were occupied with people who loved them, and who could share in the excitement of the moment. It is a moment that is shared for a lifetime, but it is one that cannot be recaptured when missed.

In that special moment the child is saying, without words, that he or she needs mom and dad to be part of the important times of their life. In the same moment the parent says that nothing in the world is more important than their son or daughter. No business meeting, no laundry, no banquet, and no work project. Nothing is more important than being with that young girl or boy at that moment.

My thoughts were on my children's moments as I was sitting in the reception area waiting for my appointment with Jacksonville Mayor John Delaney in 2000.

I had been introduced to Mayor Delaney by Governor Jeb Bush, who helped set up the meeting. Mayor Delaney had the reputation of being a very popular, successful mayor, and I wanted his advice. I was about to finalize my decision to run for mayor of St. Petersburg, but I was concerned that my job would take me away from my children. I knew that John Delaney had young children, so I decided to ask him about being a dad and mayor at the same time.

Although I had just met Mayor Delaney, he was very generous with his time, and we talked about the challenges of balancing family and a very visible job like being mayor of a large city. As I drove home from Jacksonville and thought back on the visit, I concluded that I could be successful at striking the balance. I also realized that it would not happen without a deliberate, focused effort.

Shortly after our daughter Julann was born, I read an article about being a dad that made a strong impression on me. The article said that most of us treat our work time as immovable, and treat our family time as movable. The result is that work time intrudes into family time more and more until we find ourselves missing ball games, Christmas plays, and teacher conferences. The key, according to the author, was to flip the priorities—make family time immovable and work time flexible. If work is to intrude on family, it should be a rare, significant occurrence, but family time should more easily displace work time, within reason.

Somewhere on Interstate 4, heading toward St. Petersburg, I decided that if I was elected, I would identify my priorities before I started. I knew that there would be many pressures pulling me in various directions, so if I wanted to succeed at keeping my priorities right, I needed to be extremely disciplined with respect to my schedule. Time with my children would have to be first!

Months later, I was elected. During my first couple weeks in office, I had an encounter that strongly reinforced my "priorities" decision. In fact, it produced such a vivid example that I thought of it often during my next nine years. I was on a flight to Tallahassee to lobby for funding of a drug rehabilitation center, and I happened to sit by a fellow who introduced himself, telling me that he had been on the staff of a former mayor of a major United States city. When I shared with him my desire to stay close to my children while in office, he smiled knowingly and shared a story about his former boss.

This mayor had served his first term while his son was young. The mayor had been very popular and successful, but he often stayed out late at dinners and travelled on city business, causing him to miss out on many of his son's life activities. Finally, one day toward the end of his first term, the mayor sat his young son down to share some good news. The mayor had decided to run for reelection, so he could be in office for another four years. Upon hearing the news, the young boy burst into tears, ran to his room, locked the door, and jumped onto his bed sobbing.

The mental image of this sobbing boy drove me to develop a set of guidelines for staying close to my son and daughter during the challenging years ahead. I wanted to be there for them as they grew up, and I wanted them to share in the great adventure of building a city.

Be There

It's simple. If you want to stay involved in your children's lives, then you must stay involved in your children's lives. Involvement takes place one decision at a time. One basketball game, one recital, one teacher conference, one daddy-daughter dance, one night helping your child study for a test, one out-of-town little league tournament, one summer vacation. Every opportunity missed cannot be recaptured, so it is important to handle each decision very carefully.

It starts with your schedule.

The mayor's schedule is complicated. There are countless requests and demands for time from staff, community, business, and neighborhood groups, charities, conventions in town, event organizers, and others. At times, a crisis will occur that necessitates the clearing of the calendar of prior scheduled events. Since many events involve speaking to large groups who schedule well in advance, and in some cases people who travel to the city for the mayor's meeting, it can be very difficult to defer or cancel an appointment that is calendared. Getting sick is not an option.

These factors make it necessary to calendar the family events early: youth basketball schedules, chorus performances, pageants, teacher conferences, and others. You then have to protect the dates. Generally, I tried to limit my nighttime activities to no more than two per week (including out-of-town trips) and limit my weekend events to those my wife and children could attend with me. I am thankful for the support I received from the city staff in scheduling my life and protecting my time with my children.

The responsibilities of the mayor's job are important, and I always treated them that way, but children's events are important also. My children only have one father who could be there for them at their special moments, so I sometimes missed city events as I balanced my family life. It was not only the best approach for my family, it also sent a strong, needed message to the community: it is important to be involved in the lives of your children!

Perhaps somewhat selfishly, it was also important for me not to miss out on the little parts of my children growing up. I had lunch at their school often, sang them to sleep at night, and helped with their homework. They made me a better mayor because they kept me grounded. They also helped the city. Having a young son and daughter while in office gave me a perspective on things I could not have had without my children, such as the importance of playgrounds, water slides, dog parks, bike paths, skateboard parks, and schools.

Bring Them with You

I call my daughter Julann my "go-go girl." She is always ready to go! On Saturday mornings while I was mayor, I would typically have a series of events: neighborhood picnics, ribbon cuttings, ground breakings, community clean-ups, celebrations, and speaking engagements. After getting up, I'd call to Julann to let her know that I was going out. Although my daughter typically is hard to get out of bed, she will almost always make an exception for new adventures. By the time I was dressed and downstairs she was in the car and ready to go. Only when we were pulling out of the driveway would she ask where we were going.

My son Jacob is more cautious. He wants to know where he's going, but he also enjoyed our mayoral weekend outings, especially when they involved new playgrounds, swimming pools, neighborhood picnics, or recreation fields where he could "work out his wiggles." Unlike Julann, Jacob does not care for dinner parties.

Once, when Jacob was about seven, a babysitter asked him why he didn't want to go to a dinner event that Joyce, Julann, and I were attending. He answered with a very serious face: "Well, it's like this. First you have to get all dressed up. Then you go to a big room with a lot of people who you don't know. You sit down with a bunch of grown-ups, and someone gets up to talk. They talk and talk and talk and talk; and you get tire-der and tire-der and tire-der and tire-der; and then you get old … and then you die!" I have to admit that I felt the same way as my seven-year-old son about some of the dinners I attended.

Jacob opted out of most of my banquets, but Julann was always ready to come along. One night, Julann and I attended a banquet together at a hotel in the Gateway area. She would generally accompany me to banquets if I observed two rules. First, I didn't say that she was my date; and second, I didn't call her my sweetie. Because Julann was under twelve the night of the hotel dinner, the air bag rules meant that she was in the back seat as we drove home from the banquet. During the dinner I had been at the head table, and she had been at a table in the audience, as she prefers. She generally did not care to be up front.

During our drive home I asked her how her evening went, and she said it was nice. She enjoyed the food, which she described to me in detail, and she described the various people she met at her table. She then paused and confessed that the only part of the evening she did not care for was the boring speaker. I felt like I had been kicked from behind, and I responded: "Honey, I was the speaker!" As I observed my little girl in the rear view mirror she gave me a devilish grin and replied innocently: "Well daddy, you always tell me to be honest!"

By bringing my children with me to the important events of my official life, my time was enriched, and they had experiences that are hard to replicate. Each spent many afternoons at City Hall, sometimes volunteering to do clerical jobs for the staff. They became involved in every neighborhood in every corner of our city. As we attended various events, I explained to them the importance of what we were doing to make the city better. Their experiences have ranged from witnessing crowds with picket signs to meeting celebrities like Mario Andretti, Miss America, and President George W. Bush.

Jacob was ten years old when we went to greet President Bush at St. Petersburg's International Airport. We were to meet the president as he walked down the steps of Air Force One. I had informed both kids the night before that they would be missing school so we could go meet the president. Julann was excited.

Jacob asked what time we would be getting back to school. After I told him, he got quite upset and threw a fit. He said that he couldn't go because he would have to miss physical education in school. Trying to hold back laughter at his choosing to play recess football over meeting the president of the United States, I looked at him seriously.

Although I often gave my children the option of whether to attend my events, I told him that I was going to make him go this time because Jacob would be mad if I didn't. When he looked at me perplexed, I explained that, although ten-year-old Jacob didn't want to go, years from now twenty-five-year-old Jacob would be mad if his dad didn't take him to meet the president. He seemed to buy that argument, and he went the next day without a fuss. When we arrived at the airport filled with security, police dogs, and SWAT officers on the roof, Jacob got caught up in the excitement and forgot about missing PE—although two years later he reminded me that he didn't get his perfect attendance award because of the president's visit.

As we greeted the president, Julann smiled broadly and announced that she knew his brother. This sparked a nice talk between my eleven-year-old daughter and the president of the United States about his younger brother, Jeb. They talked about what a nice man Jeb was and the fact that he was going to need a new job now that he was done being our governor. President Bush was so much at ease with my children that it made them as comfortable talking to him as they would be chatting with their uncle.

My children came to know our city through my eyes. When we drove around Jacob would point out traffic lights that were burnt out or graffiti on a sign. Together we called the appropriate person to report the problem. Julann, in sixth grade, was once asked to give an extemporaneous speech in school. Without time to prepare, she stood up and gave a twenty-minute talk on the Midtown redevelopment program and why it is so important to the children who live there. Her teacher was so impressed that he called my wife Joyce to tell her about Julann's talk.

Jacob was equally comfortable describing our efforts to bring a Post Office to Midtown, or the reasons behind building a playground within a short walk of every child. Each of our children regularly gave ideas that I incorporated into our effort, and they took pride in knowing, along with my wife Joyce, that they made their own unique contributions to the people who live in St. Petersburg.

In late 2007, the Republican presidential debates on YouTube were held in St. Petersburg. I agreed to let Jacob stay home, since he was worn out with events. Before the debate I was asked to go back stage to greet the candidates. I brought Joyce and eleven-year-old Julann along, as I welcomed each of the eight candidates and their families.

The last candidate we talked to was Senator John McCain, who would eventually be the party's nominee. After a short talk, Senator McCain excused himself and walked down the hall toward his dressing room so he could focus on the imminent debate. He got about half-way down the hall when he suddenly stopped, then turned around and headed directly toward my daughter. Something triggered a point he wanted to make to her.

Upon reaching Julann, he gently placed his hand on her shoulder, leaned down, and looked her directly in the eyes. With a smile he asked her: "Do other children ever make fun of you because you're the mayor's daughter?" "Sometimes," she smiled nervously in response. The senator, who was minutes away from his nationally televised debate, then asked: "Do they ever tell you things they think your dad should do to make the city better?" With a sigh, Julann confirmed that they did.

"Don't you worry about any of that," John McCain said with conviction. "*It's a great thing to be the mayor's daughter!*" Julann responded with a sweet smile that was a mixture of pleasure and relief; and I was amazed at the exchange that was taking place, just moments before the eyes of the world would be focused on a discussion a few steps away. I remember thinking, as I watched the presidential candidate walk toward the stage, that when my daughter and son look back to the mayoral time of their lives, I hope that they will agree with Senator McCain.

Chapter 17

Leading the City

Staying Engaged

I hear and I forget. I see and I remember.
I do and I understand.

—CONFUCIUS

Committed, passionate, competent leadership is critical to the success of any organization, including cities. Developing a strategic plan, following through on its execution, responding to the crises as they occur, and keeping the organization moving forward are critical components that are explored elsewhere in this book.

The mayor has a very broad array of constituencies, and the interaction with them is an extremely public process. The need for constant communication and interface is multi-level and hard to fully describe, but there are three activities that help the mayor stay engaged while leading the city.

(1) Listening carefully
(2) Speaking clearly
(3) Walking around

(1) Listening

Over one hundred angry people showed up for the public meeting in the college theater to discuss our new library. Before the meeting began, I looked out at the crowd and tried to understand why they were so mad. This was really a great project!

We were building a joint use library with St. Petersburg College at their campus on the west side of town. The city was to pay $2 million of the $12 million cost of the facility, with the remaining amounts coming from the college and state grants. It would be a 50,000 square foot facility to replace our present 8,000 square foot library located in the back of a middle school media center.

The new library would have a children's area as large as the entire old library, thirteen times the number of computer stations, several study areas, a public arts project, and a café. The college had agreed to operate the library, and the city's share of operating costs would be the same as our total expenses for the old library.

It was a great deal for the city and a great opportunity to build the city's largest public library in a part of the city that had felt underserved in the past. So why were these people so angry? I concluded that I needed to do a better job of convincing this audience that we were listening.

I had approached the West St. Petersburg Public Library project in much the same way I had approached projects I put together in the business world. In business, when you want to accomplish something you identify the goal, research your options, develop the strategy for accomplishing the goal, collect the necessary resources, and execute the plan. I figured that as mayor I could pretty much approach the city issues the same way, except that at the end I would announce my brilliant plan to the world and step back to receive the positive media response.

It did not work out quite that way with respect to the West St. Petersburg Library. After announcing the plan, an email and media campaign was launched from multiple directions trashing the plan. Some residents were angry that they would lose the old, small library that was closer to their homes than the proposed new site. Some were already mad about traffic issues at the college campus and felt that this would make things worse. Some feared having college students and children in the same building. Some were just mad!

I came to learn that in public projects, people who are against them will often attack on two fronts. First, they criticize the merits of the proposal—and often the criticism has some validity. It is important to be flexible in revising the plan to accommodate legitimate complaints.

Second, they will criticize the process. If someone is passionately against something, but the merits of the project are compelling, they will often look to find fault with the process. No matter when you announce the project, you should have announced it sooner, before so much planning has already been done. You should not have had any meetings until you'd first vetted the public. Honestly, I think there are those who feel the mayor should issue a press release every time he has an idea in the shower.

Ideas need time to be developed a little before commencing the vetting process, or they will never have a chance. When ideas are announced too soon, those intent on killing them are quick to point out all the flaws, to ask countless questions that you have not yet considered, and deride you for not thinking the situation through. The trick in the development of ideas within a public process is to allow the idea enough room to develop, while presenting it in such a time and manner as to enable a meaningful and transparent process for public input and approval. You then need to be willing to adjust the proposal in order to accommodate the input when constructive comments are made.

In any case, I knew I should have handled the announcement of the West St. Petersburg Library in a different manner. Those against the proposal argued that they had not been consulted and had no opportunity for input. We should have gone to the neighborhood associations and held discussions before announcing it as a project that we had decided to do.

After a few days of being publicly beaten to a pulp, I knew that we needed to reach out to the reasonable folks and let them know we were listening, and could adjust our plan to meet many of their concerns.

We started with the large forum that drew the unhappy crowd. We let everyone speak who wanted to be heard. They lined up and gave all their reasons for opposing the plan. After hours of input I spoke, as did Rick Kriseman, our city councilman who represented the west side of the city, and the St. Petersburg College representative.

During our talks we made several commitments to assure the attendees that we were listening. First, we agreed to go to the area's neighborhood associations to have further discussions and make adjustments to the plan in order to address concerns, from parking to safety. We would allow the children of the neighborhoods to design the children's area in the library. Finally, in order to further demonstrate that we were listening I committed to be the last one to leave the auditorium that night. At the end of the public comment, I sat in the front row and stayed until anyone who wanted to come up and give me their view had said their peace.

We still had a few bumps in the road, but at the end of the day we built a beautiful new library. I doubt you could find anyone now who still believes it was the wrong thing to do for that part of our city. Importantly, it is a better library because of the public input we received. The public vetting process can be time consuming and painful, but it almost always results in a better project.

And I learned a valuable lesson as mayor: while many business concepts can apply to make government run better, it is a mistake to believe that government can be run exactly like a business. Every public official must stay connected to the people who elect him or her, and the public vetting process is important.

The West St. Petersburg Library exercise convinced me to actively seek out listening opportunities. The process can be organized in different ways, such as public hearings, special topic forums, and charrettes. I generally favor charrettes over forums since they provide a greater opportunity for dialogue and idea exchange. Our charrettes typically break up a group into tables of eight to ten people, with participants at each table discussing ideas and responding to topic questions. One reporter from each table then presents the group's results to the assembly.

Part of listening is visiting the community at their businesses, civic clubs, schools, neighborhood association gatherings, and places of worship. It's good to leave opportunities for questions and comments, whether from the corporate CEO or the second grader. I liked to have informal "working lunches" at business offices around the city. Also, about every month or so, I invited neighborhood presidents, five to ten at a time, into my office for morning coffee and bagels to talk about their issues. I learned a lot about the needs of the different parts of our city, and it was a great opportunity to share with them our priorities and programs.

Listening also involves simply conversing with people when they approach, whether at a movie, park event, ice cream shop, grocery store, or on the sidewalk. Most of the time, I loved it when people stopped me to say "hello" and talk about the city. If they had a problem, I tried to address it right then, in their presence. I left telephone messages with staff members after these discussions, instructing them to call the person with the issue on the next business day. It was vital to make sure that someone followed up on the call.

People in the community also emailed, called, and wrote to City Hall with comments, suggestions, and requests. It was important to have a system where city staff captured these communications individually and responded to the citizens. Early in my first term we adopted "action on line," an online system where people could go to our website and submit requests. Whether the inquiry was the need for a pothole or sidewalk repair, the existence of drug deals, a speeding problem, or water quality issues, the concern was automatically sent to the appropriate staff person, and the sender received a tracking number to check on the status of the issue.

At our weekly Cabinet meetings, I received a report identifying the public input, both by quantity and by topic area, which had come in over the prior week. I used this report, along with time spent in the city, to keep connected to the pulse of the city and ensure that we were listening to the concerns and comments of our citizens.

Sometimes listening is simply observing. When we were developing Dell Holmes Park, a large area on Lake Maggiore at the south end of Midtown, we ran into a problem. It was pointed out to me that a portion of the land had been taken over by middle aged and senior men who were using the land to hit golf balls. Golf was not permitted in the public parks, and there were concerns about people being hit with golf balls. Some staff recommended that we plant trees in that portion of the park in order to prevent further illegal golf outings. I had driven by the area many times, and had spoken with some of the men hitting balls. It was clear that their golf outings by the lake were an important part of their social life, one which would be missed if lost. We elected to build a chipping course and putting green on that portion of the park, and we configured it in such a way that golf balls would be hit away from the rest of the park. Now I smile whenever I go by and see the fellows hitting their golf balls in the park…legally!

Another part of listening is sometimes being willing to adjust or abandon a position if it is clear that there is widespread opposition. I say "sometimes" because often positions are taken that involve integrity issues or decisions vital to the future of the city. The media have a strong influence in moving public opinion by the slant, emphasis, and content of their reporting, but they should not be the controlling voice on matters of great city importance.

At times, an elected official simply has to absorb the hits by adopting an unpopular position that he knows is best for the people he represents, but that he has been unable to fully explain due to the difficulty of breaking through the media fog. It can be hard to take comfort in the long-term view when the attacks are coming in, but this is part of the job of being a leader. Some decisions are simply hard!

Frequently, however, a mayor or his staff will make a decision that annoys the community, often after failing to fully obtain the input of those who will be most affected by a decision or proposal. Sometimes, too, the mayor finds himself behind the curve doing damage control on an issue that he may have no strong feelings about, or may not even have known about in advance, but one that staff is driving without much thought for political fallout. These issues can generate controversy and portray the government as an uncaring or abusive bureaucracy.

It is tempting to fight for the sake of fighting. No one likes to publicly admit defeat, especially when the issue has been unfairly portrayed. But fighting for fighting's sake is a waste of political capital and can result in poor decisions being made for the community. Early in the process, it is a good idea to decide whether the public outcry is based on reasonable objections to a bad idea, whether there is any hope of adjusting the approach to accommodate the concerns, or whether it is time to cut losses, abandon the direction, and move on. In the words of Kenny Rogers, sometimes you simply have to "know when to fold 'em" and absorb the one-day media story about how the city "caved in," "surrendered," or "did an about face." Two days later the community will have forgotten the issue completely, and the mayor can focus again on moving the city forward.

● ● ●

I often describe the concept of being elected as putting on the "mayor coat." While you wear the coat for a while, it is not permanently yours, and you will take it off some day. Therefore, it is important to take good care of it and use it in such a way as to benefit the greatest number of people possible while you have it on. One way to use the coat is to give people the opportunity to meet their mayor. For most it will be their first time, and they tend to remember the experience.

I believe in shaking hands. As mayor, if I attended an event, talked to a group, and then left, those attending could go home and tell their family they saw the mayor that day. But if I started by walking through the room and shaking people's hands, then they *met* the mayor. It is a much more personal interchange, and it makes people feel that they know you. It was never an ego thing to me because I knew that I would take off the coat some day. But while I had it on, I wanted to use it to give a lot of people the chance to feel more connected to their city.

While in office, I spent a lot of time shaking hands in McDonalds, Target, Publix grocery store, or just walking down the street or in the mall.

One morning, while I was having breakfast at a diner in the city, a young man who was one of the restaurant's cooks came out to my table and asked if he could talk for a moment. He said that about a year earlier he had been working as part of a convict work-release program, clearing the site for the Pinellas Hope homeless transition center, when I visited the project.

The man reminded me that I interrupted my visit to walk over to the convicts, shake their hands, and thank them for their help. He nervously exclaimed how surprised he was that the mayor of a big city would shake hands with the workers and talk to them. He wanted me to know that he had turned his life around and that he now had a job. He even asked me to look out the window of the restaurant to see the new pickup truck that he had purchased. He wanted me to know that he was going to be okay. The simple gesture of shaking hands made a lasting impression on both of us. As I was driving away from the restaurant, I realized that our encounter taught me a lot about our community. I was thankful that the young cook took the time to chat.

I participated in about thirty-five city parades while I was mayor, and I never rode in a car. I remembered President Jimmy Carter walking in his inaugural parade and shaking hands with people. President Carter's gesture seemed like a good idea, so in my first parade I left Joyce, Julann, and Jacob in the mayor's car, and I started to walk alongside the crowd shaking hands. After about a block I realized that there were parade-watchers on both sides of the street, and the people on the opposite side started to yell for me to come shake their hands as I walked. I wound up running most of the parade route going back and forth, shaking hands and taking pictures with people, while trying to keep up with the car where my family was riding.

In later parades I warmed up ahead of time, wore my running shoes, and literally ran the entire time. My children, riding in the car, would hand me water and a sweat towel as I ran. I got to meet thousands of folks, and felt very connected to the people who hired me. During my terms, children would often approach me in a store or restaurant and proudly proclaim that they had met me before. When I asked where, they would usually respond either that I had met them when I visited their school, or at a parade. The brief moment of touching their hand while running through the parade route left a memory in their mind. The bonds it built became a very special part of my life as mayor.

While shaking hands with people was a way I tried to reach out to the people I represented, it also was a great spirit-lift for me. After a school visit or parade, or simply meeting someone in line at the grocery store, I always came away from the experience with more energy and enthusiasm for my job. I felt I had a new friend with each handshake, and that I understood the city a little better. Each encounter was a special moment for me, and I was thankful that people were willing to take the time to stop, share their thoughts with me, and say hi!

(2) Speaking Clearly

One night in May 2004, I spoke to Leadership St. Pete (LSP) at City Hall. LSP is a group that trains emerging leaders in the city, and there were about fifty people in attendance that night. Assistant Police Chief Luke Williams was on the 2004 LSP planning committee, so he was at the presentation that night. When the session was over, Luke and I walked down the hall to the mayor's receptionist desk. I sat on the desk as Luke and I discussed the tension in our community.

We were in the final days of the Tyron Lewis trial. Tyron Lewis was a young African American man who had been killed by a white police officer at a traffic stop in 1996. A civil disturbance ensued shortly after the shooting, and a second disturbance came after a grand jury cleared the police officer three weeks later. The city received international media coverage for the disturbances. There were a number of injuries and a great deal of destruction of property. Later, the family of Tyron Lewis sued the city for wrongful death, and the case came to trial almost eight years after the shooting, and three years after I took office in 2001. As the trial progressed, there were warnings that another disturbance would take place if the city did not settle the case. A settlement was never reached.

As Assistant Chief Williams and I talked in the dark receptionist area, he received a call. A group had met in Midtown, rallied in support of the family of Tyron Lewis, and then begun marching down 18th Avenue carrying signs, blocking traffic, and throwing bottles and bricks at passing vehicles. It was clearly an attempt to trigger a widespread civil disturbance. Luke excused himself and left for the public safety command center that had been established at Tropicana Field.

One by one the Cabinet members began to arrive in my office as a make-shift city-wide operations center. After monitoring the activity for awhile, Police Chief Chuck Harmon and I decided to go to the Trop, leaving Tish Elston, our First Deputy Mayor, to stay with the Cabinet. Chief Harmon is an individual who possesses a calm demeanor during a crisis. It is a trait that can be mistaken for lack of strength, but I have witnessed his strong, unflustered leadership in the face of some difficult situations. That night in May 2004 was one of them.

As we arrived at the Trop, the command center scene was hectic. Media and satellite trucks were sequestered in one corner of the large parking lot, with a command center communications vehicle near the middle of the lot, and police, fire, and emergency medical vehicles stationed throughout the area. A holding vehicle for prisoners was on site. Police were dispatched, four officers to a vehicle, making arrests and then returning to the command center. We heard sirens constantly, and the feeling of urgency was persistent, but there was no chaos or panic. The police and fire personnel performed like the disciplined, well-trained organization they had become.

The protestors' attempt to create a larger disturbance failed. There was scattered damage to some vehicles and businesses. An automobile and a small building were badly burned and a motorist severely attacked, but the efforts of the police and fire personnel contained the activity to the small group who started the violence. At one point Cedric Gordon, an African American Major responsible for the southern district of the city, pulled me aside to let me know that he and Sergeant Al White had 22nd street covered. It was the core center of our Midtown redevelopment effort. I was thankful for his comment and understanding of the importance of maintaining the Midtown progress.

Twenty people were in custody by the end of the night. Sometime around 3:00 a.m., as the tension of the night lessened, I looked over at the television trucks and decided to talk to the community. I knew that most people were in bed now, but I also knew that whatever I said would greet the region on the morning television shows. It was time to deliver a clear message.

The media folks who had been there for hours scrambled to get their cameras and lights ready. In the few steps it took for me to approach the group, I developed a three-point theme that would be my consistent message to all segments of our community for the next several days. I started in a serious tone with instructions that I was going to give a statement, but I would not answer questions. I then proceeded with three concise points:

First, I was immensely proud of the men and women who served in the St. Petersburg police and fire departments. They acted with professionalism, restraint, and certainty to arrest people involved, clear the scene, and calm the area.

Second, we would not tolerate any acts of criminal violence in our city. Anyone who engaged in these acts would be arrested, and I would seek the fullest prosecution against them.

Third, I wanted to make it clear that night that anyone who condoned or supported acts of criminal violence was an enemy of our efforts to redevelop Midtown. We had made great progress, and I was not going to allow the criminal behavior of a few to stop the momentum. In fact we were going to double our efforts to ensure that the Midtown redevelopment effort succeeded.

I finished my talk and returned to the command center, where I said goodnight to the police chief. Then I drove home and went to bed.

As the three-point message spread through the media Thursday morning, the community responded with overwhelming support. Midtown residents distanced themselves from those arrested and voiced support for our Midtown efforts. Nevertheless, concern remained that a verdict against Tyron Lewis' family could invoke more violence. The trial was still underway.

Governor Jeb Bush called to ask if we needed help. I thanked him for the offer but assured him that I was confident that our law enforcement personnel could handle the situation. We spent Thursday and Friday awaiting the decision of the jury.

The verdict in the city's favor came at the time we hoped to avoid—around 5:00 p.m. on Friday night. As tension gripped the city, elected leaders from the African American community began to arrive at my office. We called a press conference. As we prepared for the press conference, someone suggested we pray as a group. We did: members of the City Council, County Commission, School Board, U.S. Congress, and Florida House of Representatives. Then we walked downstairs to speak collectively to the community.

The room was filled with cameras. It was the only time I recall during my two terms when the local television stations for the St. Petersburg-Tampa region interrupted regular programming for a press conference at City Hall. I began my talk by firmly restating the three themes that I had been repeating since the late night press conference earlier in the week, reiterating in strong terms our intent to arrest anyone who would respond to the court's decision with actions of criminal violence against the community.

Acknowledging that some in our community felt that the city had responsibility for the death of the young man in 1996, and that justice had not been served, I affirmed my belief in the rule of law. I also recognized that a nine-year-old boy, the son of Lewis, had no father. I announced my intention to raise private funds to buy a prepaid college scholarship for the boy in an effort to break the cycle that had brought us to that day. It was an attempt to begin the healing process for a city that had been experiencing the impact from this event for almost eight years. As I left the press conference, I silently wondered how the next few days would unfold.

The next couple hours were surreal. As we awaited the possibility of violence, law enforcement groups were staged at strategic places in the city. I returned home to change clothes and head to the Northeast Little League field to help coach my son Jacob's last game of the baseball season. Police had assigned security to me for the evening, including at the game and post-game pizza celebration we had outside the dugout.

I returned home to change again. I wanted to drive around the city to personally see how things were going. It had been a long, difficult week, and I wasn't looking forward to the evening as I entered my empty house. I walked by the kitchen table and found a Post-it note on which Joyce had written a scripture, Jeremiah 29:11: *"For I know the plans I have for you declares the Lord, plans to prosper you and not to harm you, plans to give you hope and a future."*

I held the note in my hand as I walked up the stairs. As I entered my bedroom, I saw a second note from Joyce on my bed stand, this time with a scripture from Esther 4:14: *"And who knows but that you have come to a royal position for such a time as this."*

I changed clothes and headed downtown. A police major and I toured the city that night, meeting with the officers staged throughout the city and observing the community to see how people would respond to the events of the day. As it turned out, the streets were empty. I remember remarking that it was probably the quietest St. Petersburg Friday night in twenty years. The next few days were the same.

We received overwhelming support both within and outside the community for our response to the crisis, including a strong statement of confidence from Governor Bush. Still, not all the comments were positive. Two council members objected to my decision to raise private money to pay for college for the nine-year-old boy. One was quoted in the newspaper as saying that "[Baker's] going to have to live with the ramifications of his decision." Most people, however, strongly supported the gesture. I recall the words of a parent introducing me at a private school groundbreaking a few days later. Emotional, she expressed pride that she lived in a city led by people who have the courage to do what's right, and the heart to heal the community.

As time went on, we redoubled our Midtown efforts, which were remarkably successful, and the suit against the city was appealed. After the appeal was finally resolved in the city's favor many months later, we quietly delivered to the son of Tyron Lewis a four-year college scholarship, which had been funded by private donors. Having spoken clearly to our community at a very critical moment, I received their support and confidence, so it was important for me to keep my promise.

The experience of the Tyron Lewis trial demonstrated that clear communication to the public is critical when there is a crisis. In those times, the community is waiting to hear how the mayor will respond. The leader's words are weighed and considered more closely, and there is generally a high level of anticipation, along with some anxiety, about how the city is going to respond. The substance and style of the communication of the mayor during these times will impact his or her ability to advance an agenda when the calm times return.

While speaking clearly is vital in times of crisis, it is also important in the normal operations of a city. When you work for hundreds of thousands of people, it is important to let them know the things you want to do and why you want to do them. In order to be successful in advancing an agenda, a mayor needs the support of a majority of City Council, along with that of a sizable portion of the community. The first step is to clearly articulate the rationale for proposed efforts. The explanation should be as concise as possible, and it is helpful if it can be reduced to a few bullet points that can be easily understood.

Once the message is constructed, it must be delivered to the whole community. This can be accomplished through speaking opportunities, online websites, city-owned television, and the media. Part of speaking clearly is developing systems where the public has easy access to information that is important to them. Like most cities, we developed an extensive website providing information on all departments and programs within the city.

Our city-owned television station produced programs that could be seen online, on cable, or on broadcast television. These programs included both documentaries dealing with our major initiatives and weekly programming on city events. We showed City Council meetings and other commission meetings. For those who could not see them on television, we video-streamed them so citizens could pull up meetings from their archive list online and watch them on our website.

Our City Scorecard used simple language without government terms so the public would find them useful.

The most common way of communicating to the public is through the media: newspapers, television, radio, and web. It is important to make every effort to maintain contact and dialogue with the media, because they are the most direct contact with the people represented. At times an issue would be so complex that it was not possible to fully explain views or rationale in sound bites or short quotes. For these times I was thankful to Phil Gailey, editor of editorials for the *St. Petersburg Times* when I took office. When I first began, Phil offered to allow me to put columns in the paper when I felt it was important. I tried not to abuse the offer, and he never turned a column away. I wrote a column every few months during my almost nine years in office on issues ranging from homelessness to crime to schools. I was thankful that Phil and *Times* editorial writer Jack Reed only modified the columns to make them flow better, without changing the substance. When Phil retired, his replacement Tim Nickens continued to allow me to publish opinions when I felt the need to communicate detailed messages. There is no substitute for being able to clearly set out the rationale for a given course of action in an unfiltered manner available to the majority of the voting public.

(3) Walking Around

During my first week of office, Andy Hines called for an appointment to come by and see me. I have a great deal of respect for Andy. One of the honored elders of our city, he served as president of Florida Power Corporation, our leading corporate citizen at the time, and as a civic, church, and community leader in countless ways. After the hectic days of the campaign, followed by the more hectic first few days of my term, I was looking forward to seeing an old friend. As Andy settled into the chair in my office, he looked me straight in the eye, gave me sort of a half smile, and delivered the message that brought him to my office in the first place: "Rick, I was successful in business because I practiced 'management by walking around.' It will work for you too!"

As is typically the case, Andy's advice was correct and straight to the point. I decided immediately to implement management by walking around, a concept originated by David Packard of Hewlett Packard decades ago. I started with work days (actually work half-days). I began a process of working the mornings at departments throughout the city. I went along for the ride in a garbage truck, laid sewer pipes, worked in the action center taking complaints, stood at the permits counter, rode with the fire trucks, assisted with summer youth programs at our recreation centers, and participated in many of the other departments that make a city work.

Through these work days, I learned the organization. Confucius' comment is correct: what you do, you understand. While I was mayor, no one needed to explain to me how a storm water backflow device works. I had been in the hole. I understood the difference in the jobs of commercial versus residential sanitation truck personnel. I knew how the police dispatch system worked, and the relationships between the permitting and inspection processes. I was aware of the fact that people are often unhappy when a codes enforcement official shows up, and I knew the balance that their job requires.

I knew these things because I had been out walking around. Another benefit of the work days is that I got to know a lot of good folks. I found that the people who work for the city, from parks workers to management, were generally hard working and dedicated to advancing our agenda of making St. Petersburg the best city in America. They were doing their jobs, raising their families, and volunteering in the community as Sunday school teachers, coaches, mentors, and tutors. They made their city better in many ways. I was proud to work with them.

The version of management by walking around that we adopted for the city was more than the physical act of walking. It was the process of becoming immersed in the organization for which you are responsible. It was learning the budgets, getting to know the management, and understanding the operations of the city. It was also being out at events, festivals, and celebrations, or just driving around. I purposefully picked different routes while going from place to place in the city in order to explore areas or check on the progress of ongoing projects. While a mayor can never fully know the details of each department, it is good to keep expanding the knowledge base. I continued to learn more about the details of our city until my last day in office.

Being out is especially important in times of natural or man-made disasters. A mayor generally does not have the luxury of managing a crisis from a distance. *He must go to it!*

I was able to be more effective by being physically at the command center during attempted disturbances relating to the Tyron Lewis trial, and during a tanker fire crisis downtown (described in chapter 4). When a major storm caused the roof of a large retail center to collapse and there were fears of shoppers being trapped inside, I joined our public safety officials in the rain.

During each of the 2004 hurricanes, I regularly gave televised media updates in order to communicate to our residents that we were prepared, and to let them know what steps they should take. During one storm, the decision to evacuate the low-lying areas came late in the evening. There was concern that our residents would not receive the message in time, so I rode with one of our police officers as he used his loudspeaker to wake up residents in the neighborhoods we drove through. Even though we had many police and fire personnel involved in the effort, it took a few hours to get to everyone. We later developed an additional contact system that allowed us to tape a recorded evacuation message and simultaneously phone it to thousands of residents based on their evacuation zone.

The importance of clear communication was reinforced to me one Sunday morning, after the 2004 storms passed, when a lady gently touched my arm as I was leaving church. She told me that she had been in a panic as Hurricane Charley was approaching, and she wasn't sure whether or not she should leave her home, even though emergency officials had ordered an evacuation. As she struggled with her decision, she saw me on television telling low-lying residents to evacuate and advising others how to prepare for the storm. Seeing a familiar face calmly instructing the community gave her a level of comfort and convinced her to evacuate to a friend's home on higher ground. "I knew we'd be okay," she told me.

Hurricane response is only one example of the many ways in which a mayor needs to be personally informed and involved with issues impacting the city. In times of calm or crisis, it is best to be immersed in the community or present at the scene in order to determine the best steps to take. In a word, leadership includes walking around.

Chapter 18

Managing the Government

All of this will not be finished in the first one hundred days, nor will it be finished in the first one thousand days, nor in the life of this administration, nor even perhaps in our lifetime on this planet. But let us begin.

—John F. Kennedy

Major cities have dozens of departments, thousands of employees, and an infinite number of potential problems. Since the responsibilities assumed by cities are extremely important to the people they serve, capable and focused management is critical. While the mayor's office is a political position, departments like parks, water, police, sanitation, and others should be led by experienced, committed professionals. Executing a strategic plan and improving government operations, topics discussed elsewhere in this book, demand that senior management understand and are committed to the mission, and are capable of carrying it out. While the city team pursues this effort, the following principles are important:

(1) Pick good people
(2) Show respect—temperament

(3) Look for opportunities to partner

(4) Think and act long-term

(1) Pick Good People

In 2007, St. Petersburg hosted the CNN/YouTube Republican Presidential Debates. It was a highly contested primary with eight candidates attending our gathering at the Progress Energy Center for the Arts. Among the participants were former New York Mayor Rudy Giuliani, former Massachusetts Governor Mitt Romney, former Arkansas Governor Mike Huckabee, and the eventual nominee Senator John McCain. With the debate featuring YouTube questions for the first time in a Republican Presidential Debate, it was a very high profile event, and the world's media were in our city.

Whenever media arrive for a high profile event, they also attract protestors who want to focus the media attention on their cause. There are few events more attractive to protest groups than a presidential debate, and ours was no exception. A few days before the debate, homeless advocate protestors established an encampment within the grounds of the arts center where the debate was to be held. They effectively challenged the city to arrest them on national news. City officials requested that the protestors move to the designated area outside the secured center, where multiple other protest groups would eventually assemble; the protestors refused, and the situation became tense.

As we approached the debate date, I was shown a clip of a television report on the latest local story relating to our homeless protest. The picture of the diverse group of characters on the TV caught my eye. The scene was a group of angry protestors surrounding Beth Herendeen, the city's director of marketing, and Goliath Davis, our Midtown deputy mayor. The city officials were patiently and firmly explaining the options to the protestors, while the "advocates" screamed and flailed their arms for the entertainment of the news cameras.

As I watched the coverage, it didn't surprise me that, although dealing with homeless protestors at a presidential debate is not within either of their job descriptions, both Go and Beth had stepped into the middle of the fire. It also did not surprise me that well before the debate day, the protestors had peacefully moved off the secured arts center property, at the insistence of our team.

Beth and Go were two good examples of our city's many problem solvers.

When you lead an organization as large as a city government, you will spend a lot of time learning about the various functions, responsibilities, and operations of the enterprise, but you will never learn it all, and you cannot make every decision. The mayor will inevitably have to count on the wisdom and judgment of the people chosen to lead the subparts of the city government. Therefore, the most critical decisions of any leader are personnel decisions: deciding who to put in an organization's leadership roles.

Before I took office, a mayor of another large city recommended to me that I require all top staff to submit letters of resignation, and then choose who to keep. The rationale of this approach is that the top leadership will have been chosen by me, and it will be clear that their loyalty is to the new mayor. While I understood the wisdom of that mayor's advice, I chose not to follow it for a couple reasons.

First, in the 2001 election I was voted into office on a Tuesday, and I took office on the following Sunday. Five days is not enough time to transition into a new government, so firing the entire Cabinet with no replacements would have resulted in turmoil. Perhaps more importantly, I was a supporter of my predecessor, Mayor Dave Fischer, and felt that he had assembled a competent group of professionals. While I hoped to add some new energy and direction to expand on past accomplishments, I decided to give the organization's leadership a chance to grow with us. As we advanced our agenda during the years that followed, we made some leadership adjustments, but most of the city's management worked well with the pace, and many thrived on the new challenges.

There are many qualities that are important to search for in the people who will assist a mayor in moving a city forward. These qualities include intelligence, work ethic, honesty, and experience, but among the most critical assets are attitude and tenacity. It is important that the people who work for the organization, especially those in the senior positions, believe in the mission and share in the vision and passion to advance the quality of life for those who live in the city. People who do not believe in the cause will ultimately undermine the effort, either purposefully or due to a lack of enthusiasm. Attitude is important.

It can be challenging for a new mayor, the elected administrator for the city, to enter as the leader of an organization with a large management team that has already worked for the city for many years. When starting, I was cautioned that I would encounter resistance to change from a bureaucracy that considered me a "tourist" just visiting for a few years, while the professional management was in place long before I came and would be there long after I left.

While it is likely that there were some in the city's organization who considered me a "tourist" when I was elected, the reality was that the team pulled together quickly to focus on achieving the great successes that were realized during the past decade. A few factors led to this attitude.

First, the establishment of a clear mission and strategies gave the team a vision to rally around. We were working together to create the best city in America, and had a plan on how to get there.

Second, the lengthy process of developing performance measures, the "City Scorecard," gave the management an opportunity to participate in establishing the metrics, and a way of defining success for both their departments and city.

Finally, the leadership style of management by walking around gave the team exposure to the top management and a greater feeling that we were in the effort together.

One of the most important qualities in transitioning a desire to succeed into success is tenacity. The city's leadership team must have the talent to accomplish an objective even when obstacles present themselves—which they always do. If anyone in management responds to a request with "I'll try" or "I'll do my best," then it is likely that they are going to fail. Even before they begin, they leave themselves a way out. It is best to find someone else to do the job.

The correct answer is "I'll do it." If a roadblock develops, it is okay to return with an update on the challenge and a request for advice. Perhaps more resources are needed, or a different strategy needs to be developed. But the critical quality for success is the tenacity to keep moving forward until the objective is reached. While all the qualities described above are important, tenacity is a key ingredient in assembling a team for the city-building effort.

During my terms, I was fortunate that most of those on the city's management team were passionately focused on improving the city. The renaissance of St. Petersburg during the first decade of this century would not have occurred without the commitment and work of all of the city's employees. They experienced many of the challenges associated with public life, but they received little of the recognition that comes to those who hold elected office. I am thankful for their friendships and for their commitment to making our city the best in America.

• • •

When you have almost 3,000 people working for you, one or more of them is going to make a mistake every day—often big enough errors to wind up in the media. Since the mayor cannot know everything going on all the time, he will sometimes find himself in the media being blamed for something he did not even know was happening.

Generally, the best approach is not to throw staff under the bus by publicly humiliating them. If the decisions made were correct, the mayor should explain the rationale to the public. At other times, the staff is simply wrong. It can take finesse to change direction without unduly attacking the employee. It is good to privately and firmly explain to the employee why a new approach is needed, but you don't want to crush them in such a way as to discourage them and others from stepping out with decisions in the future. Mistakes involving dishonesty or disloyalty will likely require a change in personnel. Similarly, judgment errors that become chronic may indicate someone who does not learn well and needs to go.

Terminating someone's employment should leave the person with dignity. To lose a job is a traumatic event in someone's life. Unless the reason for leaving involves dishonesty or other serious policy violation, the employee should be offered the opportunity to retire or resign, and in appropriate cases receive some level of severance. Respectful separations usually serve the organization best in terms of the spirit of the separated employee, the morale of the remaining staff, and in the avoidance of employee litigation.

Sometimes public employees do what they think is right, but their actions reveal a lack of understanding of the political impact. This is especially true in the budget process. While tax rate increases or service reductions may seem perfectly legitimate and reasonable while a group of professionals are sitting around a table trying to balance a difficult budget, the reality of the moves can hit the fan as the ideas get released to the public.

The will of the citizens must be factored into every decision-making process. One way to accomplish this is to choose people to serve at the organization's top levels who have both professional skills and an understanding of the political realities of the community. This is no substitute for the mayor's involvement, though; ultimately, the mayor must stay engaged.

● ● ●

As with all organizations, the mayor should help people grow. He or she should support staff when they are in a bind, and should not allow staff's mistakes to slow down the city's forward movement. It is also good to tell the staff when they have done a good job. We recognized employees at ceremonies for long tenure, through newsletter articles describing positive citizen comments, and with merit bonuses. At the top ranks of the organization, the most effective recognition is often personal.

I was in Daytona Beach once at a conference, and I had a long phone call with Rick Mussett to talk about our ongoing efforts to attract high tech research firms to the city. Rick is a solid guy who would "take the hill" when we needed the hill to be taken. He knows more about development than most people in the industry, and certainly more than I will ever know. He works incredibly long hours and has been involved in every major project in the city for the last twenty years—from the construction of the major league baseball stadium, to the development of BayWalk, to the rebirth of Midtown.

After our long conversation, I began to think of all Rick had done for the city. I recalled a conversation about Rick that I had recently had with my wife. Joyce pointed out to me that it was fine for me to tell her how good Rick was, but that I should tell him also. How else could he know I valued his efforts?

Thinking about my wife's words, I picked up the phone and called Rick back. I told him that our city has had a renaissance unmatched in its history, and that in my opinion no one had had more of an impact than he on making all the pieces come together. I thanked him for his contribution on behalf of the city, and I reminded him that he had made the lives of many people better. Rick is a person of strong faith and sincere humility—he expressed thanks for the comments, and he didn't dwell on the point. But even though the conversation took only a few minutes, I am confident that we both will remember the exchange for a long time. As I hung up the phone, I made a mental note to follow Joyce's advice more often, expressing my thanks for the many good people who are helping to move the city forward.

After all, they are our most valuable asset.

(2) Show Respect

One of the most important lessons I learned in governing a community is that most of our citizens are good people, but they generally view the needs of the community from the vantage of their own priorities. This is not a bad thing, but it can make the job of the mayor more difficult. An example was the development of the new Salvador Dali Museum. The city provided land to the Dali that was located along the waterfront between the Progress Energy Center for the Arts and Albert Whitted Airport. The location was perfect for the museum, but the use triggered conflicts of priorities between the airport, the theater, Dali, and the grand prix race that circled the entire area once a year. It took months of brokering a resolution, and I was frustrated with my inability to convince some of the individual parties to view the issue as an effort to find a solution that was best for the collective interests of the city, not just their individual priorities.

I was wrong to feel frustrated. It is actually a good thing that people feel passionate about their priorities, and it is the mayor's role to serve as the mediator to develop a plan that works for everyone. It would have been counterproductive to lose patience with people who were acting in what I thought was an unreasonable manner, especially when they made personal attacks, as sometimes happened. A sharp response from me would not have advanced our mission to move the city forward.

Sometime in the course of my almost nine years in office, it became clear that being unnecessarily drawn into public disputes makes it harder to find solutions. People get fixed in announced positions, and the media make it hard to modify or change those positions. The reward for finding common ground is headlines with words like "recanted," "backed down," or "failed." Our newspaper even developed a "Flip-O-Meter" column to highlight people who changed positions on an issue.

I came to internalize the words of King Solomon in Proverbs 15:1: "*A gentle answer turns away wrath, but a harsh word stirs up anger.*" There are many times when it would have felt good to fling a harsh word out, whether against an angry speaker at a city forum; a columnist writing an unfair piece on me or a program I was attempting to advance; or a council member quoted in the newspaper making critical comments. While it is appropriate and advisable at times to be firm and strong in defending positions, a harsh and personal response will only illicit more anger.

It was once explained to me that when someone lashes out at me angrily in a public setting, and I am considering my response, I should remember that I am not responding to the person who lashed out. It is very unlikely that I will convince him or her of anything. I am responding for the benefit of all of the observers who are watching and waiting to see how I will respond. The observers will either conclude that they witnessed two people with uncontrolled tempers yelling at each other, or they will observe that someone attacked the mayor and that he responded in a firm but respectful manner.

Temperament matters!

Lashing out, belittling people, or showing disrespect to those who don't agree with you provides no benefit. Instead, it reveals a character flaw, and it also shows a failure to focus on the large view. There will always be people who attempt to acquire political or other leadership positions by attacking and belittling others, but hopefully they will fail. It takes no talent to constantly look for bad things in order to highlight the failures of others, but it takes courage and vision to plan, promote, and lead. As President Theodore Roosevelt wisely said many years ago:

> *It is not the critic who counts; not the man who points out how the strong man stumbles, or where the doer of deeds could have done them better. The credit belongs to the man who is actually in the arena...who errs, and comes short... who spends himself in a worthy cause...*

It is okay to disagree on direction or decisions, but if the disagreement devolves into personal attacks, then it becomes very difficult to reach overall goals. In order to build on common ground tomorrow, we will need the help of those with whom we disagree today.

A related concept is to give praise both sincerely and, when appropriate, generously. There are many people to thank when success has been achieved, both those who are pulling the wagon today and those who came before us. When a city succeeds, it is because of the combined work of a great City Council, neighborhood leaders, community and faith leaders, and business leaders, along with mayors and leaders of the past. Generous praise of the efforts of all parties does not cost anything, and it builds good will in great volumes.

I came to describe the achievements of St. Petersburg as a twenty-five-year overnight success. We see the positive results now, but the seeds were planted and nurtured by many people for many years. It is important to constantly remind the community that the success of today is not the work of one person's efforts or even the work of a single generation. It belongs to, and should be shared by, everyone.

(3) Partner—Make Stone Soup

In the classic Brothers Grimm story, three hungry soldiers came upon a small village. When they had no luck finding people willing to give them food to eat, they started a small fire, filled a pot with water, and set the pot on the fire to boil. After putting stones in the pot they explained to those passing by that the stones were very special. They could produce soup when boiled. Tasting the soup with a spoon, one soldier remarked that it needed a little garnish to make it taste right. One of the villagers agreed to provide some. A soldier again tasted the soup, and again suggested that it needed something else, perhaps a couple of potatoes. Another villager offered them up. A similar process continued until the pot was filled with carrots, beef, onions, and the makings of a nourishing soup—all made from the "special stones"!

General David Petraeus, head of United States Central Command in 2009, responsible at the time for leading America's efforts in Iraq and Afghanistan, had invited Joyce and me to a dinner gathering of five couples at his home. Before dinner, we talked about the many ways that St. Petersburg had used partnerships to advance an aggressive agenda in the face of limited resources. A few weeks later, while he was speaking to an audience at a civic club luncheon, he turned to me and said, "Mayor...no one makes stone soup better than you!" I have never heard the concept of partnering to make progress explained with such simple clarity. I adopted "Stone Soup" as a metaphor for our efforts to move forward in tight budget times by calling on friends.

During my terms, we developed some very aggressive goals. My first term began with the dot-com financial crash followed by September 11, and my second term ended with the first two years of the great national recession of 2008. While we had a few good financial years in between, the fiscal realities were such that we knew we would not have the financial resources necessary to accomplish all our goals. Our options were to reduce our expectations, tax more, or identify partners and new ways to finance the projects. The first two options would have been contrary to my core principles (discussed elsewhere in this book). Therefore, for many projects we set out to find partners and develop creative ways to pay for the projects we tackled.

The approach to completing these projects was basic: identify the objective; establish the operational and financial plan using creative methods of financing; and identify and collaborate with partners who could help us meet the objective.

I learned an important lesson about partnerships in 1986 when I was a twenty-nine-year-old lawyer representing Templeton Mutual Funds in a large acquisition. After considerable negotiations for days over some tough issues, I was about to enter a room full of lawyers and business officials to close the transaction. Before entering the room, Templeton President John Galbraith pulled me aside and asked me a question that I never received from a client before or after: "Is this a good deal for them?"

My first reaction was to conclude that John thought we were giving away too much so I began to recite the reasons I thought the transaction worked well for Templeton. John stopped me and assured me that he was comfortable that it would work for Templeton. He explained that, in his experience, if the proposition was not a good deal for both sides, then no matter what we put in the contract documents, there would be a risk that it would ultimately blow apart and be a bad thing for everybody. Only after I explained to John the benefits for the other side, in addition to those for Templeton, was he comfortable in proceeding. Templeton grew to be one of the world's great financial institutions, and I learned a lesson that day about partnering: make sure the deal is fair and works for all sides.

Twenty years after that closing, when I was mayor, John Galbraith would teach me another lesson about partnering by providing St. Petersburg with a generous gift of cash and a no-interest loan to enable the city to build an airport terminal at our downtown general aviation airport. The loan was paid back with transportation grants later received by the city.

We used the partnership approach in many other of our city's projects also. We built the West St. Petersburg Library with St. Petersburg College;

developed programming for the Progress Energy Center for the Arts using naming rights to underwrite theater productions; and developed a master planned block downtown that includes the power company headquarters building, a planned hotel, and a new St. Petersburg College campus, along with new facilities for the Florida International Museum, the Florida Orchestra, and American Stage Theater.

In one case we agreed to convert two asphalt lots downtown into landscaped waterfront parks after Governor Jeb Bush signed budgets that provided $8 million in Conservation and Recreation Land (CARL) funds to help construct the new Salvador Dali Museum. The new $36 million Dali building was built between the two new parks. The parks were an "urban greenscape addition," authorized under the CARL program, and had a value far exceeding the grants from the state.

Another portion of the Dali funding came when the state university system paid $6 million for the old Dali building to convert it to a college facility for the University of South Florida St. Petersburg's downtown campus. The city had given Dali a long-term lease on the old building for nominal lease payments, and agreed to release its underlying ownership to allow the proceeds to go to Dali. Voters approved the transaction by referendum. The result for the city was a new Dali Museum, an expanded campus downtown for USF St. Petersburg, and two new waterfront parks.

Virtually all our public school support programs, downtown efforts, and Midtown programs described in this book involved partnerships. The partners included other branches of government, as well as private individuals and companies.

Our public school Business Partners program enabled us to identify one hundred businesses who stepped up to help. In turn, we reached out to these and others when we had other efforts that needed support. In baseball terms, they became our bench. When the First Night downtown-wide New Year's Eve celebration was in financial trouble, we called on the bench to find a title sponsor and other assistance. The event was saved!

When the historic tennis center in Midtown almost closed due to city budget challenges, we privatized it with local tennis players and business supporters who raised part of the funds to renovate the old facility and take over operations. It has now regained a portion of the success of a prior day, when greats like Arthur Ashe, Billy Jean King, Chris Evert, and Martina Navratilova played there. The tennis center developed thriving activities for adults and the "First Serve" program for low income children from the neighborhood. And it no longer received ongoing city operating subsidy.

When the Grand Prix needed sponsors, the bench stepped up to the plate. They also helped Pinellas Hope, our mid-county homeless center. A major grocery store developer donated their services to help establish our Midtown Sweetbay. Another company paid for the recording and sound system at Midtown's Royal Theater. Many have helped provide college scholarships for low-income children and incentive bonuses for principals. They stepped up with cash to partially fund our Gun Bounty program that helped us get violent criminals off the street.

We were careful to ensure that no one expected or received anything improper in return, only the recognition that they were helping to move the city forward. We could not have made the progress we did without their help. If a city's goal is to become seamless, it needs the help of the business community, all levels of government, neighborhoods, faith groups, community groups, and schools working together. Thankfully, we were able to field a great team!

(4) Think and Act Long Term

As I walked by my scheduling aide's desk, I glanced at her television. It was tuned to Channel 9, our local 24-hour news show, which had done an instant poll on a decision I made the day before. I was in my eighth month of office. The decision involved a very high profile issue, and the poll felt like a verdict being read by a jury foreman.

Ninety-one percent of those who responded said I was an idiot.

The poll didn't actually say I was an idiot, but it felt that way when I listened to the news anchor's report. The poll actually said that 91 percent of those who responded to the television website disagreed with my decision to fire our police chief after news accounts reported that he used the term "orangutan" in conjunction with his description of an African American suspect who had resisted arrest. In addition to the poll, there was a great deal of anger among some police officers and neighborhood leaders, who felt I was taking political correctness to an extreme. After all, the chief had apologized and attempted to reach out to those offended.

It was a hard decision to make so early in my term. I knew before I made the call that it would be unpopular to many. Only a few of my friends, including my pastor Scott Boggs, dropped by in the aftermath to express their support. Most people were either angry or puzzled. But I understood at the time that it would be vital for my administration's long-term success that both I, and our entire diverse community, have confidence in the person who leads our police department. While I knew I would have to absorb a hit in the short term, I felt that I had a much better chance of success in the long term by finding a new leader. I am satisfied that time has confirmed my call to be the right one.

When faced with a hard decision, it is good to search for a compromise that will please everyone and accomplish the city's objectives. At times a mayor is lucky and finds the common ground. Often, he discovers that there is no solution that works and pleases everyone. He simply has to make the tough choice. That is why the decision is called "hard."

It is tempting to make decisions based on what the newspaper will say the next day, or how many people will write angry emails. But there is a balance to be struck. Listening to and considering public input is critical to governing. But people voted for their mayor to make decisions based upon his judgment of what is best for the city. The mayor is expected to balance the needs of the city and gather and consider all information relevant to making sound decisions, including public input. There are times—hopefully not too often—when it is clear that a given direction is the right way to go in order to advance the long-term goals of the city, even though a majority of people at the moment disagree. It is incumbent on the leader to hear and consider all views, and communicate to the public his decisions and rationale. Yet in the end he must do what he believes is best for the city, even if unpopular with the public or the media.

If the issue is not one that is critical to the core mission of the city or the value system of the mayor, then he may choose to compromise in order to save his powder and fight another day. Still, on matters of significant importance to the city or those involving a central issue of values, the mayor should stand firm.

We often received criticism for economic incentive programs to bring in or expand companies in St. Petersburg, thus providing jobs in the city. We could easily have avoided the criticism by not pursuing the companies. After all, in many cases the taxes and jobs benefits from these companies would not be received by our city until well after I left office. But that is not the point. If a city is to grow and progress, its leadership must continue to plant seeds that will grow in later years. Few efforts are more important to a city than job retention and expansion, and we worked to do both.

We increased our water rates in order to pay for substantial improvements to our water and sewer pipes and plants. Much of the system was porous, an environmental time bomb. The voters would feel the rate increases, but few would fully understand the dramatic improvements we made to the underground and plant infrastructure, despite our efforts to communicate. Other efforts, from annexations to computer upgrades, can require an investment of large quantities of political capital without much obvious political gain in the short term. In fact, as described above, these efforts can result in political risk and harsh criticism. Still, a mayor is elected to do what he thinks is right.

Cynics will push in both directions when they disagree. They will chastise the mayor for not following public opinion at times, yet accuse him of grandstanding for the crowd at others. The mayor should listen to all sides and communicate the reasons for his chosen path. But at the end of the day, he should always take the path that he believes will make his city a better place.

Recall the television instant poll declaring that 91 percent of those surveyed disagreed with my 2001 decision to fire the police chief. Four years later I was reelected by over 70 percent of the city voters. In the long term, what mattered most was the public's confidence in my commitment to do what I thought was best for the city, and to move the city forward.

Conclusion

*For greater things have yet to come, and greater things
are still to be done in this City . . .*

—"GOD IN THIS CITY," BY CHRIS TOMLIN

hroughout this book, I have tried to provide a glimpse of our efforts to make St. Petersburg the best city in America. The strengths, weaknesses, needs, and priorities of every city are different, but the approach to improvement has a common thread: the goal must be to build the best city in the country and to make it seamless. It is an ongoing goal, and a work that is never complete. In the words of Christian contemporary singer Chris Tomlin, there will always be *greater things still to be done in the city.*

Advancing the quality of life for the people who live in any city is the core mission of its leadership. Success does not come by evolution, luck, or timing. Cities improve when passionate leaders embrace the citizens' priorities and execute a plan to make the city better. Improving public safety, economic development, schools, neighborhoods, and government operations are foundational to city progress and success. The city's goals, plan, and progress should be quantified and communicated to the people being served. Adjustments should be implemented in response to results, and the improvement effort must be continuous.

Along the way, the city leadership must assemble and utilize important tools that make the job of city development easier. Stay close to faith and family; measure progress; listen carefully and speak clearly; partner with those who can help advance the city's mission; pick good people and get to know the organization well; act for the long term, and give respect to those encountered. And always remember that improving the quality of life for the people who call the city home is the number one goal.

City-building in America is important work because the success of our country is dependent on the progress of our cities. If, some day, all children in our cities can grow up in neighborhoods that are vibrant, safe, and clean, then we will be on our way. When all children share in the pride and success of the entire community, and believe that they have a shot at achieving the American dream, then our cities will be seamless, and the greatest nation in the history of mankind will be assured of having an even greater future!

Epilogue

An E-ticket Ride

When I was reelected mayor of St. Petersburg in 2005, I considered it to be one of the greatest honors I have ever received in my life. My first election was an honor also, but at the time the voters did not know me very well. Four and a half years after I first took office, though, there had been many opportunities for the community to learn how our team would react to the challenges faced, and how we would move the city forward. So winning in 2005 made me feel a special honor and responsibility to accomplish our goals.

The job has been an e-ticket ride! In the early years of Disney World, an e-ticket was reserved for the wildest rides, like the Space Mountain rollercoaster. On Space Mountain I can remember being tossed and turned, sometimes going upside down and sometimes feeling like I had just fallen off the end of a cliff. I remember feeling exhilarated, sick, and terrified all at the same time. At the end of the ride my heart was racing, and I felt for a moment like I had lived on the edge of life. Space Mountain was good preparation for public life, with its wild and unpredictable turns, from really good days to not-so-good days.

• • •

During my years in office, I experienced the emotional pain of loss. I lost a friend and colleague to suicide, and buried many people whom I loved. The hardest loss was the death of my father, Russ Baker.

I also experienced crushing budgets, unpleasant blogs, hours of sometimes angry public hearings, a few personal threats, and many, many times of crisis. I watched an operation as a surgeon removed bullets from one of our police officers, and I responded to the community after an eight-year-old girl was killed in a senseless, cowardly, drive-by shooting.

A persistent media filed regular public records requests for my cell phone records, emails, correspondence, expense records, home water bill, and personal financial statements. It is a difficult process, but one that is a present reality for those who serve in public life. People angry with the codes enforcement department regularly checked my home for violations and filed complaints if my tree branch was hanging too low above the sidewalk or my hedge growing too far into the alley. I always instructed city staff to treat complaints about my home the same way they would treat anyone else, and the newspaper always gleefully picked up on my codes enforcement cases.

As mayor, I was the target of protestors on a wide array of topics, from union disputes to police activities to homeless issues. The pickets showed up, not only at public places like City Hall and our parks, but also at my home and in front of my church on Sunday mornings. Some swore at my young children as we left church. Others resorted to stalking my house at night and pasting stickers on my property. Once, at a City Council meeting, a fight broke out between a peace protestor and another citizen who had opposing views on the city's decision to vacate a sidewalk next to a downtown shopping center.

In addition to the hundreds of ongoing lawsuits involving the city on a range of issues, I was personally sued three times in state and federal court for matters related to my job. One of the personal suits filed against me was over the constitutionality of an ordinance that passed while I was in junior high school, living in Miami. As part of the city's litigation process, I was subpoenaed to testify at hours of depositions in multiple cases. I have negotiated with unions and given the closing argument for a union impasse hearing.

Despite the many challenges, there has been much more good than bad. I got to play softball against the *Kids and Kubs* team, players who are each at least seventy-five years old. I marched along with my family, leading the *Second Time Arounders Band* in the Macy's Thanksgiving Day parade. I played guitar and sang many times at the neighborhood festivals and the Saturday Morning Market—and a few times with the Marshall Tucker Band. And I flipped Mickey Mouse pannycakes at the annual YMCA Mayor's Pancake Breakfast fundraiser, an event established in memory of my dad who made pancakes for the Indianapolis YMCA fundraiser.

I competed annually in the Mud Wars with our city's teens (breaking my hand on the last outing); presided at the annual YMCA Mayor's Prayer Breakfast; threw out the first ball for major league baseball games several times—and once caught a Major League foul ball bare handed (even my kids were impressed). I waved the green flag to start the inaugural Honda Grand Prix of St. Petersburg. My young children sang "Back Home Again in Indiana" on a Midwest television news show before the Indianapolis 500, and I got to announce, "Ladies and Gentlemen, Start Your Engines" at an IndyCar race. My kids, Julann and Jacob, presented paper cranes in Hiroshima, Japan, at a memorial to the children lost in the aftermath of the atomic blast. Having my family join the ongoing adventure of being mayor made my job more fun and rewarding.

I talked with the president of Russia and the prime minister of Japan; had dinner at the White House twice; marched in St. Petersburg Russia's Victory Parade; spoke with two vice presidents about local and national issues; and welcomed America's president to our city many times. We had countless meetings with governors, generals, and many celebrities; and had breakfast one morning with three generations of Andretti family racers: Mario, Michael, and Marco. Months later we welcomed the World Series to St. Petersburg's Tropicana Field.

I watched the faces of one thousand low-income sixth graders receiving four-year college scholarships as their families looked on. Many parents had immigrated from Bosnia, Thailand, and Laos, while others grew up here in St. Petersburg. They all shared in a renewed hope for their children's future.

● ● ●

Our Downtown and Midtown areas emerge as success stories, and I shook the hands of thousands of our residents and visitors. I found joy in the remarkable progress of our public schools and pleasure in being welcomed by smiling faces while walking parade routes. I am thankful for the countless angels who wrote kind letters, honked when they drove by, or stopped me in a store, restaurant, or park to offer words of thanks and encouragement.

Although I don't remember all the names, I have thousands of new friends. Many of my new friends were colleagues on City Council or in other elected offices, and employees of the city of St. Petersburg for whom I have immense respect. Some protected my family, and all of the families of our city. I am grateful for their service. Other friends were children and adults whom I met only briefly, but with whom I felt a special bond.

Many new friends were members of the media who regularly reported and commented on our efforts. While we sometimes annoyed each other, I have great respect for the difficulty of their jobs. I recognize that even in a well-run city, mistakes will be made from time to time, and it is part of their job to point that out. I was especially thankful to those in the media who believed in visions like great public schools, new businesses, an improved Midtown community, playgrounds, dog parks, bike paths, a great Downtown, safe neighborhoods, and the dream of becoming America's best city. Sometimes it takes courage to report on good things, and there were many in the electronic and print media who did just that. They helped make our city better, and I am thankful.

I cherish the memories of both the good and bad days, and I am forever grateful to the people of St. Petersburg who entrusted me with their city for awhile. In life, every so often a special place emerges. If we are fortunate, we may get to live during a special time. It is a rare privilege to experience the intersection of a special time in a special place. Those of us fortunate enough to live in St. Petersburg during the first decade of the twenty-first century had the opportunity to enjoy that experience. The renaissance of our city did not result from the efforts of a single person, or even a single era. Rather, it was the result of many people during many years working together to make the place better.

My most gratifying experience has been to see the difference in attitude of the people who live in our city. We transformed from a community that, not long ago, was frustrated with what we were to a people who are immensely proud of our town. St. Petersburg residents love their city! In 2005 the reelection headline read, "A City United!" While challenges remained, we learned that we could work through them all if we focused on creating a community that is seamless, and a special place that is well on the way to becoming the best city in America!

Acknowledgments

It is a major endeavor to run for office, lead a major urban center, and then write a book about the process. There were so many challenges and successes encountered during the almost nine years of leading our city that I could not describe every one. Instead, I have tried to present those that I believe will be instructive to people in leadership positions.

The cumulative effort of writing this book required many people to join in and buy into the dream of building seamless cities. It is impossible to individually identify every person who contributed to the effort, but there are a few individuals, and many categories, I would like to acknowledge.

First, I am thankful to God for the many blessings in my life, the most important being the gift of His son Jesus Christ, whose life, lessons, and sacrifice are a constant source of comfort and inspiration.

I thank my wife, Joyce, who has been my primary source of advice, support, love, and comfort. Also thanks to our children, Julann and Jacob—they have smoothed the edges of a sometimes difficult job. Joyce, Julann, and Jacob have each lived the mayor's journey personally—the ups and downs—and have independently contributed a great deal to the future of St. Petersburg. I am also thankful for my parents, Irene and the late Russ Baker, who gave me life and lessons on how to live it—my mother remains my close advisor and friend. In addition to my parents I have been blessed with many great mentors in my life. One of the most important has been John Galbraith, who has believed in and been part of many of my efforts, including this one.

I am thankful to Governor Jeb Bush, a long-time friend and mentor, for his counsel and effort to write the foreword. Thanks also to Governor Mitt Romney, Tom James, John Avlon, Adam Goodman, and Mike Sittig for contributing comments on the back cover and inside pages.

I am thankful to the many people in the Manhattan Institute and Regnery Publishing who believed in and advanced this book, and the public policy effort it represents. This is especially true of Larry Mone, MI's President, who believed enough to support *The Seamless City*, and has dedicated his career to advocating for good government and effective public policy. Bernadette Serton from MI was my patient, encouraging, and constant advisor. MI's Howard Husock also provided much-needed advice and support. Mary Beth Baker, the book's chief editor from Regnery, walked me through the process and provided comments and advice that made the book much better. The important efforts of others from MI (Lindsay Craig, Nathan Brinkman, and Vanessa Mendoza) and Regnery (Kathleen Sweetapple and John Lalor) also helped make this book possible.

In addition to the great editors at MI and Regnery, many friends took the time to read and comment on the transcript—they all helped make the book better, and they provided critical advice and moral support: General David Petraeus, Governor Jeb Bush, Kathleen Shanahan, Curt Carlson, John Galbraith, Jack Reed, Mayor Dave Fischer, Mayor Bill Foster, Rob Kapusta, Irene Baker, John Avlon, Joyce Baker, Jim Levine, and Adam Goodman, along with others who have all provided contributions to the city.

My two successful elections resulted from the commitment of many people who volunteered for my campaign and financially contributed to the effort. It was truly a "movement" in our community that required sacrifice and enormous work by both professional talent and volunteer help. I am thankful to those who believed in me and our mission. I am especially thankful to the voters of St. Petersburg who voted two times to entrust me with the leadership of their city. I remained mindful of that trust every day.

One of my blessings of the past ten years has been the friendships I gained with the people who work for the city government in St. Petersburg. St. Petersburg is lucky to have a committed and capable City Council, along with thousands of dedicated, hard-working, passionate folks working every day to improve the quality of life for the people who call the city home—from top management to those who police the streets, answer the fire and medical emergency calls, keep the water running, make parks look great, handle traffic, keep the city clean, and do countless other jobs. Collectively, they helped put the vision of a seamless city into action and were dedicated to making St. Petersburg one of America's great cities. I miss the day-to-day interactions we had, and I am grateful for their commitment.

Our city employees were aided by an incredible team of community leaders—in other governments, businesses, neighborhood associations, civic organizations, and charitable, faith, and cultural groups. They were a very significant part of the team, and I am thankful for their friendship and their work.

The National League of Cities, led by Don Borut—and the Florida League of Cities, led by Mike Sittig—were a constant source of advice and support during my service with the city. The NLC's Cliff Johnson was a great advocate for our school and youth programs. They all provided critical support and guidance as I advanced this book.

Finally, I am thankful to the great leaders of St. Petersburg's present and past. City building is a relay race, with the responsibility for leadership being passed from generation to generation. The collective talents and energies of our leaders have built a place that is truly one of the most beautiful and livable urban centers on the face of the earth and is well on the way to becoming a seamless city.

Appendix

The city narrowed down the core City Scorecard performance measures to about 160 items. They were each presented in graph form and were broken down into the city's five strategic planning areas. They were kept online at the city's home page. The following are samples of the Scorecard items.

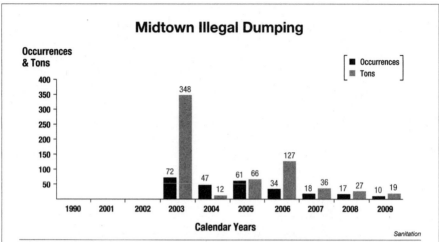

Midtown Illegal Dumping

Note: Chart represents illegal dumping in the Midtown area that was reported to the Sanitation Department. Tons collected in 2003 was based on actual weight of material collected. Tons collected in 2004, 2005 and 2006 are estimated because the materials are collected in the same truck used for special service requests for collection of bulk items. 2006 also includes 18 instances of dumped roofing material. The person responsible was arrested and his truck seized. The arrest was made by the department's Environmental Detective who was hired in October 2003.

*City performance measures comparisons are for the prior 9 years and incorporate 1990 for historical perspective; for this chart data is only available starting in 2003. Data through 2009; updated quarterly.

1-4-450-004

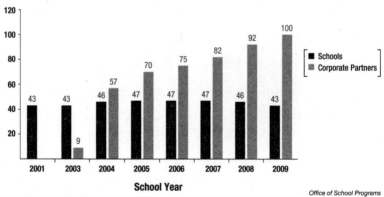

City of St. Petersburg Corporate Partner Program

*Data through 2009, updated quarterly.

*The Corporate Partners Program began with corporations matched with nine St. Petersburg public middle schools and was announced on February 14, 2003. The program expanded in 2004 to 57 corporate partners to match all 43 of our St. Petersburg public schools. The corporations provide mentors, volunteers, resouces, and/or strategic planning.

*In order to maintain quality partnerships the Mayor has capped the number of corporate partners at 100.

*School Year is July 1~June 30. The number at the bottom of each column represents end of school year.

3-1-120-010

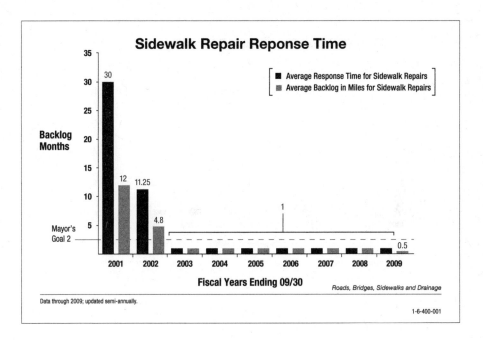

Sidewalk Repair Reponse Time

- Average Response Time for Sidewalk Repairs
- Average Backlog in Miles for Sidewalk Repairs

Backlog Months

Mayor's Goal 2

Fiscal Years Ending 09/30

Roads, Bridges, Sidewalks and Drainage

Data through 2009; updated semi-annually.

1-6-400-001

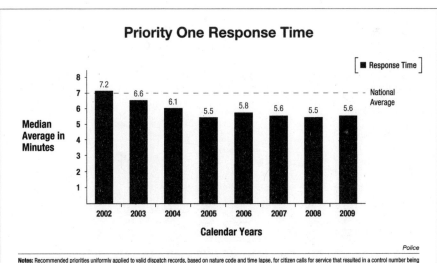

Priority One Response Time

- Response Time

National Average

Median Average in Minutes

Calendar Years

Police

Notes: Recommended priorities uniformly applied to valid dispatch records, based on nature code and time lapse, for citizen calls for service that resulted in a control number being issued. Priority one calls involve forcible felonies or calls of a life-threatening nature, where prompt apprehension is possible, or calls where serious injury has occurred or is threatened. Forcible felonies include murder, manslaughter, sexual battery, carjacking, home invasion, aggravated assault, aggravated battery and any other felony that involves the use or threat of physical force or violence against any individual. National average is 7 minutes. Data through 2009 is through 12/31; updated quarterly.

4-1-140-011

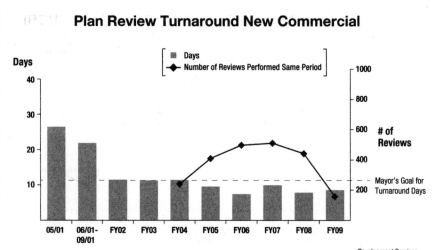

Plan Review Turnaround New Commercial

Days

Legend:
- Days
- Number of Reviews Performed Same Period

(Left axis: Days — 40, 30, 20, 10)
(Right axis: # of Reviews — 1000, 800, 600, 400, 200)

Mayor's Goal for Turnaround Days

X-axis: 05/01, 06/01-09/01, FY02, FY03, FY04, FY05, FY06, FY07, FY08, FY09

Development Services

*New building code effective 3/1/02 produced significant increase in February submittals. Plan Review Turnaround New Commercial pertains to construction of new (building from the ground up) retail, office, industrial and multifamily projects and is the number of working days between the date the application is submitted to the City and the date the first set of plan review comments is complete. Data through 2009; updated quarterly. Number of Reviews started being reported as of January 2004.

2-2-170-001

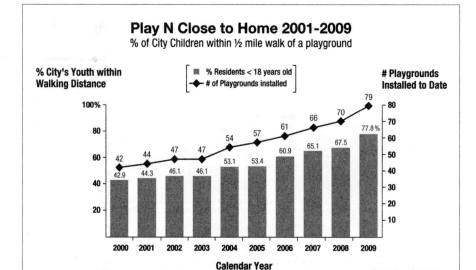

Play N Close to Home 2001-2009
% of City Children within ½ mile walk of a playground

% City's Youth within Walking Distance

Legend:
- % Residents < 18 years old
- # of Playgrounds installed

 # Playgrounds Installed to Date

(Left axis: 100%, 80, 60, 40, 20)
(Right axis: 80, 70, 60, 50, 40, 30, 20, 10)

Line values (# of Playgrounds installed): 42, 44, 47, 47, 54, 57, 61, 66, 70, 79

Bar values (% Residents < 18 years old): 42.9, 44.3, 46.1, 46.1, 53.1, 53.4, 60.9, 65.1, 67.5, 77.8%

X-axis (Calendar Year): 2000, 2001, 2002, 2003, 2004, 2005, 2006, 2007, 2008, 2009

Neighborhood Partnership

* Data based on US Census 2000 for residents under 18 years of age. Data updated annually. # Includes completed installation and new priority areas (identified).
* Data based on US Census 2000 for determination of residents under 18 years of age.

1-1-8-009

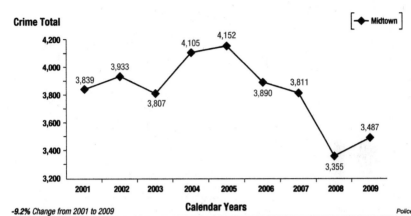

St. Petersburg Midtown Total Index Crime Totals (UCR)

-9.2% Change from 2001 to 2009

Notes: UCR index crime includes murder, rape, robbery, aggravated assault, burglary, larceny and auto theft. These are reported totals for these index crimes. Data for 1990, 1999-2007 is from the FBI's annual report, *Crime in the United States*. Data for 2008 is preliminary, and calculated with the 2007 population estimate. The 2008 population estimate, and comparative city data, is not yet published by FDLE. City performance measure comparisons are generally for the prior 5 years. UCR collects offense and arrest data according to the crime definitions provided by the National Uniform Crime Reports Program. Data through 12/31/09; updated annually.

4-1-140-016

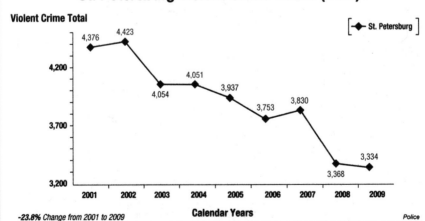

St. Petersburg Violent Crime Totals (UCR)

-23.8% Change from 2001 to 2009

Notes: UCR violent crime includes murder, rape, robbery and aggravated assault. These are reported totals for these violent crimes. Data for 1990, 1999 - 2007 is from the FBI's annual report, *Crime in the United States*. Data for 2008 is preliminary. The 2008 population estimate, and comparative city data, is not yet published by FDLE. City performance measure comparisons are generally for the prior 5 years. UCR collects offense and arrest data according to the crime definitions provided by the National Uniform Crime Reports Program. Data through 12/31/09; updated annually.

4-1-140-017

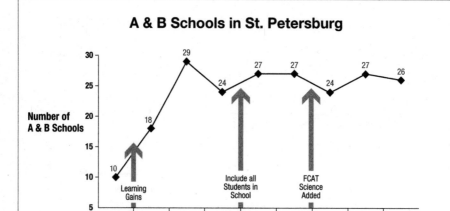

A & B Schools in St. Petersburg

Office of School Programs

*Data through July 2009. Updated annually. *School grades developed by State of Florida based on student achievement test scores. *Graph indicates a 260% increase in the number of A & B schools since 2001, the commencement of City's Mayor's Mentors & More Program. *In 2001, City of St. Petersburg worked with 37 graded public schools under the MMM Program; in 2008, 41 graded schools. *26% of St. Petersburg's graded schools were A or B in 2001- 63% in 2008. *In 2002, student learning gains were added to school grades, and in 2005 all students were included in school grades. *FCAT science was added to the school grade in 2007. *School Year is July 1 -June 30. The number at the bottom of each column represents end of school year.

3-1-120-001

Index